# THE CUTE AND THE COOL

# THE CUTE

## AND

GARY CROSS

# THE COOL

*Wondrous Innocence*

*and Modern American*

*Children's Culture*

**OXFORD**
UNIVERSITY PRESS

2004

# OXFORD
UNIVERSITY PRESS

Oxford   New York
Auckland   Bangkok   Buenos Aires   Cape Town   Chennai
Dar es Salaam   Delhi   Hong Kong   Istanbul   Karachi   Kolkata
Kuala Lumpur   Madrid   Melbourne   Mexico City   Mumbai   Nairobi
São Paulo   Shanghai   Taipei   Tokyo   Toronto

Copyright © 2004 by Oxford University Press, Inc.

Published by Oxford University Press, Inc.
198 Madison Avenue, New York, New York 10016

www.oup.com

Oxford is a registered trademark of Oxford University Press

Library of Congress Cataloging-in-Publication Data
Cross, Gary S.
The cute and the cool : wondrous innocence and modern American children's culture /
Gary Cross.
p. cm.
Includes bibliographical references and index.
ISBN 0-19-515666-8
1. Children—United States—History.   2. Children in popular culture.
3. Toys—Social aspects—United States.   4. Parenting—United States—History.
5. Children—United States—Caricatures and cartoons.
6. Innocence (Psychology)   I. Title.
HQ783.C74 2004
305.231—dc21       2003053089

9  8  7  6  5  4  3  2  1

Printed in the United States of America
on acid-free paper

*For my mother, Shirley A. Cross,*

*whose life was a passionate embrace of beauty*

*and a quiet tribute to human dignity.*

# Contents

# THE CUTE AND THE COOL

# The Irony of Innocence

When my son Alex was three years old and on vacation at his grandparents' lakeside cottage, four adults (including myself) conspired to trick him into believing that pirates had stolen his grandmother's jewels. We all went out on his grandparents' boat to a special tiny island where, aided by the pirates' map that his five-year-old sister carried along, he "discovered" the "jewels" and a sword the pirates had left behind. Naturally, we videotaped and photographed the whole event, and the boy obliged us at the end with a spontaneous outburst, "And I got a sword!" And he waved his prize proudly in the air. Our pleasure was in the deception, and we smiled at his naïveté. But we also envied his fantasy world, a place where we could only visit.

We love children for all the things we are no longer and often wish we were. We delight in the fact that they, at least, are not cynical or repressed. Even when we put them in ridiculous settings—photographing toddler boys wearing firemen's hats while clutching teddy bears or toddler girls dressed like fashion models—we admire their innocence. Small children are still capable of wide-eyed wonder at what we no longer see or of blank-eyed indifference at what frightens, distresses, or disgusts us. They are neither jaded nor obsessed as we often are about the situations, but especially the goods, around us. We love the way they look and respond, even while we feel superior. They exhibit freshness where we experience boredom or addiction. And we identify with this lost paradise of wonder because we have been so

**I.I**
A picture of orchestrated wondrous
innocence. Courtesy of Alexander and
Elena Cross.

long banished from it. Theirs is the Garden of Wondrous Innocence, the
World of the Cute.

Today, as perhaps never before, we are obsessed with kids. We come close
to worshiping them in our family photo albums, vacation splurges, holiday
giving, and even religious services. Some of us gag at the sentimental ending of *It's a Wonderful Life* when Zuzu, in her singsong voice, says, "Every time
a bell rings, an angel gets his wings." But most still get a little teary-eyed, even
if we are slightly embarrassed by it.

We love dimpled knees and round faces with bright, wide-open eyes and blemishless skin. We think cute. And we buy in the millions photos of babies and toddlers dressed as bunnies or gazing out at the sea with arms outstretched in sheer delight. Half the amateur photos taken today feature children. These homemade pictures define family. At the center are the children, the youngest in the middle, surrounded by loving parents and older siblings. In displaying these photos on fireplace mantles, on office desks, and in wallets, we tell ourselves and anyone who will look our ideal of family life. Images of babies and toddlers, so much alike, and so little like the way our grown kids look today, make us feel as if we have captured time in our children when they were still all potential and no accomplishment. In fact, we have snatched innocence out of the air. Pictures of small children make us feel so good that advertisers are forever featuring them in their ads. Despite their irrelevance to the function of computers or financial services, ad makers think people will favorably associate their products with images of children, and so they use them in about one-third of their commercial messages.[1]

A child makes a couple into a family. Childlessness is, for many, a tragedy; and having a child is so important that Americans spend $2 billion a year on fertility drugs and test-tube fertilization. In a culture in which most people find happiness only in private life, giving birth is the supreme proof of self-realization.[2]

We worship beginnings of life and hide from the endings. Husbands take videos of their wives spread-eagled giving birth, and expectant couples gush over the grainy and clinical ultrasound images of their three-month-old fetuses. The "unborn child" has become holy. Babies no longer represent the Fall from grace as they did for most of Western history. Newborns, despite their natural vulgarity, symbolize today the purity of innocence. They are "fresh from the hand of God," in the words of the romantic poet William Wordsworth, who anticipated modern feelings by a century. Childhood has become a time to cherish and to protect from the modern Fall of growing up. No longer are the aged those near God who have climbed the hill of life's pilgrimage to glory. Rather, children are gifts sent down from God, divine lights, all too soon extinguished by life itself.

A few years ago I attended a quite ordinary church service. It not only included a children's sermon (as preschoolers gathered near the altar to hear a simple lesson illustrated with a popular toy) but also featured a children's choir (in which my children participated) singing an upbeat calypso hymn. Everyone smiled. We also heard a long recitation from the minister, reminding us that we must be as little children to enter the Kingdom of God, that the young know trust and do not know possessiveness, status seeking, and greed. Yes, we adults are the fallen; we need to see the world once again with the innocent eyes of youth, those angels fresh from God. In this mainstream Protestant church as in so many other modern institutions, the innocence of childhood is one of the few beliefs that all share.

Our holidays have become celebrations of childlike innocence—Easter, Halloween, even summer picnics. Memorial Day and Labor Day have become the bookends of the summer season of family fun. Christmas, celebrated by the religious and secular alike, glories in the wonders of childhood and the promise of reliving it. The only major holidays that we have not turned over to children are Thanksgiving and New Year's Eve. We build our vacations around the pleasures we give the young: In the 1990s, Walt Disney World became the greatest single tourist draw in the country, attracting more than twenty-eight million to share family times for nearly a week per visit.[3]

Despite the haunting image of JonBenet Ramsey, the six-year-old beauty queen murdered in her parents' comfortable suburban home the day after Christmas in 1996, a few of us, at least, still enjoy kiddie beauty pageants. We find it cute for the young to pretend to be adults, their faces made up with rouge and mascara, hair tinted, dressed in miniature strapless gowns. Nevertheless, we are confused about what it means: Are we turning kids into sex objects, targeting them for perverts? Are we exploiting babies by toying with their innocence, forcing them to play out our adult fantasies of glamour, depriving them of a childhood? Innocence is so empty of positive meaning and yet so alluring that it has become intertwined with much that seems to be the very opposite of innocence.[4]

Over and over, we find salvation in the naive joy of the child. Each generation has its own child movie and TV stars: Jackie Coogan, Shirley Temple, Freddie Bartholomew, Judy Garland, Elizabeth Taylor, Jay North, Jodie Foster, and Macaulay Culkin. Ideals of innocent beauty and the adorable have changed little in a hundred years or more. The look has persisted from its origins in eighteenth-century romantic paintings, through nineteenth-century prints and illustrations, to twentieth-century advertising and amateur photography.[5] Many today share with the Victorian middle class an attraction to the blond, blue-eyed, clear-skinned, and well-fed child and are appalled by, uninterested in, and even hostile to the dark, dirty, and emaciated child. Even when humanitarian groups try to shame us into giving money to support poor peoples far away, they usually show us an image of a smiling, olive-skinned (not black) girl, a close copy of our ideal of innocence.[6] Western society seems to require an image of purity. When the feminist revolution of the 1960s and 1970s removed that burden from women, it was shifted to the child.

In the film *Nine Months* (1995), a sophisticated, selfish, professional man drives away his pregnant wife because he fears impending fatherhood. Only when he sees his unborn child's ultrasound image does he learn that he would "win back his youth" rather than lose it with a baby. In *Baby Boom* (1987), a hardworking but unfulfilled thirty-something professional woman finds true happiness when a distant cousin, killed in a car accident, bequeaths to her a baby girl. In this movie the innocent child brings not perpetual youth but another, perhaps higher, goal—an escape from the rat race for the yuppie New Yorker. Through her child, she learns how to live simply in Vermont and find success starting a company that makes gourmet baby food. Whatever the problem, the child is the solution that brings the "happy ever after."

Our fascination with the pure child leads us to look for it within. It seems that the innocence deep in our psyches needs to be freed from the barnacles of life. To get in touch with these children within, we have to think, feel, and be like a child. This theme has long been a staple of pop psychology as, for example, in Hugh Missildine's *Your Inner Child of the Past* of 1963 and John Bradshaw's *Homecoming: Reclaiming and Championing Your Inner Child* of 1990. Regression is the only way to feel alive—to feel free to hate an abusive father and to freely love a mate. As the saying goes, "It's never too late to have a happy childhood."

Still, the innocent are more than "pure." Today they are also cute and spunky. Sitcoms often put the funniest lines in the mouths of four- or six-year-olds, leaving the wise adult to play the straight man. Even *I Love Lucy*, the most popular TV comedy of its era, could be improved with the naive, seemingly unintended humor of Little Ricky. More recently, a whole movie could be built around the irony of a baby made to speak wisdom to the adults (*Guess Who's Talking*). For years, baby boomer parents have enjoyed the wisecracking Bart Simpson on TV and kids in movies like *Matilda* and *Home Alone* who get the best of cynical and stupid adults. Many drew the line at *South Park* or *Bevis and Butt-Head*, whose youthful characters went too far by discarding the cute and instead becoming cool and rebellious. But most delight in seeing the adult "humanized" and even humiliated by the child.

Innocence, however, has always been fragile—like the proverbial "blossom of youth." It inevitably ends—until fairly recently, often in sudden death or by the need to work. For the most part, modern parents in the rich countries have been able to protect their young from premature maturity. No one wants their children to remain forever childlike—we hope that our Wendys eventually leave the nursery—but we do not want to rush the process. Today, however, we feel tremendous forces pulling our kids into adulthood. This comes not so much from the dangers of death and labor as from the commercial culture from which there is no escape: "latchkey children" watch late afternoon shock TV where transsexual "trailer trash" fight onstage over their lovers before cheering crowds. In 1996, notables from both the Right and the Left demanded that the television industry stop targeting adult programs to youth and instead help parents monitor kids' viewing with content warnings. They even demanded that the networks restore the family hour in prime-time evening schedules. Whereas local authorities once required that *Playboy* and *Hustler* be shrink-wrapped and displayed above the sight line of children, on-line cyberporn has become a click away, accessible to any kid who can spell "sex."[7]

Over the years, we have witnessed wave after wave of fearful warnings that someone or something was threatening the innocence of our children. In a recent study, nine out of ten Americans said it was harder to raise "good people" today than it was twenty years ago, and two in three felt that they were doing a worse job as parents than had their own mothers and fathers. We are anxious for children's safety and future, and we try to protect them from molesters in our neighborhoods: Megan's law, a popular regulation named after a victim of molestation, forces convicted child sex offenders to register their movements after prison. We use computer programs to shield the young from sex on the Internet; we insist on posted warnings to protect minors from sexuality in music and movies; we demand "V-chips" in new TV sets to block out offensive programs from the eyes of our kids. Some subscribe to William Bennett's weighty moral ballasts against the decadence that threatens the young.[8] Outsiders seem to prey on our children's imaginations and desires. Conservatives like Michael Medved attack secularism in the media and the breakdown of parental authority; libertarians and parent advocates call for homeschooling; and liberals like Cornel West and Hillary Clinton insist on more gun control.[9]

At times this impulse to protect has taken extreme, even bizarre, forms. Recall the 1983 McMartin day care case in which a mother (later to be diagnosed as suffering from acute paranoid schizophrenia) accused a male child care worker of sodomizing her son and forcing him to participate in satanic rituals. Egged on by police and child welfare investigators, youngsters from this day care center led authorities to file 353 counts of alleged abuse. A series of trials lasted seven years but produced no convictions.[10] This extraordinary witch-hunt may not have resulted in anyone being burned at the stake (just lengthy imprisonment for some of the accused), but it was an embarrassment to American justice. This case and others like it produced a healthy skepticism about investigative methods used to evoke horrid memories in toddlers. It also revealed a deep anxiety about predators lurking out there beyond the loving care of the family and home. Even though the most common abuse came from within the family, Americans could and did believe these outrageous stories. This is not really surprising given the sharp increase of children in day care, a practice that broke so sharply from traditional parenting and caused so many to feel guilty.

More often, we see a threat to innocence in media violence. There certainly is nothing new about exposing children to murder on the screen. How many space aliens or Indians did today's parents and grandparents see killed on TV and in the movies? Naturally, we insist that the media violence in the past was tame, even harmless, because the bad guys always lost and good prevailed. Today, media and video game violence seems to be pure mayhem, a deadly mix of blood, sex, and humor that desensitizes and/or makes the young feel the world is a cruel and dangerous place.[11]

While we long to protect the young, sometimes we also fear them when they do not fit our image of innocence. We have such high expectations that when children do not conform, they become fallen angels. For decades we have tried to shelter our children from the temptations of the street (or more recently TV and computer screens); but we also want to shield them from other young people who have given in to those temptations. Very often we see danger in the faces of poor and minority teenage males (whose lack of self-discipline all too often, we believe, is the cause of their failure to climb out of poverty and discrimination). While many whites fear young black males on the street, adults in general are almost as uneasy near teenagers of whatever race when they gather in crowds. In the 1990s the Mall of America, in Bloomington, Minnesota, responded to this anxiety by requiring children less than sixteen years old to be accompanied by an adult on weekends. To break up a throng of kids congregating at the entrance to a mall in Australia, management continuously played a Bing Crosby song![12]

Talk shows and popular magazines tell us that most sex offenders started as teenagers and that teens are the main drug pushers. To nip this danger in the bud, state legislatures have mandated lengthy suspensions for children bringing pocket knives or even fingernail files to school. High school girls have been suspended for carrying Advil or Midol in their backpacks (for violating drug rules). One six-year-old received the same punishment for kissing a classmate on the cheek (deemed to be sexual harassment).[13] Schools today may less often use corporal punishment to control the puerile mob, but they have "zero tolerance" for policies for almost anything that even remotely suggests sex, drugs, or violence.

This overkill is in part a response to a wave of seemingly random acts of violence perpetrated by kids. It was easy to see the brutal murder of a toddler by two ten-year-old boys from Liverpool, England, in 1993 as an "inexplicable act of evil." A few years later, in Norway, three six-year-olds battered to death a five-year-old girl, and in Chicago, boys of ten and eleven years dropped a five-year-old fourteen stories to his death after he refused to give them candy. And then there were the school shootings. In 2000 a boy shot a girl in a first-grade classroom. In the United States in 1997 alone, twenty students were killed and forty-seven wounded by classmates. Few cared about street killings (the 11,000 suicides or homicides in two years involving American children), but guns in school represented a defilement of the nation's secular temple.[14] We resent and fear the young when they threaten our illusions about the purity of childhood, and it has become easy to react with calls for old-time discipline. In the wake of a mass killing of high school students in Littleton, Colorado, the state legislature of Oklahoma passed a bill reminding parents of their legal right to paddle their children.[15] Spare the rod, spoil the child—and make them into killers!

As if to protect our image of the innocent child, we purge ourselves of the young who do not fit that ideal. Thus, authorities send children as young as fourteen to adult courts for violent crimes. It has become easy to see "the face of Satan" in teenagers who kill parents or classmates. Since the 1970s a steady stream of stories and movies about young people possessed by the devil (*The Exorcist*, 1973; *Carrie*, 1975; and *The Shining*, 1980) has resurrected the archaic idea of the "bad seed," a dark and scary version of the religious idea of original sin. These monsters are somehow unique—an inexplicable and rare evil—and have nothing in common with our innocent kids despite their tender years.

Even when we affirm childhood innocence, we find ourselves utterly confused about when it ends and who has it. Up to what age should a child be protected from the temptations and manipulations of adults? When is a child responsible for his or her actions? Answers seem to be shifting, without any really clear rationality. Increasingly, children are given the rights of adults in child custody trials (as in the well-publicized case of Kimberly Twiggs, who switched between natural and adopted parents in the 1990s); they are assumed to be free agents like consumers with rights of choice; and, of course, they are held responsible for violent crimes. Far less often than a generation ago do juvenile courts act as substitutes for the loving arms of parents, showing care and understanding for the wayward child. In today's radically individualistic society, no one is spared the cold wind of equality before the law. You do the time if you do the crime, even if you are a child. At the same time, the underaged are protected from sex, tobacco, and alcohol.

Thus a fifteen-year-old boy having sex with a female teacher is a victim, whereas the ten-year-old killer is a criminal. The former is a child; the latter is not. Does this make sense?

Our confusion about the dividing line between childhood innocence and adult responsibility permeates contemporary culture. Especially problematic are the "tweens," those children between eight and fourteen years of age who are neither dependent children nor relatively autonomous teenagers. We read about how ten-year-olds who once frolicked at hide-and-seek or played with dolls or toy trucks now try to look like a Lolita or street toughs —the child's version of the cool. In the past we might have expected this from working-class or minority neighborhoods, whose parents presumably failed to protect their children from evil. Today, it seems, we see the same kind of rebellious behavior of children from college-educated, even church-going, suburbanites. The rush into the peer and consumer culture of the teenage years excites marketing executives, who lust after the increasingly generous allowances of the twenty-seven million tweens in America. In 1999, ten-year-old Americans spent nearly fourteen dollars a week on themselves. Marketers have decided that the best way to reach the tweens is to assume that they want to be like their cynical, rebellious, sexualized older brothers and sisters. And they may be right, no matter what parents might think.[16]

Busy parents, guilt-ridden for spending so little time with their kids, often spend money on them instead, accelerating the rush into "tween" consumerism. While parents may be proud that their children know what they like at the mall, social critics wonder whether cultivating this skill may give the young a false sense of power, a distorted view of money, and, most of all, a jaded understanding of life and thus a premature loss of innocence. Similarly, adults push children out of childhood and live through their successes. We have only to recall the tragic death in 1996 of a seven-year-old girl urged by her father to break the record as the youngest person to pilot an airplane across the country.[17]

Ironically, noted an English journalist, "children may hurdle into a fake adulthood, grow old without growing up, and look back sentimentally at the childhood they never had." Many adults admire the freedom of youth and turn it into a lifestyle rather than a life stage. The childlike persona of the veteran rock star Michael Jackson may seem extreme to many. Still, an ad for a sporty car in 2003 promises to be "there" for boylike men "on that long road to maturity." And so these adults delude themselves into thinking that youth can be bought and preserved with Oil of Olay age-defying beauty cream or even regained with Rogaine to restore lost hair. Yet, as adults long for their carefree youth, kids often pine for the security of family and the attention of grown-ups. Thus, we have created a curiously contradictory culture of "jaded children and youth-hungry adults."[18]

How do we grapple with our confusion about what innocence really is and how to protect it? Surely we must begin with a more serious understanding of childhood and how modern culture has influenced it. Cultural critic Neil Postman provides one interpretation. He argues that modern society has eliminated the distinction between children and adults, thus reducing life stages to three—infancy, child-adults, and senility. When kids and grown-ups share a common culture through TV, movies, and the Internet, the enchantment that childhood once held disappears. Postmodern culture is propelling us back into the Middle Ages, where kids were precocious and adults childlike. Postman insists that the mark of the modern world—literacy and the barrier that it created between children and adults—has declined with the coming of electronic media. No longer must children wait until they have learned how to read to gain access to adult "secrets." The young seem to have lost their sense of wonder and curiosity, becoming jaded and cynical at increasingly early ages, and have failed to develop the self-control and responsibility that presumably formerly defined adulthood.[19]

One of the most sophisticated explanations of lost innocence, Postman's theory goes beyond the self-serving blame game in the culture wars between the secular Left and religious Right. He sees the problem as more complex than too many guns or video games. And he recognizes the powerful implications of a culture that no longer shelters the young from that culture. Nevertheless, Postman still assumes that the threat to childhood comes primarily from outside forces. He finds the culprit in the dark depths of technological change and mass media. And, by implication, the only way to protect innocence is to severely limit the influence of these forces outside the home.

This is a natural response. The media and politicians have long fed our anxieties about sexual predators, peddlers of violent video games and real weapons, and pushers of drugs, tobacco, sex, and other commercial addictions. They aggressively publicize dramatic, but rare, outbreaks of youth violence like the killings at Columbine High School in 1999 or the abduction of Elizabeth Smart in 2002. Moreover, these concerns are real in a mobile society, where parents have little control over their offsprings' contacts, and markets for almost everything are practically unrestricted. Inevitably, we ask: How do we protect children's innocence when they face so many external threats?

The problem may be the question itself. It assumes that "innocence" is a self-evident characteristic of children and that forces outside the family threaten it. In fact, we adults and parents have created the idea of the innocent child, and we undermine it with our very own actions. Our dilemma goes way beyond the threat of the pied pipers of a popular culture who peddle disrespect, violence, crude sexuality, materialism, and unchained desire. The solution certainly cannot be found in merely purging youth of the bad apples. The difficulty lies much closer to home. Ordinary well-meaning adults are part of the problem and any solution.

Let us begin by looking at our contradictory behaviors: We see childhood as timeless, yet we shower the young with fads and innovation. We take delight in the dependent, sweet child and despair when our indulgences seem to create the independent, jaded teenager. We buy more things for the little ones at birthdays and holidays than research shows they want, and then we fret when older children seem so insatiable.[20] We fill children's rooms with TVs and other electronic gadgets and then wonder that we have little knowledge of what they do behind closed doors. We keep our offspring off the street and give them TV and computers instead. We want kids to be kids, and yet we force our young into early adulthood when we introduce them to the consumer market. We enjoy some children's fantasies, like those presented by Disney and Children's Television Workshop, but find other kinds bewildering or even threatening, like the dark violence of many action-figure lines and video games. We forever look for threats to innocence, and yet we are not sure just what innocence is.

How can we be so confused? One obvious problem is that innocence has different meanings and origins, leading us in very different directions. First, an older view that I call "sheltered innocence" is that children are "blank slates." This provocative and slightly condescending image of the pure child was popularized by the seventeenth-century English philosopher John Locke. It undermined the Christian doctrine of original sin and transformed child rearing from an alternatively neglectful and oppressive regimen into a systematic effort to isolate and train the young. Locke still thought that children were susceptible to temptations and to corruptions.[21]

Schools, along with many parent and youth groups, have adopted this strategy of sheltered innocence. Scout camps and educational toys, as well as children's museums and churches, are all supposed to build skills and character while isolating the child. Today, organized play dates, Little League, ballet, and computer camps may seem to undermine playfulness. Still, parents are merely trying to protect innocence by walling off childhood from the threat of the Other, those kids who cannot and will not fend off the allures of unfettered and purposeless pleasure.[22]

We have a stake in this idea of sheltered innocence. It is the foundation of a proven way of rearing self-disciplined children. By regulating their access to a commercial popular culture that by its very nature encourages immediate gratification and prematurely introduces the young to grown-up desires and behaviors, adults try to prepare the young later for rational self-restraint. Sheltered innocence even helps adults protest the impersonal market and imagine a world beyond buying, selling, and producing. Children, by their inexperience, represent a cherished world free from the calculating domain of commerce and compulsive work. By protecting them from that world, we preserve a bit of time and (in the child-focused home) space where that realm of rational and selfish modernity does not intrude. Children remind us that "Yes, Virginia, there is a Santa Claus." They can inspire us to seek a higher value than free markets, and so we try to protect the young from drugs, violence, and tobacco. But the idea of sheltered innocence also makes it easy for us to delude ourselves into believing that threats to this ideal come from outside our homes and ourselves.

Most important, the sheltered child explains only part of our feelings toward kids. It is challenged by a more modern meaning of the unsullied child that fits less comfortably with our cherished views and is far more troubling—innocence as wondrous desire. This is a vision of childhood that denies self-mastery and development; most important, despite the influence of mass media and commercial culture, it comes not from outside but ultimately from within the home in the attitudes and behaviors of parents. Its origins lie deep in the emotional needs and desires of parents to find joy and pleasure in the delight of children who by their fresh (innocent) encounter with the world recall the wonder that adults often feel they have lost.

There seems to be a shift from sheltered to wondrous innocence. Since the eighteenth century, adults have found psychological refuge in the mystique of childhood. The romantic image of timeless youth is a lasting legacy of Victorian culture. From those times, we learned to believe that children see with different eyes, that they, unlike jaded adults, recognize nature's beauty and can teach us a simple and true sympathy for God's creation. The fact that this image of the wondrous child coexisted with much overwork and neglect of real Victorian children only confirms that it was a cultural ideal, constructed by adults seeking to recover wonder in their own lives, not necessarily to preserve it for all children.

However, the twentieth century redefined the meaning of wondrous innocence in important ways. The romantic's pure child became cute. First, it was no longer confined to romantic art and literature or to the lives of the privileged minority. It became an essential part of the rituals of middle-class child rearing. Most important, more indulgent styles of parenting and new kinds of consumption increasingly shaped what was innocent and wonderful about children. Earlier beliefs in the child's capacity for seeing the delights of nature took on new meanings when those delights became the pleasures of encountering a fantastic world of new goods and entertainments. Inevitably, childhood wonder and spending on kids became the same thing. The child's "secret garden" of innocence was increasingly filled with the images and values of an emerging consumer culture. And, like the Victorian's natural world of the child, this new world of fun and fantasy became a place that adults wanted to enter, too. Parents indulged their young with an ever-changing and growing array of toys, dolls, and storybooks, but they also fulfilled their own needs for release from the constraints of work and responsibility by viewing and vicariously enjoying their offspring's carefree play. Through spending on children, parents temporarily entered an imaginary world of childhood fantasy free from the fear and tedium of change. They recovered their lost worlds of wonder through the wondrous innocence of their children's encounter with commercial novelty. Adults found refuge in the mystique of childhood, but a very special kind of childhood, defined and experienced through consumer culture.

The merging of children and consumption challenged and transformed the older image of the sheltered child. The young became a reason to spend, but they also became a caution against an overcommercialized society. Children had to be sheltered from excessive commercialism and its moral dangers not only for their own sake but for society as a whole. Without realizing it, children became a kind of "valve" for adults, both opening and restricting consumption. Wondrous and sheltered innocence coexisted in an uncertain balance. The desire of adults to escape into a world of childish wonder and to embrace the image of the cute ultimately meant that adults lost control of that wonder and led them to frustrating efforts to shelter the child.

Wondrous innocence had several meanings and ramifications. First, it meant finding, even awakening, wonder and desire in the young. One of the greatest pleasures of modern parenting became the act of giving children fresh and unexpected pleasures—handing an ice cream cone to a surprised toddler in the 1900s or taking a youth on an adventure to Disneyland in the 1950s. This joy became the centerpiece of Christmas and birthday giving. In return, the giver expects to feel pure delight, an emotion long lost in his or her own encounter with consumer goods. While consumer culture constantly produces the new and exciting, it also generates boredom and disappointment in the fashions or flashy cars that the consumer had once so longed for. Its goal is not to satisfy so much as to create the need for more, potentially leading to obsession or even addiction. Ironically, by introducing the child to consumption, adults overcome, if only temporarily, their own frustration with that very culture of spending. The awakened look of wondrous innocence in the "gifted" child returns adults to the Garden of Eden of pure desire, a dreamworld where no one is jaded or obsessed. Unfortunately, the wide-eyed innocent quickly became the bored and unappreciative brat when repeatedly exposed to the wonders of modern consumption.

Second, parents' gifts introduced their young to a fantasy world that realized adult needs for coping with change. Wondrous innocence often meant cloaking children in the mysteries of timelessness. The camera, for example, promised to freeze time in the snapshot of the child. The teddy bear suggested a "natural," unchanging realm of childhood. At the same time, adults offered youngsters gifts of novelty—the latest toy or media fad, the pogo stick or talking doll. Innocence implied fresh encounters with the new and adults celebrated the fact that children were the future by giving them playful novelties. Adults learned to cope with the new by giving it to their children. All this brought together opposites—timelessness and hypertimeliness—between which adults were unwilling to choose. As a result, wondrous innocence became boundless fantasy, fixed by neither the real past nor the probable future, an escape for adults, but also often a confusing way of introducing the young to the real world.

Third, the look of wondrous innocence or the cute came to imply a new tolerance for the "naughty" child. The mischievous Peter Pan in Neverland offered adults the vicarious joy of temporary freedom from the rules and routine of everyday life. The Kewpie and other "New Kid" dolls that parents gave their children in the early twentieth century featured eyes turned askance to suggest a slight naughtiness but also showed dimples and rosy cheeks that affirmed their basic decency. Parents accepted, even encouraged, their children to test boundaries when this meant naive and spontaneous play, thus allowing adults to vicariously participate in the "anarchic moment" of children's exuberant play. The naughty-but-nice theme is an old one, but it became more important in the twentieth century with more tolerant, indeed permissive, views of children. Everything from Freudian psychology and child-rearing manuals to family comic strips and Norman Rockwell illustrations encouraged this perspective. It reflected a new acceptance of the complexity of children and a more subtle reading of their developmental stages. But the secret power of the innocence of the naughty-but-nice youngster was that it gave vicarious pleasure to adults while giving kids freedom from adult control. The seldom acknowledged fact is this: Parents introduced kids to a fantasy world of desire, unbounded freedom, and even rebellion. Over the decades of the twentieth century, parents unwittingly became pied pipers to their own children, serpents to their little Adams and Eves.

An even more frustrating problem was that wondrous innocence slipped out of the control of parents. The images, goods, and rituals of a commercialized childhood led very subtly to a fantasy culture from which parents were excluded and which appeared to be anything but innocent. In effect, kids took over the secret garden and, with the help of fantasy merchants, largely locked their parents out. Fantasy, fads, and fascination with the boundary combined to transform children's culture. What had been the cute, ultimately controlled by parents, became the cool—the opposite of the cuddly and delightful. The first clear signs of the cool appeared among older boys in the 1930s with the appearance of dark science fiction stories and then in the 1960s and 1970s, when the cool look of Barbie and monster figures replaced baby dolls and Tinkertoys.

Adults responded to this apparent subversion of innocence by attempting to draw a line between permissive and dangerous fantasy and pleasure. Across the twentieth century, this took many forms—from regulating movies and enforcing dress codes and attempting to ban comic books and toy guns to protecting children from ad campaigns for alcohol and cigarettes. Often these "moral panics" were directed against minority or working-class "threats" to middle-class white youth, with their presumed taste for violent comic books and sensual rock music. At other times, efforts to shelter the innocent from pornography, tobacco, and even excessive advertising were a way of constraining the larger permissive and consumer culture.

The different meanings and rites of affirming childhood innocence inevitably produced confusion and conflict. The idea of innocence as shelter led to the removal of children from the workplace, the extension of compulsory education, and constraints on markets to protect the vulnerable young. This doctrine of sacred youth entitled parents to exercise a firm if gentle control over the culture and experience of their children. At the same time, however, the idea of wondrous innocence and the cute pulled children into the very heart of a new consumer market with few ties to the worlds of parents. This, in turn, unleashed a hedonistic spirit that often contradicted the developmental goals of the educator. Wondrous innocence met parents' (and often children's) emotional needs, but ultimately challenged adults' values and control. Adults looked for playmates in young children. But when kids no longer wanted to play their games and tried to be cool, parents saw them as troubled and potential victims of troublemakers.

"cool"

Adults face many questions: What is innocence? Why are they obsessed by it? When does it end, and when should it end? What does the fact that we ask these questions say about us and the culture we live in and create? Let us look for answers to these frustrating questions in the story of childhood innocence in this age of consumption.

# The Two Faces of Innocence

T oday's newspapers and magazines regularly feature stories about schools—reports on test scores, changes in the curriculum, proposed laws to raise academic performance—and the latest child-rearing findings, such as the impact of reading stories or playing classical music upon the later success of toddlers. An ad appearing in the summer of 2000 jokingly contrasted twin males separated at birth, one sent to a home where he was exposed only to fishing magazines, the other to parents who daily read to him the *Wall Street Journal*, with obviously contrasting results by the time they became adults. The first never left home (or fishing), and the second made millions and was surrounded by beautiful women. Everyone appreciates what children are exposed to.

At the same time, children's TV, beyond the toddler years, has been largely shorn of "educational" content and has little to do with growing up to success. From *Rugrats* to *SpongeBob SquarePants*, Nickelodeon and other TV channels offer children frenetic fantasy, where wisecracking characters bounce from one wild adventure to another with hardly an adult in sight. Kids today seem to live in a disjointed world of purpose and play, of preparation and personal gratification. Perhaps this is no different from how adults combine in blissful contradiction sobriety and seriousness in their daily business of making a living with an equally obsessive "childlike" joy in collecting dolls, playing kids' games, or listening to the popular music of their adolescence the minute they leave work for the day. But parents are disturbed when the contemporary standards of undirected consumption or violent play seem to overwhelm children's educational "work." They are frequently confused about how to balance serious effort with fun in their children's lives, especially when the ubiquitous commercial culture is so successful at the serious business of promoting fun. And, if they were honest, many parents might admit that they often do not want to assume this role. Let the schools do it!

In fact, these battles between consumerism and education have been with us for generations. Novelty toymaker Louis Marx said in 1955, "I don't go along with psychologists who want to sneak up on [children] and jam education into them through toys. . . . [Only] spinster aunts and spinster uncles and hermetically sealed parents who wash their children 1,000 times a day give educational toys." Marx was voicing the bias of a lifelong manufacturer of windup boxing Popeye figures and "Fort Apache" play sets. But millions of adults who identified with Tom Sawyer against Aunt Polly would have agreed with him.[1] They want their children to excel like Lisa Simpson, but they might secretly identify with Bart. Modern parents are continually torn between the "improving" and the playful image of the child.

In part, this fissure in the modern soul is simply part of what sociologist Daniel Bell called the "cultural contradictions of capitalism," a division between the work ethic and hedonism that has long been essential to the success of the modern enterprise economy. Modern economic progress has depended on both effort and desire, reason and imagination, work and gratification. But parents are still frustrated when they see this division in their children. That is nothing new, since these opposed cultures of training and play have battled for more than a century for the soul of the child-centered family. Adding to the confusion, training and indulgence have often been hard to distinguish. And the frustration is amplified by the fact that, at least at home around the TV, computer, and toy box, the improving ethic has largely fallen to a fun morality. In the process, the very meaning of innocence has changed: the idea of sheltered innocence, with its insistence on effort, reason, and work, has ceded much influence to wondrous innocence, with its appeal to desire, imagination, and gratification. While this is especially the story of middle-class families, it shapes also the expectations of many other Americans.

## The Shaped Child

In 1900, Ellen Key declared that "through our posterity, which we ourselves create, we can . . . determine the future destiny of the human race."[2] Key was a widely read Swedish advocate of a controversial list of "progressive" ideas: wages for mothers, homeschooling, and even eugenics. For her, the future depended on society recognizing the possibility of transforming humanity into a race of confident, competent, and contented people, not through religious conversion or political revolution but through the careful nurture of children.[3] She was a militant in the church of the sheltered innocent.

Emphatically, Key argued, child rearing required the full attention of mothers, who should not divert their attention with outside jobs or social or political activities. Key insisted on "teaching the child to get him under control." But, like many advocates of the trained child, she was no strict disciplinarian and opposed the repressive attempt to "root out passions altogether." Instead, the child must have the freedom to "enter into relations with his own infinite world, to conquer it, to make it the object of his dreams." The child should not be subject to adults' petty tyrannies. In fact, "only the people who can play with children are able to educate them," she insisted. "The mother should feel the same reverence of the unknown worlds in the wide-open eyes of her child that she has for . . . heaven."[4] For Key, the child was to be trained for a glorious future but also allowed to find his or her own way to that future. If this was not a contradiction, it certainly suggested a very difficult balancing act. It required the parent to mold the child like clay but also to let the child blossom like a flower. This encouraged a willful individualism in both the parent and child, often with conflicting results.

Key's dual ideal was a culmination of a historic campaign for the child-molded and child-centered family. It is useful to return briefly to the oft-cited founders of the idea of the innocent child, the philosophers John Locke and Jean-Jacques Rousseau. In his famous essay *Some Thoughts Concerning Children's Education* (1693), Locke insisted that adults set examples for children "of those things you would have them do or avoid." He recognized the cognitive and emotional differences between adult and child and yet believed that children could be reasoned with at their level. He also held that children should learn through play: Parents should encourage "gamesome humour," well adapted to the child's "age and temper." This appeal to reason and play challenged the traditional view that children were born into original sin and had to be broken like animals to serve the needs of adults. Nevertheless, Locke hardly argued that children were inherently good or without antisocial desires. Rather, he insisted merely that they were at birth intellectually blank slates that could be written upon with selected lessons of experience. He still believed in the old doctrine that the young seek "dominion" over others, evident in the smallest infants: Obstinate behavior or crying "should by no means be permitted because it is but another way of flattering their desires and encouraging those passions which it is our main business to subdue." Far from assuming that the young knew their own needs and that parents were obliged to let them express them, Locke held that the young must be shaped and sheltered: "Children must leave it to the choice and ordering of their parents what they think properest for them. . . . [T]he wants of fancy children should never be gratified in." Even play, he believed, "should be directed towards good and useful Habits."[5]

The eighteenth-century French thinker Jean-Jacques Rousseau, often seen as the father of permissive parenting, insisted that children be sheltered from sexual and other desires so that they might learn to raise impulse to a higher cultural level. According to this view of innocence, children must be isolated so that they can follow their inner talents. Rousseau rigorously contained liberty within the walls of the home, nursery, school, and supervised play. Sheltered freedom, he insisted, taught the young self-mastery and allowed them to learn nature's law of freedom within limits.[6]

According to Locke, Rousseau, and their followers, the young needed to be sheltered from disorder and bad people in order to learn how to function effectively in the adult world. Purposeful play facilitated these goals. Later disciples like Maria and Richard Edgeworth promoted the use of balls, kites, pasteboard, and other "toys which afford trials of dexterity and activity." Still, these authors opposed filling children's heads with the dreamworlds and violence of fairy tales. In the 1820s, the American author Samuel Goodrich reinforced this emphasis on rationality and useful knowledge with a series of books featuring the geography and history lessons of the grandfatherly Peter Parley. This belief in the need to shelter and cultivate the child meant not freedom but adult manipulation and even repression in the name of preparing the intellectually malleable, but willful and vulnerable, child for a morally upright and socially useful adulthood.[7]

Locke's developmentalist view prevailed over more traditional religious views in the early decades of the nineteenth century. Evangelical Christians, then as now, insisted that a child's will be broken, not bent, because they still believed that infants were born with original sin. From the 1830s until the 1860s, child-rearing manuals told parents that the young were plastic creatures who could and should be strictly trained to religious uprightness and rational habits with the use of the rod, if necessary. However, the admonition to break the child's will with strict discipline and religious indoctrination gradually gave way to the ideas of reformers like the American Protestant theologian Horace Bushnell, who believed that the nurturing moral and religious example of the "genuinely Christian parent" would create a generous and sympathetic as well as upright child."[8] Personal happiness and material success gradually displaced religious concerns in child rearing, and by the 1870s, authorities insisted that parents try to understand their children's inborn personalities in order to shape them and win their obedience.[9]

This change was more than a victory of an educational philosophy. It reflected new middle-class family goals. Beginning with the bourgeois Victorian, parents saw childhood as too precious to be squandered at wage work. Adults had to protect their innocent offspring from public life. Only after protracted training could the young avoid the pitfalls of, and gain the skills necessary to succeed in, that adult world of the market. This transformation was subtle and gradual. In the middle class, the age at which a child was expected to work outside the home had already risen into late adolescence and beyond by 1900. The number of Americans attending high school rose from 110,000 in 1900 to almost 4.4 million by 1930.[10]

Caring parents, who by definition kept their offspring off the job market, said to themselves that their children brought not money but meaning, love, and vitality to the home. Sheltered innocence guaranteed that the home was a refuge from the cash nexus. Society increasingly condemned as cruel and selfish those parents who forced their offspring to take jobs. This attitude reflected more than the fact that children (especially in the middle classes) were less necessary in the industrial economy or that additional schooling was becoming essential for success. Rather, the middle-class rejection of child labor reflected a profound cultural shift— the sacralization of the youngster at home.

This view of childhood advanced on many fronts: Between 1880 and 1930, states raised the so-called age of consent for girls from as young as ten to sixteen or even eighteen years, extending the presumed age of innocence and making even "voluntary" sex below that year "statutory rape."[11] Similarly, juvenile courts, instituted first in 1899 in Illinois, made the state a superparent. The same movement for protecting children led to a federal law in 1916 banning children less than fourteen years old from factory work (even though this law was soon overturned in the courts). Far from the workplace, in the warmth of the domestic circle, the child would become the parents' handiwork, chiseled into a secure and unique individual, free from the premature influences of the market.[12]

## The Romantic Ideology of the Wondrous Child ②

A still more radical view of the child paralleled and ultimately challenged the goal of sheltered innocence. A far more romantic perspective emerged when painters and poets saw children as fonts of a joy and wisdom not found in the adult world. The young had become the embodiment of a positive natural life, a force to be evoked and captured, not merely a potential to be shaped. Rather than reason with the child and devote young life entirely to training in good habits, the child should be allowed to explore feeling and, most of all, be happy. Although an advocate of the sheltered and shaped child, Rousseau also shared much with this romantic tradition when he wrote: "Why rob these innocents of the joys which pass so quickly, of that precious gift which they cannot abuse? Why fill with bitterness the fleeting days of early childhood, days which will no more return for them than for you?"[13] In his "Ode on Intimations of Immortality from Recollections of Early Childhood" (1804), William Wordsworth boldly proclaimed, "Trailing clouds of glory do we come from God who is our home: Heaven lies about us in our infancy!" But soon that blessed state fades:

> The Youth, who daily farther from the east
>     Must travel, still is Nature's Priest,
>     And by the vision splendid
>     Is on his way attended;
> At length the Man perceives it die away,
> And fade into the light of common day.[14]

Newborns were no longer "blank slates" to be guarded from dangerous desires and prepared rationally for adulthood, or children of Adam to be broken, but, in the words of historian Hugh Cunningham, "the spring which should nourish the whole life. If adults do not keep the child in them alive, they will become dried up and embittered."[15] Adults must go to these purifying waters of youth regularly to be renewed. The doctrine of original sin was transformed: The expulsion from the innocence of the Garden of Eden no longer takes place before birth in the disobedience of Adam and Eve but "happens" to the innocent child when the young person is corrupted by the "fallen" world of adults. The young still need to be protected, of course, but less against inborn antisocial desires than from the dulling effect of ordinary life that deprives them of a divine vision of the world. No longer are the mature sanctified through their years of struggle against temptation and drawn close to God as they successfully climb the long hill to salvation. Rather, children reflect the countenance of God with what William Blake calls "visionary simplicity." American essayist Henry David Thoreau made the same point a half century later: "Every child begins the world again."[16] By the nineteenth century, children's birthdays became times of celebration in the middle-class home. Parents were expected to actually enjoy the company of their children. This romantic view made the "naturalness" of the unsullied child the model of happiness for all.[17]

The message was clear: Adults must cherish this revelatory image of the child in paintings and literature and capture and even evoke it in the joys of child-centered family life. The image of the delighted child increasingly delighted adults. From the mid–seventeenth century, Dutch paintings of family scenes had begun to feature ordinary children in real-life situations. For example, Jan Steen's *Eve of Saint Nicholas* showed the glee of children receiving gifts of toys and candy—and the horror of a bad boy given a birch rod. With the paintings of William Hogarth in the 1730s and those of Thomas Gainsborough and Joshua Reynolds somewhat later, images of youngsters playing with kittens and bringing joy in informal family settings became common in Britain. No longer were children portrayed simply as small adults or seen only in allegorical roles (as angels, mythological figures, or the baby Jesus). Instead, they were lovingly shown as distinct personalities with their own "innocent" looks of wonder and affection. Commenting on the new style in family portraiture, English historian J. H. Plumb notes, "The implied happiness of the husband and wife with their children [marks] a vital social change in eighteenth-century life."[18] Increasingly in the nineteenth century, artists celebrated children in their "natural" pursuits—laughing, blowing bubbles, even fighting with each other. John Millais's *Bubbles* and *Cherry Ripe* were perhaps the most famous of these paintings—and the most often copied.[19]

What made the "natural child" so compelling? William Blake offers us a clue when he wrote that children are born "in pleasure which unsought falls round [their] path."[20] The innocent know the pure delight of the senses not simply because they are free of knowledge and prejudice but because this pleasure is "unsought." They experience nature beyond desire, and their feelings of wonder are thereby free from the obsession and disappointment that come with the older person's real experience of longing. What makes children attractive is their ephemeral joy, their delight free from desire, but which, as pleasure, inevitably creates desire. This was the essence of wondrous innocence.

The look of the child became the look of wonder. Lorraine Daston and Katharine Park tell us that the Enlightenment and its scientific view of nature and bureaucratic vision of society greatly narrowed the feeling of wonder. The Latin equivalent, *mirabilia*, which became both the marvelous and the miraculous in English, has roots in the Indo-European verb *miror* (smile). The look and feeling of wonder encompassed a response to the "outmost limits" of knowledge and possibility that rejected any distinction between the natural and supernatural.[21] Because wonder was lost when the natural world became the object of control and systematic reason, the look and feeling shifted to the child. Wonder became less an encounter with the uncommon or novel in the world (insofar as these became ordinary for most moderns) and more the response of the innocent to that world. Jaded adults can recover the lost magic of wonder in the "smile" of the child as she or he encounters nature. That look can lift the weight of dullness and boredom in adults and liberate them from obsession and fear. The child has not yet learned to split the sacred from the profane and thus can still see the supernatural in the natural world. Children's images in the nineteenth century were "otherworldly," notes art historian Anne Higonnet, in part because children could still enjoy an "untrammeled intimacy with nature."[22]

In the nineteenth century, as wonder was banished from the world of adults, it gradually became infantilized. Literary fantasy, which adults had traditionally enjoyed, was increasingly shifted to children. These stories challenged the moralistic and didactic literature that warned and informed the child. Beginning with fairy tales, American children obtained access to a world of pure fantasy. Much of this came from Europe. Grimm's stories were translated into English in 1823, and Hans Christian Andersen's in the 1840s. Time was ignored in the "imperishable world" of fairy tales, where the supernatural became natural, and even death was mere "sleep." Nothing was hidden, and all problems were resolvable. Of course, fairy tales were not mere wish fulfillment because cruelty and betrayal were common themes. But, if Cinderella was rejected by her stepmother and sisters, she was comforted by animals and trees, and evil like the witch in the tale of Hansel and Gretel ultimately consumed itself.[23]

The secret garden of children's fantasy reached its zenith in late Victorian literature: Lewis Carroll's *Alice in Wonderland* (1865) glorified a child's world where adult pretensions were mocked and a comic literalness was featured. A new acceptance of fantasy in children's literature emerged fully after 1860, paralleling a critique of industrial society. Think of *Treasure Island* (1883), *The Jungle Book* (1894), or *Pinocchio* (1883). And, at least in rich families, children increasingly had time and space for such stories.[24] In fact, the accounts of traditional folk heroes like Robin Hood and Saint George became enchanting when they were told to children. Similarly, mechanical figures, miniatures, and even ball games that had once edified or amused adults became the playthings of young people. Even the often violent and sensual rituals of carnival and mumming were tamed and then passed down to children. When adults abandoned these toys and games, their daily lives became more "serious." Still, on special occasions they could escape the world of rationality, competition, and achievement by joining their children in a world of play that had been transformed into innocent delight. Wonder was saved from rationality and progress when it was given to children. When parents said yes to fun for children, they accepted play that had a new purpose: It no longer had to teach discipline and skill, nor was it a carnivalesque disregard for rationality. Play instead could capture the essence and spirit of a youthful wonder that adults themselves desired.[25]

Children also represented wonder because they were still free from the flow of change. Wonder was "lost" over time (both as the individual matured and as "progress" disenchanted the world) but was continuously recovered in the eyes of each young child. The wondrous innocent gave delight and assurance to the anxious adult, fearful of the future and alienated from the past. As John Gillis has suggested, the timelessness of the young attracted a culture that had discovered the benefits of rational linear time but still wanted a refuge from the rush and uncertainties of the day-to-day. Adults projected onto the young a wondrous world that was an escape from the boring and often stressful realms of markets and work, the rationalized worlds of science and business.[26]

Inevitably, adults were attracted to the image of the wondrous child as savior, liberating the old from the sins of aging. In books like *Little Lord Fauntleroy* (1886) and *Rebecca of Sunnybrook Farm* (1903), adults embraced the idea not only that childhood was holy and should be preserved as long as possible but also that children were redeemers: The "Lord" Cedric is a plucky but lovable child with the spontaneous naturalness of his working-class upbringing on New York's Hester Street. He alone can make his crabby English aristocrat of a grandfather into a real human being.[27] The wondrous child was privileged—both more natural and closer to God than adults. The young were gatekeepers to an imaginative but simple world that contrasted with the daily experience of adults confronting routine and compromise. Adults projected onto the young a wondrous world that was, in reality, an escape from their boring and often stressful modern lives but that also renewed their sense of wonder.

This romantic image of the child did not stick simply because of its emotional appeal. It was the ironic product of modern capitalism and was nurtured by a relatively small number of propertied and professional families. As the modern factory, office, and store gradually pulled work and business out of homes, family residences became retreats from income-earning work, and children's labor became irrelevant to the family's survival. Inevitably, parents reduced the size of their brood: In 1800, American mothers bore an average of 7.04 children. That number dropped to 5.42 by 1851, to 3.56 by 1900, and

**2.1**

Little Lord Fauntleroy, dressed in adult-pleasing finery, softening the hard edges of his aristocratic grandfather with a natural act of kindness. Frances Hodgen Burnett, *Little Lord Fauntleroy*, 1913, 95. Reginald Birch, illustrator.

to a mere 2.9 children by 1930. Smaller families meant mothers could devote more time to nurturing each offspring. But at the very moment when serious attention to child rearing became a possibility, nurturing became problematic. Why should a couple have children when giving birth was increasingly a choice? The old view that offspring simply arrived disappeared in an age of "voluntary motherhood." Inevitably, child rearing became a "creative" project, especially for the mother, and, for some women, a compensation for a diminished role in economic and political life.[28]

This ideal of a nurturing, perhaps even indulgent style of child rearing conformed with the popular and growing belief that childhood should be a time of refuge from the pressures of industrial life. As the home became a less crowded workplace, it could become a retreat from neighbors and markets, and parents kept their children close to home and away from other adults.[29] No one thought it wrong for Wendy in *Peter Pan* to remain in the "nursery" until she was ready to leave it. This identification of the child with a retreat from the hurly-burly of public life was a long process that began with rich American-born whites and continues to this day. In working-class and especially immigrant and black families, children's income was vital for family survival, and thus the child-centered home remained unattainable. As late as 1900, working-class or African-American childhood frequently ended by age ten, when children were sent out to work. Nevertheless, the long-term trend for all American families was toward fewer offspring more protected from the world and thus fostering childhoods of wondrous innocence.[30]

Starting with the mid-Victorian middle class, parents, especially mothers, realized that their increased comfort made unnecessary some of the rigidity and austerity of their own childhoods in the new generation. Some mothers began to counter the competitive and materialistic ways of their husbands by embracing these romantic ideas about childhood as a time of imagination and freedom from the real world. As a result, childhood inevitably became more playful and centered on celebrations of fantasy as the nineteenth century wore on. Late Victorians, who felt uneasy about enjoying pleasure themselves, experienced it through their children. Parents could escape the outside world of economic calculation when they showered their children with gifts.[31]

## Consumption and Childhood Wonder ③

The late Victorian middle classes found a place for both sheltered and wondrous innocence. This dual relation with the next generation was given fresh meaning in the twentieth century, especially when childhood delight was wed to the world of consumption. At the same time as children were sheltered and removed from the producers' market, they became an essential part of the market of consumers, a world of delight. This was because parents began to use gifts of entertainment and goods to express the pricelessness of their children in their love and care for them. As Viviana Zelizer notes, couples chose to bear offspring as emotional assets that could best be "valued" when showered with things that evoked in children a response of wonder.[32]

One sign of this revolution in attitudes can be seen in what kind of child was desired in adoptions. Traditionally, couples preferred to take in an older, often male, youngster; they could be reasonably well assured that he was free from mental or physical "defects" and, even more important, could put him to work on the family farm or in the family business. The adopted child was an economic investment. A major change occurred when adoptive parents began to seek newborns. The demand for infants rose from 19 to 21 percent of adoptions during the 1930s to 48 percent in 1950, 68 percent in 1960, and 98 percent by the end of the 1970s. Increasingly couples wanted a baby who was "cute and cuddly," not an older child who might have been emotionally damaged by an orphanage or foster home. Adoptive parents tried to form a close psychological bond as early as possible and desired the emotional experience of caring for, and especially giving to, an infant. This shift reveals the influence of psychological expertise but also the changing purpose of children in adult lives. By the twentieth century, babies had to fulfill the deep emotional, even spiritual, needs of parents. They were no longer treated as deficits (burdensome expenses) or investments (future helpers and workers). Affluence created the opportunity for adults to protect the child from premature exposure to adult life. At the same time, this wealth encouraged parents to indulge their own fantasies through their children. In the process, children became increasingly expensive objects of affection—objects of spending, but with the goal of evoking innocent wonder.[33]

On its face, this trend might suggest simply a logical completion of the ideal of the sheltered child. But the sacralization of the young did not mean merely the child's exclusion from helpful labor or the cash nexus. It entailed a new relationship between parent and offspring. The purpose of the money exchange *between* adult and child changed but was not eliminated. In the nineteenth century, the "piggy bank" had been favorite gifts to children, a perfect expression of an older idea of childhood innocence; the piggy bank taught the cardinal virtue of thrift and prepared the young to enter the responsible adult world on terms "appropriate" for a child. In the early twentieth century, a new custom, the allowance, took the relationship between money and innocence in a new direction. Ostensibly, this weekly allotment to the child was supposed to teach money management, but it also suggested that the child had the right to "little pleasures" that parents had to provide. Money no longer was just about growing up (saving for the future) but also about immediate gratification, meeting desire, and even parents enjoying the satisfaction of the child's pleasure. The sheltered child became the wondrous child.

More important still, parents reintroduced the child to the economy via consumption that used the young to fulfill adult emotional needs. In many subtle ways, love and affection for the young were expressed through spending. This had been true generations before the modern consumer society. Anthropologists have long recognized how peoples of all cultures have exchanged material things to cement relationships. In the twentieth century, however, sentiment, always difficult to express without aid of ritual and special objects, found an outlet in consumer spending. Curiously, at first blush, intimate relationships, presumably the very antithesis of materialism, can be confirmed through the exchange of goods. This is no less true in the affection between parent and child. Adults love children, at least in part, because they love being loved by children, and, like it or not, that exchange of feeling is realized in material gifts. The distance between giving delight to the child with a birthday present and giving delight to oneself as the beloved parent is a short one.

This new role of consumption and affluence in twentieth-century American families transformed the nineteenth-century romantic idea of wondrous innocence in distinct ways. First, the romantic version that stressed the child's fresh encounter with nature became increasingly a response to consumer culture, in effect, a "second nature." If nineteenth-century romantics needed to see flowers or cascading waterfalls through the fresh eyes of the child, it was because their adult eyes had grown dull. Likewise, twentieth-century consumers needed to consume through the wondrous innocence of the child because their desire for things, even new and improved things, had grown flat. Thus, it may make sense that modern economics, first developed in the 1870s, was based on the declining "utility" or desire for things. Consumer goods, no matter how exciting and desirable at first, inevitably disappoint or, at least, lose their appeal with familiarity. Adults used the child to awaken their desire for desire itself in a consumer culture that ironically suppresses desire by its constant attempt to awaken and expand it. Youthful desire had not yet succumbed to the adult's descent into satiation and addiction. The child became the Edenic consumer, a reminder of a paradise lost to adults and redeemable only through the child. As the sociologist Colin Campbell notes, romantic ideas (expressed especially through the imagining of self in new and exciting situations) easily shifted to consumer longings (imaging oneself possessing or experiencing a commodity). The child's wonder of nature became the wonder of consumption to which adults introduced the young on a nearly daily basis by 1900.[34]

At the same time, by the end of the nineteenth century, the romance with children's fantasy began to reflect more than a longing for a refuge from change. Although a quest for timeless innocence hardly disappeared, the identification of the young with novelty and the future added a new feature strongly linked to consumerism. Adults continued to pass down toys, games, and holiday rituals from their youth to their children. They even dressed children in archaic clothing for special occasions.[35] Nevertheless adults tried to share with their children the excitement of participating in the here and now and in dreams of progress. The association of the young, especially those of reading age, with the timely was increasingly made in the late Victorian period. Board and card games, once moralistic or educational offerings like "The Mansion of Happiness" or "Authors," by the 1880s became expressions of the "latest thing." Many games celebrated contemporary world and travel themes. "Around the World with Nellie Bly" of 1887 drew on the famous young journalist's successful effort to circumnavigate the globe solo in fewer than the eighty days of Jules Verne's story. Fad toys and games have a long history, but there was an abundance of them in the early twentieth century. Ping-Pong, appearing in 1903, Diablo in 1907, and Rook in 1910 were not designed for children, but manufacturers often adapted them for the young, responding to a new willingness of adults to share novelty with their children.[36]

The romantic idea of timeless childhood and the commercialized timely fad for children were not always contradictory and sometimes even coincided. One example is the Brownies, Palmer Cox's Scottish elves, who first appeared in 1879 in an illustrated poem in the children's magazine *St. Nicholas*. Mary Dodge, the magazine's founder, rejected the old practicality and didacticism of the Peter Parley stories and instead published the playful Brownie stories, believing that a "child's magazine is its pleasure ground." Cox and Dodge straddled the moralistic past and the commercialized future. The Brownies, according to Scottish tradition, inhabited houses and expected treats in lieu of tricks. Rooted in folklore, they had an aura of timelessness. Yet, in Cox's hand, they were transported to urban America as pleasure-loving boylike figures and he made them into the subject of a commercially successful series of story books, dolls, toys, and novelty items. With their oversized heads and sticklike legs, they represented ethnic and other stereotypes (Irishman, Chinese, Arab, Dude, and Cowboy) who, resolved their differences in the shared boyhood joys of bicycling, canoeing, and ballooning. Despite their mythological origins and appearance, they were up-to-date adventurers flying airplanes and joining Teddy Roosevelt's Rough Riders. They might get into trouble, such as tipping over boats or falling into icy rivers, but they did good deeds and, through their adventures, taught children about geography and history. The end of the story often included a little moral "tag": "Both life and honor surely wait on him who's early at the gate."[37] Still, in a

**2.2**

The Brownies in all their modern variety, showing the magical fusion of the timeless past and exciting future as they venture onto new and dangerous flying machines. Palmer Cox, *The Brownies' Latest Adventures*, 1909, 44.

fantasy world, free of adults, they lived as a "gang." Cox blended many contradictory appeals, but he especially conjoined the traditional world of nostalgia and moral rectitude with the progressive realm of the new, the playful, and ultimately the commercial.

Another impact of early twentieth-century affluence and consumerism was a new more tolerant attitude toward children's behavior. At the end of the nineteenth century, the ideal of the angelic child certainly persisted in portraits of girls framed in oversized chairs, as a "doll-like bundle of white," and even boys were pictured in the formal dress of Little Lord Fauntleroy or archaic sailor suits. As historian Paula Fass notes in her study of kidnapping, the vulnerable child became the basis of a deeply emotional narrative in American culture.[38] Gradually, however, this image became more nuanced, incorporating more ambivalent and more rebellious streaks, even integrating a more "realistic" image of the child into the complex. Especially in boys, the ideal of the Little Lord Fauntleroy was hard to live up to, and that name became equated with the prissy, sissylike boy, like the expression "goody-two-shoes." In fact, years before the publication of *Little Lord Fauntleroy* in 1886, American literature openly acknowledged a boyhood far from angelic. Thomas Aldrich, in his nostalgic *Story of a Bad Boy* (1869), celebrated his own youth as a good-natured, disobedient child, "an amiable, impulsive lad, blessed with fine digestive powers, and no hypocrite." During summer vacations in New England, he learned from other boys that childhood was about vitality, fun, innocent enthusiasms, and affections that got him into trouble yet "naturally" led him to a successful and decent adulthood without formal "training." Mark Twain's *Tom Sawyer* (1876) and *Huckleberry Finn* (1884) also abandoned the old formula of moral improvement. Tom and Huck were "good bad boys," crude jokesters always getting into trouble. Tom had affection for his Aunt Polly but never let that determine his actions. His village classroom was in constant war between the schoolmaster and the pupils; even the church, like home and school, was the source not of value but of confinement. Tom and Huck possess an instinct for doing the right thing without any moralizing adult telling them what to do. A more open and affluent America made Twain's boys acceptable.[39]

These stories expressed more than increased adult toleration for the fantasy or even willful defiance of the child. They tell us about adults' nostalgia for the imaginary freedom of the child. As Jacqueline Rose notes, J. M. Barrie's *Peter Pan* began as an adult novel, and the play was at least as popular with grown-ups as with children through the 1920s. Pan recalled a Greek god of nature—half boy, half animal, a playful and adventurous antidote to the cramped reality of urban life and commerce in the 1900s. He was a wish fulfillment to millions of adults, especially men. The amoral celebration of chaos and rebellion in stories like *Peter Pan* was not cynical or even naturalistic. Because they take place in a child's world, these tales did not challenge the moral order. Instead, they were merely an "innocent" escape from traditional notions of sheltering and guiding the young.[40]

Subtly, Victorian attitudes toward the disobedient (especially male) child changed. He became less a rebel against heavenly or earthly fathers and more a curious, sensuous, unassuming boy behaving like most other boys. By the beginning of the twentieth century, the idea of wondrous innocence had shifted from the romantic infatuation with nature to the delights of consumption, from a fixation on a timeless past to a fascination also with the future, and from a vision of the angelic child to a recognition of the naturally impish youth.

## The Dilemma of the Child-Rearing Expert: 1900–1980 ③

Both the sheltered child advocated by Ellen Key and the wondrous youth of Peter Pan competed for the allegiance of American parents in the early twentieth century. An emerging group of child development professionals, however, saw this parity as a challenge and battled against wondrous innocence in the name of the shaped and sheltered child. Especially between 1900 and 1930, experts questioned the romantic and commercial implications of wonder, seeing them as threats to the rational development of the child. They called for the withdrawal of young people from the labor market but also resisted their introduction to the consumer market and tried to teach youngsters to be rational and adaptive within the laboratory settings of schools, professionally managed playgrounds, and properly equipped homes led by trained parents. While many middle-class parents embraced this strategy, they also introduced their offspring to a consumer culture that finally undermined this developmentalist ethic. In fact, far from defeating the romantic and commercial ideas of wondrous innocence, by the middle and late twentieth century, child care professionals like Benjamin Spock and Penelope Leach made concessions to wonder when they advocated "permissive" child rearing.

Emerging groups of professionals in the psychology and education of children were determined to reform child-rearing practices and enlisted parental allies in their quest for the well-trained youth. From as early as 1888, G. Stanley Hall's Child Study Association trained small groups of mothers in the science of child rearing.[41] This and similar groups insisted that children needed more than a loving caregiver who relied on traditional folkways to raise the next generation. Only a well-informed parent, trained by the professional, could successfully prepare small children during those critical years before they were turned over to the teacher. The U.S. government joined this effort in 1912 when it created the Children's Bureau, a research office that distributed large numbers of booklets on the most up-to-date methods of baby and child care. Aspiring immigrant and middle-class mothers embraced this information, eager to prepare their offspring for the modern competitive world. Popular women's magazines featured the latest in serious child-rearing advice, and in 1926 a group of child development professionals founded *Parents* magazine to popularize scientific child-rearing information to mostly middle-class Americans.[42]

This movement for sheltered innocence had a modern cast, emphasizing the roles of professionals and specialized sites of child formation like kindergartens, but it still relied on traditional home-based child training. The White House Conference on Child Health and Protection of 1930 idealized the mother at home who was to isolate but also expand the horizons of children, molding them for future success. Its "Children's Charter" insisted that the child should be protected from "labor that stunts growth" and be provided with an education that teaches the domestic virtues of "successful parenthood" and "homemaking." By their own example at home, parents must give children "training in the control of desires and appetites."[43]

In a complementary way, the progressive recreation movement tried to isolate and prepare the young in the regulated playground. From the 1870s, a small number of philanthropic men expressed concern that the new generation of youth (especially boys) growing up in unprecedented affluence was no longer being raised to be rational, self-controlled, and adaptive. As a substitute for the traditional challenges of a hostile natural environment, reformers advocated adult-managed play that would direct the potentially disruptive energy of youth into "productive" endeavors.[44] By 1900, reformers insisted that sports and other forms of directed recreation were no longer simply childish diversions set apart from the real world but were vital tools for preparing youth for adult life. This idea lay behind the curious practice of "preparing" boys and youth to become leaders by playing childish games like baseball and football or camping with the Boy Scouts. Square in the Lockean tradition of the sheltered and shaped child, the recreation movement assumed that training for modern adulthood was to take place in a world of youth, separate from real life.[45]

Both the child study and recreation movements danced on a narrow ledge: They encouraged parents to impose indirect and positive controls over their children but did so in order to develop the "unique" and "vital" personality of each child. They affirmed the Enlightenment ideal of the innocent child, sheltered from, and only gradually introduced to, the adult world. Only this protected youth could adjust with integrity to a demanding and changing world. Ideal places to realize these complex goals were home playgrounds with protected sandboxes, swings, and playhouses or playrooms with hygienic bare floors and walls painted in cheerful colors. Children with these sheltered play places and lots of good toys would not want to venture out to join street gangs or stray from becoming productive fathers and nurturing mothers.[46] The free child was to play, but with objects and in places selected by parents. The guiding concepts were indirect control and sublimation, not intrusive regulation. But play was only a means to an end, never the goal itself.

Given these views, then, how did child-rearing experts respond to the romantic and commercial image of "wondrous innocence"? Inevitably, they saw the commercial side of the child-centered culture as a threat to their vision of the developmentally protected child. They believed that advertisers of sweets, toys, and comic books violated an implicit contract with the parent to protect the sacred childhood of sheltered innocence. But they were not rigidly didactic and austerely rationalistic. Their challenging task was to teach parents to distinguish between productive imagination and commercial fantasy, between "constructive" and "escapist" play.

Adding to their difficulties, the experts revealed an often confused blend of up-to-date psychological theory and Victorian morality in teaching these lessons of good parenting. An influential English authority, Beatrix Tudor-Hart, insisted that a single doll or teddy bear, from which the child could not be separated, fostered the imagination and depths of feelings. Giving more toys might serve a parent's desire, but it frustrated the child's true needs for developing strong attachments and identity. The pioneer of the modern kindergarten movement, Patty Smith Hill, warned parents in 1914 that they should dole out playthings to meet changing developmental needs throughout the year, not lavish them at Christmas or birthdays.[47] The objective was to develop complex skills, independence, and tenacity, all of which challenged the emerging commercialism that encouraged "excess." In 1934, educator Ethel Kawin feared that consumerism and the novelty culture that it engenders "does not tend to produce rich, dynamic personalities or develop . . . socially constructive behavior."[48]

These experts fostered the modern psychological ideal of the integrated, adaptive personality, but another underlying value was the traditionalist doctrine of simplicity, an ideal that ran against the promises and temptations of an affluent age. Typical was this warning: If children were given too many toys, "their precious ability for enjoying the little things of life may be taken from them and a life of discontent is likely to follow." This thought echoes the traditional religious doctrine of concupiscence, the theory that individual desire grows out of control when a person is exposed to temptation.[49] In 1924 psychologist Benjamin Gruenberg defended the virtue of simplicity when he attacked the "acquisitiveness" of youthful collectors: "The collection may be the nucleus of a museum or of a competence; it may also be the beginning of a barbarous junk heap, or of miserliness." Too often, "false standards of value through the artificial emphasis upon rarities" led the child into a life of obsessive accumulation and other distorted values.[50] Only the developmental strategy could help children overcome their innate weakness and shelter them from temptation.

This stress on the old and on simplicity reflected the persistence of a Victorian and bourgeois ideal—that children should learn the virtue of caring for and respecting property, especially "quality" goods. The "right kind" of toys—simple, utilitarian, and "educational"—were simultaneously markers of scientific knowledge and middle-class taste. Middle-class professionals assumed that the unlearned masses were attracted to the cheap novelties of the new consumer culture and that middle-class children should be sheltered from its influence. Opposition to that culture blended bourgeois disdain for the mass market for novelty with desire to inculcate in children a love of the unique and lasting. The complex goals of modern psychological integration and Victorian ideals of simplicity, quality, and separation from the common culture inevitably confused and compromised the advocates of sheltered innocence.[51]

Equally contradictory was the simultaneous effort to shape the child and let her or him blossom according to her or his own inner self. This conflict was often resolved when the experts encouraged parents to indirectly control their children through playthings. The trained parent was to program play by preselecting toys and books that led children to develop specific skills and behaviors without constant parental coaching. After "careful observation," Patty Hill advised, adults could introduce appropriate items when the child was ready for them. These wisely selected toys allowed adults to rule while minimizing their confrontations with children.[52]

Experts were very suspicious of any objects that undermined the essentially manipulative, if benevolent and rational, relationship between adult and child. The problem was that consumer culture seemed to threaten this goal at every turn because it inevitably favored immediate gratification of the child, not the presumed developmental goals of parents. Moreover, commercialism appealed to emotions—the parent's as well as the child's—essentially subverting rationalist restraint implicit in the goal of sheltered innocence.

Child development experts relied on parents and the modern home to carry out their reform program of child rearing. Nevertheless, they realized that parents undermined their program of reform when they embraced consumerism. The experts expected adults to shelter and lead their children to the promised land of maturity. Still, consumerism encouraged adults to abdicate this role and to join the child in a fantasy world. Child-rearing manuals repeatedly warned against fathers playing with their children's toys and insisted that novelties were bad because they appealed not to the child's imagination but to the adult's amusement. They even disapproved of parents

**2.3**

The 1960s culmination of the ideal of play as an educational venture, an appeal against the commercialized fantasy of most toys of the time. Lego ad, *Parents*, Dec. 1966, 43.

and children playing together for the sake of togetherness rather than a developmental goal.[53]

Despite gallant efforts, this rationalist view of child rearing, with its ideal of the sheltered and shaped child, was never able to defeat the ideas and practices of wondrous innocence in the world of consumption and home life. Its inherent asceticism and elitism, shared with the wider culture of gentility, gradually lost its hold on its middle-class audience.[54] This was in part because economically secure parents wanted both to join in childhood fantasy and to enjoy the emotional relationship with their children that wondrous innocence brought. As important, most of the experts were themselves torn between the rational culture of the nursery and the spontaneity and pleasures of youth. They advocated a delicate balance that was easily tipped.

The half century after 1930 saw just that shift when experts abandoned the doctrine of rational child rearing for permissiveness, tilting away from the shaped and sheltered child for the wondrous child of the modern consumer culture. At the beginning of the century, child rearing was anything but indulgent or romantic. Through the 1920s, most professionals affirmed a rigorous regimen of scheduled feeding, early toilet training, selective response to crying, and a distrust of emotional attachments to babies and small children.[55] Mary Read's child study movement went so far as to propose that mothers regularly place a newborn over a "small (warmed) cuspidor" and then work up to a toilet by eight or ten months. Early toilet training practices surely reflected the fact that mothers at the time lacked disposable diapers and automatic washers. Moreover, the experts still believed that the child needed a proven procedure of care to reduce the still high infant and child mortality rates. The central issue remained biological, not psychological.[56]

This obsession with order, however, also revealed an archaic fear of infantile desire. Like Locke, L. Emmett Holt, author of the widely read *Care and Feeding of Children*, insisted that mothers should respond only to infants' moaning and sharp cries. Holt held to a traditional view: "What is the most certain way of causing a child to develop the crying habit? By giving him everything he cries for." This only makes a "spoiled, fussy baby, and a household tyrant whose continual demands make a slave of the mother." Psychologist John Watson may have been extreme when he advised in 1928 that mothers should "never hug or kiss" their children or even "let them sit in your lap." Still, the Children's Bureau 1914 edition of *Infant Care* warned that "much of the play that is indulged in [between parents and children] is more or less harmful."[57] Children's desires were insatiable, domineering, and antisocial, and they had to be controlled.

Signs of more positive images of the child's nature began to emerge in professional thinking by the end of the 1920s. In 1925, when pediatrician Arnold Gesell of Yale University found that naughty behavior was often, in fact, "typical" for very young children, he reassured parents that their children were merely "going through a stage" that was natural, harmless, and even necessary.[58] By the 1940s, *Infant Care* had abandoned the demand that babies be toilet trained by eight months, allowing this traditional marker of self-control to wait until the child was two years old. While this change reflected improved diaper services, it also suggested a shift to accepting children's desires as natural and good. Benjamin Spock's *The Common Sense Book of Baby and Child Care* (1945) insisted that kids would, without prompting by parents, select the best food in the proper amount. By the 1980 edition of *Infant Care*, all concern about indulging a domineering child had gone: "Don't worry about 'spoiling' the baby. . . . Giving the needed attention during the first year will help build the trust which will help him or her learn more 'grown up' behavior later on." The experts no longer saw the child as a contrary creature who had to be coerced into accepting rational family routines and needs. Rather, the young person was a self-regulating natural organism who cried only to signal parents of physical and emotional needs. Freud's stress on the sexuality of children certainly threatened the romantic ideal of angelic innocence, but, as presented in child-rearing manuals after 1930, it also affirmed that infant sexuality was natural and that sexual urges became obsessions only when parents interfered.[59]

Now the child rather than the father knew best, affirming the basic doctrine of wondrous innocence. The mother was obliged to discern the child's every want or need and immediately meet it. The new view abandoned the traditional goals of sheltered innocence—to affirm the traditional distinction between needs and wants and to favor deferred over immediate gratification. Those distinctions disappeared in the new child psychology. As media scholar Henry Jenkins notes, by the 1960s the child-rearing ideal was simply this: "The body doesn't lie; if it feels good, it can't be bad."[60] ©

An even more subtle change was a dramatically new strategy for coping with children's desires. In a Children's Bureau's pamphlet of 1930 we read, "The best way to break up a bad habit in a child is to keep the child so busy with interesting things to do that he forgets the old habit." Instead of resisting a child's desire, the parent should diffuse or displace it. Replacing the traditional religious fear of concupiscence was a new approach. Giving in to the child would satisfy her or his longings, preventing a "fixation" that led the child to lifelong obsessions. Replacing the fear of "Give an inch and he will take a mile" was a new attitude toward children's desire: Give the baby the whole and he'll only take a part. As anthropologist Martha Wolfenstein put it in 1955, "We developed (without conscious calculation) a new kind of defense against impulses. . . . This defense would consist in diffusion, ceasing to keep gratification deep, intense, and isolated, but allowing it to permeate thickly though all activities, to achieve by a mixture a further mitigation." Thus, the child would never become obsessed by a frustrating desire if impulses and longings were allowed to be expressed widely.[61] The culmination of this trends can be best summarized in the words of the famous baby doctor Penelope Leach in 1977: "You and your child [should be seen] as a unit of mutual pleasure-giving." The parent role was no longer primarily to represent "reality" and the "future" to the offspring but to share the immediacy of enjoyment with the natural child.[62]

The permissive revolution represented several distinct trends. New research in child psychology promoted indirect ways of shaping and directing desire. After 1945, child-rearing experts tried to substitute more democratic family styles for the authoritarian and patriarchal practices that presumably had bred the militarists and racists of World War II.[63] Probably even more important is the simple fact that parents not only followed the advice of the child development experts and their model of sheltered innocence but also embraced the romantic and ultimately commercial idea of the wondrous child. As we shall see in the next chapter, advertising taught parents that children had the right to have their desires fulfilled and that it was the parents' role to make them happy. Merchandisers instructed parents on how consumer goods could displace and defuse children's desires without repressing them. Spending could end family conflict and even help parents bend their offspring's wills while apparently giving in to them.[64] Most important, indulged children became an opportunity for parents to indulge themselves.

The child development specialists, in effect, reluctantly caught up with a commercial culture that for at least a generation had been teaching permissiveness. This did not mean the defeat of the ideas and practices of the sheltered and shaped child of the experts. Instead, both wondrous and sheltered innocence battled for the right to raise the child. While sheltered innocence thrives today in the classroom, library, and child-rearing magazines, wondrous innocence prevails at the mall, in the movie theater, and on most holidays. The result of this stalemate is a curious set of contradictory meanings of the innocent. Children today are protected from premature contact with the calculating world of work and markets but also are invited to delight in the continuously changing offerings of the consumer market. They are sheltered from dysfunctional desire and shaped into productive citizens in school, church, and other improving institutions but also are encouraged to express personal longings through consumption. Children are pushed back and forth between these two definitions of their innocence, to the confusion and frustration of all.

# 3

## The Cute Kid *Images of a Wondrous Childhood*

What a cute doll! What a cute child! The modern notion of the child as "cute" as opposed to merely adorable or even charming crosses a boundary. A word with changeable meanings, its origins are revealing. Until the twentieth century "cute" was merely a shortened form of "acute," signifying "sharp, quick witted," and shrewd in an "underhanded manner." In American slang of 1834, it came also to mean "attractive, pretty, charming" but was applied only to things. The original meaning of the "cute" person was interchangeable with "cunning," a corruption of "can," meaning clever and crafty.[1] Significantly, both words shifted meaning by the 1900s (though only briefly for cunning), from the manipulative and devious adult to the lively charm of the willful child, suggesting a new tolerance for the headstrong, even manipulative, youngster. Today, the little girl who bats her eyes to win favor or the little boy who gives his mother a long look of desire at the candy counter is called "cute." This suggests that the attractive, bubbling enthusiasm of the child is no longer seen negatively as manipulative or devilish, but positively as charming and even desirable. The cute became the look of wondrous innocence.

What changed, of course, is not the child but how the adult sees the child. The cute represents positive emotional response to all that a small child often is—dependent and imitative, but also spontaneous, demanding, and even disruptive. Modern parents surely try to control the negative emotions of children—jealousy, envy, and anger—using techniques advocated by child-rearing experts. But parents also bundle children's feelings and be-haviors in a ribbon of cuteness.[2] The cute child's desires no longer appear so selfish or devious, nor does fulfilling them seem so irresponsible and fraught with future danger. They are natural. The cute child is naturally a little naughty but always nice, radiating not a naive look of youthful beauty but energy, spunk, and friskiness. The cute can steal cookies from the cookie jar but do it without real malice or greed. Cuteness takes both the child and the adult to the edge of the acceptable, even across the line of self-control, to a playful, unserious anarchic moment. Inevitably, the cute was gendered, draw-ing on the characteristics of animals and urchins for boys and angels and co-quettes for girls. Despite the best efforts of child-rearing experts, the image of the cute child defined the American love affair with wondrous innocence. Even more, cuteness itself, even separate from the child, became desirable as the look that we want to purchase and possess. The cute became a selling point (especially when associated with the child in ads) and an occasion for impulse spending.

## Origins of the Cute, 1880–1910

When and why did the child become "cute"? Searching for images of the child in the increasingly more visual media of American magazines and advertising offers some clues to its origins. Activities today associated with the fun-loving and playful child were not necessarily linked in the nine-teenth century. For example, pictures of the new and exciting sports of roller skating and bicycling showed no children in *Frank Leslie's Illustrated Weekly* in 1885 and 1896.[3] Moreover, late Victorian advertising generally did not use images of the sweet child to sell goods as it incessantly would in the twenti-eth century. In 1885, Pear's soap (later famous for its child icons) featured a stately image of a young woman with endorsements from a countess and a pro-fessor. Eleven years later, Quaker Oats offered a ghostly figure of the "Auto-crat of the Breakfast Table," the aged Quaker, to sell its cereal.[4] In magazines, children appeared in limited but revealing settings—the pitiful street musi-cian; shoeless, but clean, urchins given ice cream by charitable uptowners; cautionary images of newsboys up to no good at the seashore; and poor face-less youngsters dragged to the Bowery museum freak show by thoughtless par-ents. These were moral tales that stressed middle-class charity and the dan-gers of the neglect of the innocent. Images of ideal middle-class childhoods also appeared: troops of Sunday schoolers visiting Grant's tomb or boys pa-raded in britches and fancy wide collars and girls in frilly dresses with wide-

JACK-IN-THE-BOX.

**3.1**

An image of fright, not delight, as an adult springs a jack-in-the-box
on two Victorian children. *Harper's Weekly*, 7 Dec. 1870, cover.

brimmed hats.[5] These images revealed sweetness, but little cuteness. Even
subjects that might be ideal opportunities to display the delighted or emotional child produced very different images: A *Harper's Weekly* cover illustration of 1870, portraying a father turning the crank of a jack-in-the-box with
his toddler on his lap, shows a frightened child, not a delighted one. The toy
let adults feel powerful and superior, but it also gave them a way of evoking a
dramatic response from children that also made the young and vulnerable desire the adult's love and protection. Fathers and other male relatives surely
found this a way of relating to the innocent. Still, it was a long way from contemporary rites of evoking wondrous innocence. "The Little Mischief Maker"
(1885), from *Frank Leslie's Illustrated Weekly*, shows not the impish child but
a girl looking angelic and even devoted. The older image prevailed even in a

**3.2**
This image of the mischief maker, the girl disturbing
a bird's nest filled with eggs, has none of the look of
the twentieth-century impish cute child. She almost
looks angelic. *Frank Leslie's Illustrated Newspaper*,
12 Jan. 1885, 261.

context that modern artists would make cute. Only images of children's "discovery" of Santa's filled stockings on Christmas morning even begin to ap-
proximate the wondrous child.[6]

Formal paintings of children continued to feature traditional themes. For
example, portraits showed children holding birds on a string (symbolizing the
strong possibility of early death when the bird would become "free"). Pictures
of mischievous children did not glorify youthful exuberance and freedom but

condemned their parents for poor supervision. Images of the urchin suggested the need for charity but also unrealistically presented a romantic view of innocence, marked by tender youth, even effeminacy, and cleanliness.[7]

Gradually, these images of the child underwent a change. This transition can be seen in trade cards, colorful images produced by manufacturers and retailers to advertise their products and stores, which had their heyday in the generation after the Civil War. Consumers and their children often collected these cards as a form of popular art. Although pleasing images of nature or informative illustrations of landmarks and tourist sites were common, many trade cards featured pictures of children.[8] In one striking image, we see a child's delighted face emerge from an advertising sheet for San Francisco's White Department Store. This association of the wondrous look of childhood with consumption would anticipate much twentieth-century advertising. But most cards were much more subtle, with no direct reference to the "sponsor" except for a discreet printing of the company's name and address. More important, sentiment, rather than the child's wonder or desire, was the overriding theme. One card featured an older girl playing the piano while her little sister looked on in awe and admiration; another illustrated a toddler girl lovingly leaning her head on her loyal dog. Even Pet cigarettes offered a sweet scene of two loving sisters in white winter clothes, the younger with a doll (1890). Some were obvious copies or imitations of popular artists or illustrators. Millais's sensuous girl in the illustration Cherry Ripe was borrowed, as was the image of the three Muses in a card featuring bonneted girls with flower baskets.

Specific children's themes were repeated over and over in trade card series. Children were often used to symbolize a romantic view of nature. For example, red-cheeked five-year-old girls with bonnets and flower baskets playing on swings represented spring. In another, children's faces were framed in petals representing different flowers. Often the theme was nostalgic, such as boys in fishing scenes or sailing Dutch shoes on ponds. Children were dressed in archaic clothing (seventeenth-century ruffled collars or eighteenth-century powdered wigs and britches, for example). The A & P Tea Company presented a bold series of children all looking alike except for their different national costumes and flags. These images associated the child with preindustrial life and a changeless and harmonious world. They remained within the world of the romantic and sentimental.

Other trade card images of the child more directly anticipated the modern idea of the cute and commercial. Many cards show children in comical situations, with amused looks of friskiness or even naughtiness on their faces. A few take delight in the humiliated youngster, as in the card that shows a

THE WHITE HOUSE

J. W. DAVIDSON & C?

**3.3**
A trade card for a San Francisco Department store (ca. 1870), an
early example of selling the delighted child as she breaks through
what appears to be wrapping paper. "Scrapbooks of American Trade
Cards," Courtesy of the Bancroft Library, University of California
at Berkeley.

baby (dressed as a catcher) hit in the face by a baseball. Others have a more
benevolent message: a shoeless boy standing with baseball bat in hand saying, "Ain't she a beauty." More common, however, was a card that humor-
ously shows two boys sewing the tails of a cat and dog together on a new
Singer sewing machine. The naughty boy theme became even more prominent at the end of the nineteenth century.[9]

**3.4**

Two in a series of trade cards provided by a San Francisco domestic goods store portraying children in archaic clothing of the gentry, an example of an emerging definition of the cute. "Scrapbooks of American Trade Cards," Courtesy of the Bancroft Library, University of California at Berkeley.

Part of the emerging image of the "cute" appeared in playful images of kids in unusual and unnatural situations, suggesting a world of desire and fantasy that transgressed the passive innocence of the angelic child. Sometimes children appeared with objects of unnatural proportions: children in peasant costumes rolling a huge egg in an ancient barrow or toddlers clad in archaic clothing trying to wind a toy top twice their size. One especially striking series of cards featured East Asian children wearing oversized gloves, socks, or top hats. Others featured children dressed and playing adult roles—adorned for an elegant eighteenth-century French banquet or dueling for a "lady." Babies were dressed up as Scots highlanders or other old-fashioned soldiers. Other kids were portrayed as inattentive "jurors" in the box declaring their "verdict" for Clark thread. Occasionally, we find a girl in a provocative prone pose with a sensual look on her face. But more common are the silly illustrations of a baby pulling petals in a series of cards with captions, "He loves me," "He loves me a little," "He loves me passionately." Adults delighted in the baby in a topsy-turvy world free from nature's restraints. They enjoyed the absurdly imitative child. But in all these familiar images of the child, we still do not get the whole painting of the cute.[10]

By the last decade of the trade card's prominence, there is a more dramatic change that points to a new view of the child's will and nature. In one card, two sweet little girls appear to read a book labeled on its cover "Imperial granum medicinal food," directly linking the child's desire to a commercial breakfast food. Another shows a girl in an archaic costume exclaiming, "What! Never Tasted Hires' Root Beer: You've Missed a Treat." In a 1896 card for a cocoa drink, a sweet, pensive girl surrounded by kittens and a toddler sipping from a cup says, "I want a cup of Huyler's Cocoa too!" Finally, the romantic child was given a will and no longer simply provided a sentimental aura around a product. The most abiding theme of this form of commercial art, however, was not that of desire but of health. Note the picture of a girl of about seven on a sled with a bird fluttering about—this one with no string.[11]

The image of the robust and vital child helped create more optimistic and playful approaches to child rearing. The makers of the Kodak snapshot camera (invented in 1888) picked up this idea. George Eastman made personal photography a reality with roll film that allowed amateur picture taking on the go. Eastman's slogan was "You press the button, we do the rest." In 1901, Kodak offered customers "Pocket Kodak Portraiture," a free booklet promising guidance about snapping photos and capturing "charming studies of child life." Eastman's company even suggested that children "capture fantasy in taking pictures just as adults capture the child as fantasy by taking pictures of them." In 1909, author Philip Hale noted with slight disapproval that "nowadays fond mothers are constantly taking their children to the photographer . . . [and that children are] photographed much more than their elders."[12]

By the 1900s, Americans were ready for a new image of the child—one expressed in the word "cute." In *Harper's Weekly* from 1857 to 1913, the word appeared repeatedly to refer to the clever (as in a sneaky "Cute Yankee land-lord" in 1857, "cute miser" in 1867, or even "a cuteness for which widow mothers are proverbial" in 1875). Animals could be "cute," too (in reference to pug dogs and kittens in the late 1880s and 1890s). An ad for a watercolor picture of a "cute chinee kid" appeared in 1900. Only in 1909 was that word applied to the American child: "I like cute little girls that look up at you and take your hands and cuddle right up to you—they are so much sweeter than the other kind."[13] Finally, the child had become the wondrous innocent. By becoming cute, the youngster had that special look that evoked all the feel-ings and desires that were so important in shaping the modern image of the child and modern consumer culture.

## New Kids on the Block

A new "look" to the child became ubiquitous in American consumer cul-ture in the first two decades of the twentieth century. This so-called New Kid image appeared on dolls, in illustrated stories and comic strips, and on trademark icons and advertising, popularizing the look of the cute. Like the trade cards, the cute images on dolls, toys, and illustrated children's books were designed to appeal to adults who purchased these items for children's use.

The change in the look was most dramatic on the faces of dolls after about 1900. European designers rejected the highly stylized "doll face"of the Victorian china doll, with her pursed lips, high cheeks, small straight eyes, and adult body, creating instead a far more natural and playable representa-tion of the child. European doll makers like Kaethe Kruse crafted dolls to ex-press real children's emotions (especially the look of pain or fear). American New Kid designers featured dolls' faces with large, round, wide-open eyes, "full of child-like humor." They no longer represented the miniature adult, or even a naive innocent, but a child with a slightly impish or coquettish look to them.[14]

Dolls' names (Miss Mischief, Naughty Marietta, Miss Coquette, or Flossie Flirt) openly appealed to the adult's admiration for the spunky, even slightly manipulative and self-centered child. Desire in the child had become desir-able to the adult. A "cunning" look (an early equivalent of the cute), unac-ceptable in the adult, was amusing and charming in the innocent youth. The visual clue was eyes askance or even eyes that "naughtily roll from side to side in that delightful flirting way."[15] Sometimes this appeal was more subtle: ads for the popular Patsy doll line (appearing first in 1924) insisted that Patsy was

3·5
This New Kid doll, "who gayly rolls her flirty eyes from side to side in the most delightful, mischievous way," was supposed to appeal to parents as much as to children in the 1920s. Sears catalog, fall 1929, 639. © 1929 Sears Brands. LLC. Used with permission.

a "loveable Imp with tiltable head and moveable limbs." The attraction was made even stronger when she was paired with her "family" of sisters: Patsy Ann, Patsykin, Patsyette, Patsy Joan, Patsy Lou, and a baby sister, Patsy Babykin, each with her own personality. Patsy "is so cunning and adorable you just want to hug her"—and buy her.[16] Adults' attraction to the New Kid reflected their new, more tolerant view of the child and their identification with a more vital, exuberant image of the young.

The cute always seemed to make adults buy. The earliest and best known examples of the New Kid look were originally designed to sell new consumer goods in the growing areas of magazine advertising and package and trademark design. Grace Drayton's Campbell Soup Kids, those two pudgy, apple-cheeked youngsters in overalls, graced an advertisement in the *Ladies' Home Journal* in 1905 and soon thereafter postcards, lapel buttons, and dolls. The image conveyed health and vitality in a time of concern about food purity and the need to take positive steps to improve the life chances of offspring with good nutrition. The Kids immediately became the spokespeople for Campbell's, as did other New Kid foods and soaps (selling, for example, Morton's salt or Fairy soap). Like the Campbell Kids, these images of cute children associated their products with cleanliness and robust good health, sometimes linking these traits with Dutch or Japanese cultures. Other trademark New Kids included the grinning boy in the sailor suit on Cracker Jack boxes and "Sunny Jim," with his exuberant face selling a breakfast food and later peanut butter.[17] The image of the cute delivered positive associations with new products just as it conveyed new attitudes about the child. The New Kid look crossed many symbolic boundaries and took forms that stretched its meanings and allowed playful, even contradictory, associations.

The image was expressed differently for male and female New Kids, but often in surprisingly gender-blended forms. Girls were no longer portrayed merely as passive and pretty. They had a vitality that edged into the impishness that female New Kids shared with boys. Still, cute girls as represented in literary characters and images remained "helpers" while boys were more commonly good-naturedly selfish and naughty.[18] The cute child was associated with both the angelic (usually portrayed as female) and the animal (with mostly male associations), allowing adults to embrace both the darling and the impish, the child as savior and as free and even wild.

## Animals and Angels

B ambi, especially in Disney's animated incarnation of 1942, expresses perfectly the romantic ideal of nature's innocence and thus its association with childhood. In a forest where wise owls, fun-loving rabbits, and beautiful butterflies live in harmony, the blissful romp of the fawn Bambi is only disturbed by the predator, the human hunter, who heartlessly deprives the deer of his loving mother. From the Victorian Water Babies to the contemporary Muppets, the animalization of children's stories reinforces a common theme: the contrast between the enchanted world of nature's childlike creatures and the selfish and cold realm of human adults. By the 1930s, animal characters were beginning to replace silly and marginal ethnic stereotypes in children's literature, thus making these images more acceptable in the modern world.[19]

Most important, anthropomorphized animals express the modern adult's complex feeling about the child, especially the male, by giving play to a range of natural but innocent qualities.

The linkage of the boy with the animal is perhaps best seen in an early twentieth-century fad, the teddy bear. In the nineteenth century, the bear was a frightening image and used in toys to scare children (similar to the jack-in-the-box). By contrast, the teddy bear had become a cuddly New Kid doll that, when associated with a real boy, became a veritable emblem of cuteness. Parents gave small boys teddy bears on the boardwalk on the New Jersey shore in the summer of 1906, and within a year the now common practice of photographing them grasping their stuffed bears had become a fad. This snapshot image amused adults for its absurdity, but they also found it endearing for the unassuming child's trusting embrace of the harmless animal. Unlike the doll, long linked with girls' gender role-playing, the bear had wild and primitive "boyish" associations, thus making it appropriate for male companionship. At the same time, in the "teddy" form, the bear had been domesticated (linked with the story of Teddy Roosevelt's protective act of sparing a cub bear on a hunting trip in 1902). Moreover, the gentle teddy bear took a new physical form when made out of huggable soft plush (the material of modern upholstery and pillows) instead of hard wood as had been the usual material of toy animals. While the earliest teddies sometimes had sound boxes that growled, they soon represented anything but the frightening. The teddy bear became, like the boy, a domesticated primitive. So appealing was this image that the teddy bear became the object of numerous novelties and toys. He appeared on target and board games, water pistols, tea sets, pedal cars, and rubber stamps, and even in songs and a teddy bear movie.[20]

Less well known, but equally illustrative, is the Billiken. This creature in plush took the form of a monkey with feet and hands of fur, but it had the face of an impish boy with East Asian features. First appearing in 1907, the Billiken briefly competed with the teddy bear as an icon of the tamed animal. While certainly racist in its association of the Asian with the simian, the Billiken was a New Kid boy—a beast with the mind of a male child—who was also a "god" with the power to bring good luck and good moods. He stretched the imagination in other ways, too. Unlike the teddy bear, the Billiken was grotesque, rather like one of P. T. Barnum's freaks in his American Museum and circus sideshows; and, like the dwarfs and pinheads that American peered at, the Billiken attracted adult's pity and sense of superiority (much as do "ugly" misfit dolls today).[21]

The Billiken and teddy bear were the first of many examples of this modern need for the childlike animal (reflected also in the obsession with small

**3.6**

One of many storybooks featuring the teddy bear. Here the cute
(boy) animal is paired with the cute oriental girl image, representing
the full range of the wondrous child. S. W. Scull, *The Teddy Bear
Story Book*, 1908, cover. Courtesy of the Allison-Shelley Collection,
Special Collections, Pattee Library, Pennsylvania State University.

and "toy" dogs). Perhaps the most striking and obviously successful successor
is Mickey Mouse. In his original form, he had a long rodent nose and body
and was malicious to boot.[22] In "Steamboat Willie," the famous cartoon of
1928, Mickey was an irreverent, even anarchic, figure who hit a parrot and
used the backbones of animals to play music. He very much followed the pattern of a comic strip figure, Ingnatius Mouse, who regularly struck Krazy Kat

(Ingnatius's admirer) with a brick but never got punished for it. These cartoons were in the tradition of the European Punch-and-Judy shows that featured an enraged Punch killing a policeman. By 1934, Mickey had changed. He grew plumper and shorter, with a much more subdued nose and rounder, more prominent ears. In fact, he came to resemble a sweet-looking toddler more than a pesky mouse. Mickey's new personality and roles appealed to parents upset by the "amorality" of cartoons and comic strips of the era. Mickey became the symbol of the charming child who was not too independent to learn a boy's lesson. His most memorable role was perhaps in the moralistic tale "The Sorcerer's Apprentice," in which Mickey discovers that he should not tempt fate by even dreaming of using the sorcerer's wand before learning its proper uses. Mickey also became an All-American boy. According to a Disney studio handbook written in the mid-1930s, "Mickey seems to be the average young boy of no particular age; living in a small town, clean living, fun-loving, bashful around girls, polite and as clever as he must be for the particular story."[23] He wins a "girl" in Minnie Mouse and a dog in Pluto. As the domesticated animal, Mickey had become the very image of an idealized childhood.

If the cutified primitive defined the New Kid boy, the angelic imp represented the New Kid girl. The image of an angelic female youngster was repeated endlessly in portraits and films well into the twentieth century. The vulnerability of the innocent angelic child had made the abducted child a deeply sympathetic story in the popular press by the end of the nineteenth century. The protection of the angelic child remained a major theme in early films. For example, in Edwin Porter's feature *The Life of an American Fireman* (1902), the central dramatic scene was the rescue of a child from a burning building. The vulnerable angel was also a savior, as in Eleanor Porter's *Pollyanna* (1913), the story of an orphaned girl sent from the Ozarks to live with and ultimately humanize her prissy, cold aunt. Still another version of this theme was *Little Annie Rooney* (1925), whose tomboy heroine saves everyone with her naive trust.[24]

Celebrities of stage and screen from Mary Miles Minter and Mabel Norman to Lillian Gish and especially Mary Pickford built careers on their "doll-like" appearance. Using kittens and bird cages as props, accentuating youthful poses and wide-eyed looks, and hiding her woman's body with rags or pinafores, Pickford played child roles into her thirties. Shot with cleverly orchestrated camera angles that stressed her under-five-foot frame, Pickford became the ideal child character. Pickford's blond hair, long associated with the angelic, delighted an audience of millions on the screen, even as she anticipated a more sensuous image with her ringlets. Again stretching her image, she combined the angel with the gamin when she played the waif from the shantytown in *Tess of the Storm Country* (1914).[25]

Perhaps the best known New Kid girl was the angelic Kewpie created by Rose O'Neill. The Kewpie doll's image first appeared in an illustrated story in *Ladies' Home Journal* in December 1909. Kewpie recalled the cupid, though O'Neill's character, instead of tricking humans into falling in love, got people out of trouble and assuaged the sorrows of the urban slums. This image was in the Victorian tradition of the chivalric innocent, the savior in a child's pure body with a baby's topknot, wide eyes, snub nose, shy expression, outstretched arms, and round belly. Kewpie was angelic but also impish. "See their plump bodies, roguish eyes, and smiling faces. Everybody loves a Kewpie," trumpeted a Sears advertisement in 1919. The contradictions continued: the Kewpie had traditional female virtues but was physically neither a boy nor a girl. As historian Shelley Armitage notes, "Kewpie was the ideal American child—it had no genitals" and thus seemed innocent. It represented a fun-loving urchin, the authentic, as opposed to the formal, dull, and arrogant upper class.[26]

Toy makers adopted the Kewpie by 1912 and immediately gendered it, selling "bashful girl" Kewpies and (more rarely) comical boy Kewpies, dressed as policemen or soldiers. Kewpie danced back and forth between ads, dolls, and illustrated stories in *Ladies' Home Journal*. At first a fad, the Kewpie remained popular for years and appeared in many forms: dolls of all sizes, on a talcum powder container, a camera, beach ball, and at the end of O'Neill's career, in 1940, even as a Buddha. While many New Kid images started as commercial trademarks, the Kewpie went in the opposite direction, shifting from savior to sales, hyping chocolate, soap, and especially Jell-O. This infinitely plastic image tapped into contradictory adult longings and, despite much character and gender stretching, remained the classic image of the New Kid girl.[27]

The angelic New Kid look continued in the early 1930s with "America's Sweetheart," Shirley Temple, who at the age of five began her remarkable film career. Jackie Coogan had proved in the early 1920s that a very young child could play in the movies. Previously, children's roles in the theater were played by adults because directors believed that real kids were incapable of enduring the pressures of live (or even film) performance. By the 1930s, thousands of parents, dreaming that their toddlers would become the next Jackie Coogan, sent them to dancing school and groomed them for cast calls. Shirley was one of the few lucky ones. Not only could she dance and sing, but in her looks and manners she epitomized the angelic imp on the screen. In *Little Miss Marker* and *Stand Up and Cheer*, she played the role of the orphan who reformed adults with her naive, big-hearted optimism. In fact, she was a New Kid doll in the flesh, with her short legs, dimples, sweet smile, and "bright eyes." Like all New Kids, she was also spunky and able to get things done, a gift to a "weary old world," as one actor noted. The "cuteness" of Shirley was not narrowly defined; an essential part of her appeal was the fact that her image slid between the naive/dependent and the wise/vital. Shirley Temple was innocently sweet but also "very precious when she tightens her jaw." As film historian Norman Kline noted, in the movies of the 1930s "children are powerful enough to force adults to stay moral." At the other extreme of the image was Jane Withers, a more realistic, even bratty child in her film roles who, like the naughty boy, got into "fixes." But she also saved the day with her tomboyish solutions to problems.[28]

Through these images of the domesticated animal-like boy and the angelic impish girl, adults gendered childhood. They also blended extremes and thereby expanded what they found delightful about children. Parents sought in children much of what they felt they had lost as adults in their secular workaday worlds: the natural, the pure, and most of all wonder.

## Urchins and Coquettes

Underlying the domesticated animal and the impish angel is the idea of the naughty-but-nice child, willfully but naively on the moral boundary. Again, gender difference comes into play. Despite overlap, images of boys as urchins and girls as coquettish define their respective kinds of "naughtiness." The street child, though never exclusively a boy, had long been a stock character in novels (such Charles Dickens's *Oliver Twist* and Horatio Alger's *Ragged Dick*). In various ways, the urchin suggested an innocence of childhood that prevailed over wretched conditions outside the protection of middle-class home life. Even more, the urchin reflected the adult longing for the natural life beyond the comforts and constraints of bourgeois domesticity. The urchin, associated with the free and untamed life, was easily assimilated to all boys.[29]

By 1900, this theme became a daily encounter in the new popular genre of the comic strip. It appeared first in 1895 in Joseph Pulitzer's *New York World*, with the publication of Richard Outcault's "Yellow Kid." Dressed in a yellow flour sack nightgown, this streetwise, parentless child, vaguely oriental in appearance but Irish by intent, lived in Hogan's Alley, where he created mischief at every opportunity. Outcault's vision coincided with a trend in newspapers to sensationalize the gritty reality of urban life and appealed to popular audiences with little patience for genteel stories and values. His comic strip character would have been a familiar image to readers of irreverent humor magazines like *Wild Oats* and *Life* in the 1880s, which through the urchin mocked the pretensions and foibles of bourgeois life and culture. Outcault stood apart from the self-assured middle-class readers of Palmer Cox's Brownies (whom he parodied). The "Yellow Kid" was also a part of the ethnic humor of the popular newspaper. Readers were amused by the satirical play on cultural differences and prejudices (especially waged against African-Americans) and the appeal to the white ethnic underdog.[30] Despite his devilish charms, Outcault's Yellow Kid was too rough talking and slummy to appeal to a wide American audience and soon disappeared. Still, many other comic strips shared the mischievous child theme. The *World's* "How Kelly's Kindergarten Class Was Broken Up" was typical, with its chaotic scene of the classroom from which the kids had driven the teacher. A weekly feature in 1909 was "School Days," built around this gag and a spunky streetwise girl named Ophelia. Others featured boys playing mean jokes on their fathers or, as urchins, joining with adult tramps and failures (as in a 1907 comic strip version of "The Kid"). Some even highlighted the child's view of adult life or fantasy image of the world (as in "Little Sammy's History of the World" or the famous "Nemo's Dreamland"). For a time the child theme seemed to predominate: In early 1907, five of seven strips in the *New York World* featured children.[31] Many of these strips in effect made the child the symbolic agent of anarchic cultural protest (serving as the stand-in for working-class or ethnic minorities). But this theme had its limits. Adult, especially middle-class, comic strip readers longed for an image of the (mostly) boy child that addressed the changing roles of parents and home life. The "acute" child at the "edge" of the acceptable was changed into the "cute" child—willful, even selfish and devious at times, but ultimately good at heart.

Outcault met this need with the strip "Buster Brown," his 1902 replacement for "The Yellow Kid." Buster was a mischievous lad, but he was protected from growing up too fast by a bourgeois home. He was portrayed in the familiar image of the Little Lord Fauntleroy suit and haircut, completing the wholesome image with loyal bulldog Tige. Yet he was anything but a goody-two-shoes when he played tricks on piano movers, his tutors, and his dog. He had the good fortune, we are to believe, of having parents willing to "correct" him with a spanking when his pranks got out of hand. Outcault repeated this theme over and over, ending with a moral lesson given by a contrite Buster. In one strip, when Buster's mother warns him not to touch the seltzer water on the table, he immediately feeds it to his dog, which is furiously buffeted

**3·7**
An example of Richard Outcault's Buster Brown
comic strip, one of the famous "resolutions" of Buster
after a naughty adventure. Richard Outcault, *My
Resolutions Buster Brown*, 1906, np.

about the room as the gas explodes from his mouth. Upon discovery Buster
is caned, but, with a pillow on his backside, he concludes the strip with a
homily on optimism and not being able to be an optimist while he cannot sit
down.[32] This naughty but nice boy, with his slightly crooked bow tie, wide,
round eyes, and cheerful grin, was a domesticated urchin, the very image of
the "cute" boy. Buster appealed to all regions of the country (as the urban Yellow Kid did not) and thus easily found his way into syndication. Outcault established an ad agency to sell and license the Buster image and, according
to historian Ian Gordon, had before Buster's retirement in 1921 accumulated
ten thousand copyrights for his image in ads and on products. Like the Kewpie, Buster Brown became an appealing endorser of new consumer goods—

selling cigars and whiskey to impish males, as well as shoes to parents of toddlers who recalled the "good" side of Buster in his famous homey "resolutions" on how to improve oneself and get along in life. In all his contradictions, Buster was the classic expression of the domesticated urchin.[33]

Buster Brown was not, however, the final word on the cute urchin. Only gradually would this image of the mischievous boy be tamed, and then only by conceding that the boy was naturally unable to conform to the domestic order. A more outlandish competitor to Buster was the "Katzenjammer Kids" (1897). In this strip, adapted by Rudolph Dirks from the German Wilhelm Busch's Max and Moritz stories of 1865, we see the same story repeated endlessly: The Kids steal Mama's pies or play tricks on the Captain (and the Captain's sidekick, the Inspector). Beginning with the title, "Katzenjammer" (meaning, in German, "cat howling," a colloquial expression for hangover), the strip is consistently irreverent. The reader sympathizes with the incorrigible Kids, who steadfastly refuse to be good. The obvious implication is that boys must be naughty to be "real" boys. The Captain and the Inspector (ironically a school official) sometimes play tricks on the Kids, proving that males, no matter their age, naturally rebel against the stultifying order imposed by female domesticity. Although the adults repeatedly thrash the Kids (though this declines by the 1920s with changing sensibilities), the boys never learn their lesson. The general impression is of a never-ending "war" between the generations as the adults get even with the Kids for their wily pranks by spanking them. The message is anything but didactic. It lets the "child" in the reader identify with the boys' anarchy and sheer willfulness. Many strips find the Kids triumphant, laughing at the gullibility of the adults falling for their endless pranks. The strip is set in alien environments (Africa and other foreign places), and the characters speak English in German dialect, all the better for middle-class readers to distance themselves and their families from the story. The message is clear. Adults recognized and were fascinated by the seeming fact that boys have no control over their impulses. In fact, boys' innocence is expressed through their impulsiveness.[34]

There were many variations on the Buster Brown and Katzenjammer theme: Little Jimmy (who repeatedly got sidetracked when sent on an errand) or Tim and Tom the Terrible Twins. As a gender variant, there was sweet-looking Little Lulu, who was "always in and out of trouble, but mostly always in," as her trademark song went. Created by Marjorie Buell in 1935 for the *Saturday Evening Post*, Little Lulu went on to fame in movie cartoons, with her imaginative pranks and endless struggles with neighborhood boys led by the dullard Tubby.[35]

Perhaps the best known derivative of Buster Brown was "Skippy" by

3.8
A version of R. Dirks' Katzenjammer Kids showing Fritz and Hans up to no good. *Hans and Fritz*, Saalfield, 1917. Courtesy of the Allison-Shelley Collection, Special Collections, Pattee Library, Pennsylvania State University.

Percy Crosby, a fixture in Hearst newspapers from 1926 to 1945. The character starred in a radio show in 1931, and child actor Jackie Cooper played Skippy in a movie in 1930. Crosby went on to produce a number of comic strip books and even a Skippy novel. Here was a still more gentle image of the impish boy. Like Buster, he was anachronistically dressed in an English schoolboy costume with bow tie and short pants, but his true character was revealed in his shapeless hat, deviously slanted over his eyes. In one story, Skippy uses his slingshot on other boys in the library and justifies it by saying, "School ain't so hard if you balance it with a little pleasure." As a Skippy book notes, "Skippy's hands were opened for friends and knuckled for enemies." But Skippy lacks the Katzenjammer Kids' malice, and his opponents were all fakes and snobs. Although he eats his mom's freshly baked cake and blames it on the flies, he is not punished, nor does he have to carry a moral message at the end. After all, he tries to be good, and everyone knows he is just too much the true boy to succeed all the time.[36]

By 1951, Hank Ketcham's "Dennis the Menace" is no longer even slightly to blame. Dennis is merely "curious" like the little monkey George in H. A. Rey's *Curious George* (1940). Often it is only the adult's fussiness (as in the encounters with the neighbor Mr. Wilson) and Dennis's natural spontaneousness and honesty in speech that get him into trouble. And he is never punished. By 1953, this four-year-old had his own comic book, dolls in his image, and a line of boys' clothes. Few adults found Dennis so menacing that they would not buy his image on a product for their own toddlers.[37]

Just as the boys in the comic strips became less threatening, the fathers and other adults were becoming more bumbling. In 1905, George McManus, a newspaper illustrator from St. Louis, arrived at the *New York World*, eager to make a name for himself in comic strips. His first effort, "The Newly Weds," featured a young couple's firstborn, Baby Snookums. The comic strip repeatedly had the overexcited father lose the baby or otherwise stumble in every situation he met (for example, in giving away Snookums's toys to the maid when the baby appeared bored only to have them return the next day with the maid's child, leading to a very upset Snookums). At the same time, the dad was convinced: "Why Snookums can do anything but speak," making the case that kids know best. Briefly, Baby Snookums, with a trademark smile showing one front tooth, was a commercial fad sold as china figures and dolls. The name survived into the 1930s as a term of endearment for a girlfriend. In 1912, McManus went on to produce "Bringing Up Father," a long-lived strip that featured Jiggs, the nouveau riche Irish patriarch who stumbles through his new social status while his all-knowing daughter, Nora, looks on. At the same time, his incompetent son, Junior, gets into his own scrapes. *The Simpsons*, the popular TV cartoon from the 1990s, was only an update of this theme. While Homer Simpson is a caricature of the bumbling father, Bart, the mischievous son, is certainly less innocent than Dennis the Menace and Skippy, but he, too, remains good at heart.[38]

The theme of the domesticated urchin went well beyond the imagination of cartoonists. Charlie Chaplin was, both in his own childhood and on the screen, a modern version of the plucky street child. In 1921, Chaplin teamed with Jackie Coogan in *The Kid*, a story of an orphan who is befriended by "The Tramp." Their antics in coping with an indifferent world offered audiences both pathos and comedy. When the Kid is sent to an orphanage, the Tramp frees him. Even when the boy is reunited with his wealthy, long-lost mother, the Tramp comes back to visit. The domesticated Kid still needed to recall his urchin past. Movie audiences shared with Chaplin an affection for Coogan's "whimsical wistful quality, a genuineness of feeling" that came through in Coogan's urchin roles. In the film version of *Peck's*

**3.9**
Jackie Coogan, the instant child star, as his urchin
character in *The Kid*. The key to the cute here is his
sad, languid eyes. *Motion Picture*, Jan. 1922, cover.

*Bad Boy* and *Skippy*, Coogan again played the boy free of female domestication who was somehow the better for it. Following on the cute urchin theme
was Hal Roach's extraordinary run of 221 episodes of *Our Gang* cinema
shorts. Between 1922 and 1944, this series featured a group of naive but independent neighborhood children. The Gang's members were "just kids, tat-
tered and full of spirits"—hardly parentless, much less homeless—but with
lots of time and freedom to play and get in and out of scrapes. *Our Gang* was
supposed to be about real kids' thoughts and actions, not the mama's boy image of Little Lord Fauntleroy or the rich, bored, stilted child that obsessed
mothers and nannies made from once naturally high-spirited boys.[39]

Probably the most famous of the domesticated urchins, however, was
Mickey Rooney, who stretched the role into his teenage years. Part of a
vaudeville family, Rooney was featured in 1939 at MGM movie studios as the

exuberant boy "born to be Huckleberry Finn," even though he was already eighteen years old. Movie ads noted his "wholesome personality and essential boyishness" that "will make you a child again" and "make you forget the hustle and bustle of the world we live in." In 1938, he made three movies that spanned the range of the domesticated urchin. He played the street tough made into a Christian boy hero by Father Flanigan in *Boys' Town*, the stableboy who rehabilitates the washed-up bum in *Stablemates*, and the exuberant but obedient teenage son of a small-town judge in *Love Finds Andy Hardy*. The last was one of fourteen formulaic episodes featuring the "straw haired, kazoo-voiced adolescent" whose enthusiasm for life sometimes left his mother bewildered and his father obliged to give him some sorely needed advice. While in *Love Finds Andy Hardy* Rooney finds himself "in love with three girls at once," his essential naïveté and good-naturedness prevailed.[40]

While it was "cute" for boys to deviate from domestic propriety (perhaps a rebellious streak secretly shared by their dads), they were saved by their "natural goodness." For girls, the naughty-but-nice theme was modeled less on the urchin than on the coquette—a difference that was ultimately more dangerous, and thus less acceptable to adults. Shirley Temple is once again a good illustration. In addition to the angelic imp, Shirley's image had another dimension that linked her to the previous generation's female star, Mary Pickford. Shirley was a nymphet, an innocent who imitated the sensuous woman, just as Mary was the sensuous woman who turned herself into the cute child. At three years of age, Shirley Temple acted in a series of shorts called *Baby Burlesks*, in which little children played the roles of famous adult stars, wooing each other with romantic poses and songs. Following the path of other would-be child stars who started in vaudeville dressed as fan dancers or brides, Temple did an impersonation of Marlene Dietrich. In Shirley's later movies, she often played the motherless girl who apparently is cared for by, but in reality takes cares of, a lonely bachelor (for example, hard-bitten male leads like Lionel Barrymore in *The Little Colonel* or Adolphe Menjou in *Little Miss Marker*). Although, in contrast to the later films of Brooke Shields, there is no overt sexuality in Shirley's performances, there is coquettishness enough that novelist and critic Graham Greene wrote an article condemning it. So offensive was Greene's claim that he was sued for libel by Temple's mother. Shirley's flirtatious innocence appealed to middle-aged men, both to their memory of their first desire for females and to their desire to protect a dependent little girl. The image survives today in kiddie beauty pageants, as toddlers dress up in obviously seductive clothes and strut in front of judges and smiling moms.[41]

Even as Shirley became too awkward at age twelve to continue to appeal to this curious combination of longings, the image was perpetuated by Margaret O'Brien in the 1940s by and many others down the road. Moreover, the ambiguous presentation of maturity and innocence worked in the teenage girl in the 1930s. Judy Garland became famous for her childish clothes and hairstyle but also for her mature singing voice and self-assertiveness in *The Wizard of Oz* (1939). Less well known today are Deanna Durbin's teenage musical roles. In the 1940s, Durbin cultivated a youthful look (white anklets, bows in her hair, and an angelic face) with a grown-up operatic voice and roles that stressed her mastery of the situation. Like Shirley Temple, Judy and Deanna, with their innocent and natural tomboyishness, took charge of the men around them.[42]

The boy as domesticated urchin and the girl as innocent coquette presented the two faces of the cute child. Inevitably, the coquette was less often seen and more subdued that the urchin. She was, in effect, too threatening to innocence. Sexuality was a form of rebellion and manipulation that parents (and an obliging media) feared and wanted to suppress more than the antidomestic defiance of boys.


## Galleries of Wondrous Innocence: Magazine Cover Art

The New Kid version of cuteness turned up in many places in early twentieth-century American culture, even on the covers of new general interest magazines. A brief look at these covers, especially from the *Saturday Evening Post* between 1900 and the 1960s, reveals much about the impact of wondrous innocence in American popular culture. At the turn of the twentieth century, Cyrus Curtis's *Saturday Evening Post* and other magazines (especially *Collier's*) were beginning to publish colored illustrations on their covers, usually featuring images of major public figures or themes from lead stories.[43] Gradually, however, in the first two decades of the century the child began to appear on weekly covers entirely disconnected from any editorial theme within. Obviously, the cute sold magazines. Picking up many of the themes from the old trade cards, at first sentimental images dominated. The earliest cover of the *Saturday Evening Post* featuring a child occurred in December 1904. It was a picture of a boy reading a book while surrounded by classic Christmas toys of the period: a train, sword, and jack-in-the-box. Reminiscent of the themes of trade cards, magazine images of children often symbolized nature and seasonal changes. One portrays a little girl to commemorate Valentine's Day; another shows toddlers at the beach listening to shells to mark the coming of summer. The number of weekly illustrations of children on *Saturday Evening Post* covers increased to 11 in 1905, peaking at 24 in 1915 and averaging almost 16 per year during the second decade of the century.[44] The message also became less innocuous with the rise of New Kid themes: The impish lad sets off a firecracker under a standing policeman, or boys go skinny-dipping in a forbidden swimming hole. The daring, willful child is also often frustrated (for example, the boy who is obliged to hold his sister's doll while she is at bat, the toddler trying to shave, or the seven-year-old dreaming of joining the circus).[45]

In the two decades following 1920, images of children on the covers of the *Saturday Evening Post* were less frequent (averaging 14.3 per year in the 1920s and 10.1 in the 1930s). But the formulas of wonder became more obvious. Pictures of children continued to introduce the seasons, but no longer was the child merely a symbol. He or she displayed wonder at the seashore or delight on Christmas morning.[46] Covers of *Collier's* and the *Saturday Evening Post* tell "amusing" stories of willful boys innocently trying to cope with authorities (teachers, doctors, mothers) or to accomplish some daring deed that they were not quite ready for, very much in the mold of the naughty but nice New Kid boy. In *Collier's* (1923), a boy with goggles and a huge pipe wrench and oil can "works" on repairing his toy race car, and on the 1930 New Year's cover, a red-faced baby with boxing gloves winds up to take a swing at a punching ball in the form of the globe while his dog cowers in the corner. In 1933, a middle-class mother has her toddler boy over her knee. With hairbrush in hand and surrounded by evidence of the boy's misdeeds (a broken vase, mirror, and clock on the floor with a hammer nearby), she looks puzzled as she tries to find permission to spank in a child psychology book. The humorous message is that the "experts" sometimes are wrong and that naughty children need to be domesticated now and then. Still, the tone is never violent or vindictive; instead, children, especially boys, are portrayed as feisty, not bad. And the fun-loving spirit, even naughtiness, of the "older" boy is well illustrated with the scene of a grandfather gleefully riding his grandson's rocking horse as the little boy holds on in terror.[47]

The cute girl seldom appeared as the urchin. Occasionally we see the tomboy girl playing marbles. More common were illustrations of girls gathering springtime flowers or bringing their dolls to the doctor's office for checkups. Girls were shown in slightly coquettish but still nurturing roles (holding small dogs and cats), while a female toddler was pictured getting ready for bed with toothbrush and dog in tow, admiring her mom as her mother admires herself in the mirror. As in so many other images of the girl, the "cute" is contained, more nurturing and narcissistic rather than sexual.[48]

In the *Saturday Evening Post*, the childhood theme declined in the 1940s

**3.10**
A classic cover illustration by Norman Rockwell of the cute girl,
learning narcissism from her mother. *Saturday Evening Post*, 21 Oct.
1933, cover. Printed by permission of the Norman Rockwell Family
Agency Copyright © 1933 The Norman Rockwell Family Entities.

(dropping to merely 5.8 cover illustrations per year), partly due to the war. In
the 1950s, with the rise in the baby boom, the themes of childhood wonder
revived (for an average of 17.9 child images per year, peaking at 23 in 1955).
Old themes reappeared: kids sneaking a peak at Santa, girls in romantic
meadow scenes, boys at the swimming hole, even a tomboy waiting outside
the principal's office, proudly wearing a "shiner" from a fight. On a 1952
cover a toddler boy is "curious" as he empties the purses of all the women
guests at his parents' very formal party. Norman Rockwell created many of

these covers, but he was working in a well-developed and beloved genre conveying themes of good natured, willful boys and mostly sentimental, narcissistic, and occasionally coquettish girls, two sides of wondrous innocence.[49]

## Children and Permission to Consume

The New Kid image slid across the pages of storybooks, the trademarks of new brand-name goods, the crude newsprint of comic strips, and the faces of toys, stuffed animals, and dolls. It reappeared in the perky look of Shirley Temple and Jackie Coogan on the movie screen and was imitated in commercial and amateur photographs of children found in living rooms in millions of American homes. Perhaps most significantly, this look of wondrous innocence also found its way into the pages of advertising, in copy that associated a product with an appealing child. The New Kid image in all its forms shared a common theme—the innocent on the frontier of change and desire.

The mass circulation magazine advertisement, as it emerged shortly after the turn of the twentieth century, became the chief example of the selling power of wondrous innocence. Practical advertising copy writers appealed to the concerns of their readers and adapted the themes and language of the child-rearing articles in magazines like the *Ladies' Home Journal*. Inevitably, ads reflected the ideology of the sheltered and scientifically raised child. More interestingly, however, the ads also challenged the assumptions of child development experts by making central the seemingly natural desires and delights of children rather than their developmental needs.

Early twentieth-century ads often showed children needing health-giving products. Ads could even preach against "rich, heavy food" at the holidays, as did one for Fleischmann's yeast. "Instead of overindulging" children, this advertisement advised, "give them plenty of bread and milk for the best gift of all—health."[50] This appeal hit a very hot button in the early twentieth century, when infant mortality rates were dropping sharply but memories of the sickness and death of young children were still strong. Prudent parents could make the difference. Child-rearing manuals of this era emphasized the physical care of the young and monitoring of their demands. In 1925, a Lifebuoy soap ad captured this well: "It's so natural and vital, like air and sunshine, this splendid health of our youngsters that one often forgets how easily it can be lost—and yet how easily safeguarded"—by using good soap, for instance, to ward off germs. In 1913, a Ralston Wheat Food ad sermonized: "Your child's future health is your present responsibility." By the 1920s and

1930s, ads insisted that only the father's foresight in taking out life insurance could guarantee his child a proper education or even protection from a miserable life in an orphanage.[51]

These ads tell us about more than the need to protect and guide the child. They also embodied something that the child-rearing manuals did not stress—the desire to make children glow with longing and wonder. The purpose of modern radiators, according to ads, was not merely to ward off colds but to make children beam with comfort. One extraordinary ad showed sad and sickly children pass through a set of American radiators to emerge with that fresh and healthy look of the Campbell Kids. An ad for Westinghouse's heating lamp was rescued from the humdrum by featuring a blissful baby rising warm and cozy from her bath in the glow of the new Westinghouse appliance. Denton's child sleepwear promised "warm" feeling on the baby's skin. A Lysol ad featured not simply a healthy child on the disinfected floor but a father happily watching his delighted child at play. Health-giving products produced a payoff not merely in doing one's duty to save and protect but also in personal delight in seeing the happy child.[52]

Ads suggested that babies embodied delight, perhaps even were the very source of wonder. Their desires were thus natural and good, and thus it was natural for parents to want to give them delight in the magic of modern commercial goods. No longer seen as either "mouths to feed" or "assets" to train and exploit, children gave parents pleasure through the "sacrifice" of parental largesse. This was a particular form of vicarious consumption—adults enjoying spending through spending on their offspring. It was surely a morally acceptable materialism because it was focused on the dependent and remained within the confines of innocence. Buying toys and providing a comfortable house with a play set in the back yard was good; by contrast, spending money on Scotch in a nightclub or on the latest fashion to display oneself at a party was suspect. The look of the child, of either happiness or disappointment, weighed heavily on the new consumer.[53]

In many ads, that look seemed to be what was being sold. A favorite setting was, not surprisingly, the wondrous child entering the living room on Christmas morning to see the presents under the tree. So appealing was this scene of anticipation and delight that it was used to sell products that one normally did not associate with this main event in modern consumer fantasy. For example, Sun Maid raisins were portrayed as "ideal" stocking stuffers in an image of toddlers casting their gleeful eyes upon those red boxes of raisins peering out from their stockings hung by the fireplace. An ad for Spencer heaters shows a similar Christmas morning scene with the caption promising that the company's heater "keeps bare-foot treasure hunters warm."[54]

The purchase of the look of wonder was even more explicit in the ads for snapshot and movie cameras in the early twentieth century. At first, Kodak ads insisted that the company's cameras provided an "education in taking pictures" (especially for children behind the lens). By the 1920s, Kodak's ads were focused on the look of the child: "A story that never grows old is the picture story of the children—your children, to-day it is filled with the charm of human interest. To-morrow, when the children have outgrown their childhood, it holds you fast—brings back again and again, as you peer over the pages of your snap-shot album, the vivid story of the children *as they*

3.11
An image of the mother ready to capture the wonder of childhood with her Kodak camera. From an early 1920s ad. Reprinted courtesy of Eastman Kodak Company.

*Let Kodak keep the story*

Autographic Kodaks, $5 up

Eastman Kodak Company, Rochester, N. Y., *The Kodak City*

were." When Bell and Howell introduced its home movie cameras in the mid-1920s, the company's ads warned parents not to "wait and wish" but to take movies of the children now. "The alchemy of time is changing them day by day—under your very eyes. There is only one way to preserve their present appearance, fleeting expressions, mannerism, gestures—all the sweet and impish ways that endear them to your heart. That way is through your own Motion Pictures." To reinforce the message, the ad showed an emotional scene of a pleased dad and his teenage son watching the movie of the boy as a toddler dressed in a sailor suit playing with his electric train. *Parents* magazine reinforced this message with articles advocating monthly snapshots of each baby, even if the family's budget might be strained in the Great Depression. Better still was to "train your own cinema star" in home movies that could record "the animation, the aliveness, the untiring energy and vitality of the child."[55]

The advertiser's romance with the wondrous child declined somewhat during the Depression, when new magazines like *Life* began to shift toward sexual titillation to attract consumers. Suggesting this change is a Bell and Howell ad for movie cameras from 1937. Instead of featuring a child, it presents readers with a sexy blond woman. Still, the familiar image of the delighted child's encounter with the promise of consumer culture remained a major selling point in ads, and never more so than in the postwar generation of baby boomers. Some ads drew on the familiar scene of Christmas delight, for example, a 1959 issue of the *Saturday Evening Post* that featured a little boy joyously catching Santa sneaking into the family's refrigerator for a Coke. Others drew on memory of lost wonder, as in the imaginative AT&T ad of a granny calling her granddaughter long distance to "listen to her smile."[56]

The commercialization of wonder went beyond attaching delight to the natural desires and desirability of young children. It suggested that children were the portals to the new world of consumption and "naturally" knew what goods were best for them and everyone else. Youth, especially in its New Kid form, represented health and purity. Note the "Dutch Boy Painter" selling house paint; the rosy-cheeked, pug-nosed Campbell Soup Kid who brought a wholesome basket of vegetables to the "hot, stuffy crowded city"; and the coolly smiling boy dressed in a yellow rain slicker who heralded the waxed-wrapped freshness of the new Uneeda cracker.[57] Children repeatedly "showed" adults new products. Images of youngsters "learning to cook" with Cleveland baking powder or GE's efforts to sell the electrified home with an image of a boy playing with an electric train set up around a Christmas tree became commonplace in family magazines by 1910. In one ad, a seven-year-old girl shows her mother the "hi-lo" brush control on a new vacuum cleaner, telling her, "See Mother! This makes the new Bissel better!" The girl knows how to find the "new and improved" and encourages her mother to give up her "old servant," her outdated cleaner.[58] This image appeared over and over, even in settings that seemed to be very distant from children. For example, an ad for Chevrolet in 1937 featured a boy and girl in bright new outfits, their faces shimmering with delight as they are introduced to the "completely new" line of cars.[59]

These images communicated to very receptive middle-class families that children naturally embraced the new, and that the new was natural. As silly as it seems now, in 1916 a Pearl's soap ad featuring a crying baby with the caption "He won't be happy 'till he gets it!" turned the traditionally willful or simply troublesome child into a self-assured consumer. Ads for Mennen's talcum powder even gave the baby a voice: "Hurry up with Mennen's," a naked baby shouts as she impatiently waits for her nanny's attention. Ads repeatedly claimed to read the minds or dreams of children and invited adults to do the same by anticipating their offsprings' desires in wise purchases. Typical was an ad about a little girl, "Dorothy, whose birthday is to-morrow," who "dreams that fairies bring a big Jell-o dessert for her party, and wakes to find it is true." The notion of getting inside the head of the child is taken to an absurd extreme in Johnson and Johnson's comical ads, appearing from the mid-1930s into the 1950s. An especially striking series of ads showed a baby that had grown to gigantic size lecturing a baby-sized mom. In one ad, the roles are completely reversed; the mother, pictured as a baby, asks her oversized child for "more than lullabies to sooth me." The baby responds: "Maybe now you see that a baby's skin needs plenty of Johnson's Baby Oil and Johnson's Baby Powder!" Ads did not challenge rational and scientific authority; rather, they put the child's natural desires and tastes on an equal footing. Children became experts not in the nutritional or economic value of a food but in what they knew best, what tasted and felt good. This is why they longed for puffed rice.[60]

Ads celebrating children's desires in turn glorified desire itself. A Kellogg's Corn Flakes ad from 1911 featured a cherubic child in glowing light cradling a box of cereal in her arms. The caption reads, "You'd be selfish too." A pure desire for corn flakes and much else is more than "understandable"; it is natural and thus good. In another Kellogg's ad, two children, a girl with her mother and a boy alone on a shopping errand, pass each other on the street with the "right" corn flakes under their arms, simply giving each other telling looks.[61] Kids have a semisecret world, where they are in the know, and, as with their secret gardens, adults too should want to go there. Now that garden is filled not with flowers but with consumer goods.

3.12
An extraordinary appeal to American parents' efforts to learn the natural and thus authoritative needs of the child as the mother becomes the baby and is lectured to by her offspring. Johnson & Johnson ad, *Ladies' Home Journal*, Aug. 1948, 49. Courtesy Johnson & Johnson.

**3.13**
One of a series of Kellogg's ads subversively appealing to the natural
desires of children and, by implication, the naturalness of
possessiveness. *Ladies' Home Journal*, Mar. 1911, back cover.

Ads promoted a related theme, that children are naturally demanding and impish. This idea was expressed in ads featuring young children, especially in trademark images: from the Campbell Soup Kids (who looked as if they were just about to steal from the cookie jar) around 1910, to the impish cartoon figure of Little Lulu serving as a spokesperson for Kleenex in the 1940s and 1950s, to Bart Simpson warning us much more recently "not to lay a finger" on his Butterfinger candy bar. Occasionally, ads copied the images of the impish gang of boys so often celebrated on the covers of magazines in the 1920s. A *Saturday Evening Post* ad for a simple tire pressure gauge illustrated the dangers of underinflated tires by showing a gang of six rowdy but essentially good-natured boys perched on the back bumper of a family car, to the surprise of the couple inside. An ad for Listerine mouthwash insisted that mothers could spare their "ball-playing boys" sore throats and thus "stop stay at home days" even in winter with ample doses of the company's antiseptic.[62]

If some consumer products were supposed to make being a "real" boy easier, others were designed to fill his naturally insatiable needs. When the boy's body screams, "Eat some more food quick," that urgent need must be filled with Beach Nut peanut butter, according to a 1913 ad. Boys were described as "hungry as little bears" in a Swift meat ad published in early spring (1919), a time in the year when "the children are like young animals let loose after the long winter's cold." This idea that children had animal-like desires applied mostly to boys, but like the tomboy New Kid, a spunky girl could appear in a peanut butter ad, asking an adult, "Guess how many I've had?" The reader is informed that she has eaten three peanut butter sandwiches and is told: "Why shouldn't they like it? No reason in the world." The delighted naughty boy eating jam off his fingers scooped directly from the jar feels no guilt. He has only to say, "Hey Mom! The best ever!"[63] The New Kid boy, in all his natural naughtiness, was a natural consumer.

The boy is supposed to want new and playful products, as does the older boy of the house, his dad. This natural longing becomes the basis for father-son bonding, a common theme in ads from the early twentieth century. An ad for Post Flakes shows a father and son in suits, suggesting that both boys and men need "bulk." Later, in 1948, the image has become more childish: "Little injuns (big chiefs too) call Kix cereal 'heap good.'" Another setting for fathers and sons to share delight was in playing together with the electric train: "To the luckiest men in the world, a Father and Son who are pals" with Lionel trains. Ads like one for the Daisy air rifle warned: "It's surprising how fast boys grow. . . . Don't put him off needlessly. . . . Wont' he be a better man, with the training in clean manly sport that he can get from a Daisy Air Rifle." Other ads encouraged the father to recall his happy times

**3.14**
We hear the boy's voice of vital and almost animal
need that must be satisfied. Beechnut ad, *Youth's
Companion*, 7 Oct. 1920, 590.

with the Daisy (a commonplace toy in middle-middle class boys' culture
since 1888). Ads for construction toys like Meccano or Erector repeatedly
claimed that there was really no difference between boys and men: "Boys of
5 or Boys of 50 all find fun in Meccano. The Meccano Boy grows up—Meccano helps to make a man of him—but he never outgrows his liking for Meccano." Similarly, Kodak drew on the common image of male cuteness—the
boy and his dad throwing a football. The mom takes a photo that shows dad
"bursting with pride" in seeing his son in his first football suit. The mother,
"with a little sigh for the baby he was," dutifully, if wistfully, takes the picture,
signifying her son's passage into the boisterous world of men.[64]

Similarly, the girl was represented in ads in ways that largely mirrored
the popular cultural image of the cute and coquette. Pearl soap (1919) of-

**3.15**
This ad for the Meccano toy construction set is an early example of the appeal
of cross-generational male bonding through play. *Saturday Evening Post*,
5 Dec. 1914, 50.

fers a picture of a baby with hair high on her head captioned, "The beginning
of a good complexion." The baby is already an attractive female who needs
to protect her beauty with this newly formulated complexion soap. Mom and
daughter share a mirror in an ad for Fairy soap, as the copy advises both to
"let your mirror frame a lovely face." Little had changed by the mid-1930s.
Ivory soap this time advised the mature woman, "Don't envy a baby's skin"
but have it for yourself with the right soap.[65] No better could this link between the wondrous female child and the presumed consumerist desires of
women be established than in an ad for Cheramy perfume that answers the
question "What is Youth?": "It is charm . . . not quiet, unresponsive charm;
but charm that is vivid, bright, changing, always alive, always different. . . .
It is charm that can stir hidden depths, and create memories, that can turn
back years in seconds, yet make seconds pass as years. . . . It is charm that
comes in a breath, and breathes spring when it is autumn."[66]

The girl's "charming" look mirrors adult longing—even narcissism. The
message was plain: The adult woman was to imitate the innocent but coquettish *look* of the female child. Girls, in turn, were supposed to imitate
mother's *work*. Especially after the war, manufacturers of women's home per-

manent hair products, sewing machines, cleaning supplies, and much more featured child-sized copies to promote their goods. Girls were supposed to play with these miniature tools of domesticity and femininity, and ultimately to develop brand-name loyalty. While dads were expected to play with and like boys, girls were supposed to imitate women's work and values, even when adult women were supposed to look like girls. Women in ads sometimes seemed to be in competition with their daughters, but occasionally they could bond not in play but while sharing a moment of rest from housework with a 7-Up or a Coke.[67]

Taken together, these ads celebrated an image of childhood that one would seldom see in the child-rearing manuals, with their call for firm guidance through the stages of youth to the promised land of adult rationality and self-control. Yet copywriters recognized that parents were torn between the appeals of indulgence and child worship, on the one hand, and the developmentalist-rationalist ideology (and their own convenience), on the other. In fact, ad writers solved the problem by claiming that modern goods provided an effective compromise between these competing ideals. Many promised parents that new consumer products would ease strained relations by reconciling the inevitable conflicts between the child's desires and the parent's convenience and duty without either having to give in.

Merchandisers instructed parents on how consumer goods could displace and defuse children's desires without repressing them. Typical was an ad for a presumably well-built Mallory Cravenette (a man's sport hat). Jokingly, a boy "sails" it along the shore of a pond, but not to worry: "Papa won't care. It's a Mallory Cravenette." More commonly, in the 1920s, ads for new boys' clothes featured images of "happy go lucky youngsters" playing in "rough and ready clothes." No longer would active boys be burdened with "elastics, button bands," or "dangling draw strings."[68] An ad for Quaker Oats offered this parenting advice: "Are you still telling your children, 'eat this, it's good for you'? Please stop—it's so much better to give them the food they need in a form they love!" No more mushy rolled oats but "puffed" wheat or rice could get them to eat right. When parents bought puffed cereal, they made "their breakfasts a delightful game. Children think these fairy grains are confections—you know they're rich grain foods." Chocolate-flavored vitamins let the child be a child (enjoy chocolate) while a parent could still be a "good parent." Lifebuoy soap took this principle to school by offering elementary teachers "Washing up Charts" to make a "jolly game of keeping clean" as children were encouraged to compete to be the cleanest. Mother and teacher no longer needed to cajole or spank. The imp or brat became merely playful and self-expressive with the help of modern consumer goods. The necessary and unpleasant no longer had to be sternly instilled as habit but could instead be given in stealth as pleasure. The unstated assumption—that childhood should be a time of innocent pleasure—ran through all these ads that on the surface seem to be so pragmatic and parent oriented.[69]

In the final analysis, ads told adults what they wanted to hear—that if children with their "natural" needs wanted something, then adults had the right to indulge them. The New Kid permitted fun, giving adults permission to delight in their children's desires and to do so without guilt. Children showed the way for the adult to return to wondrous innocence. Most important, indulging a child not only satisfied the young but also became an opportunity for a parent to indulge his or her own "inner child." By the 1950s, parents "desired their children's desires" even as they were anxious about these longings.[70]

Permissiveness was not invented by Benjamin Spock, Penelope Leach, or any other modern child care guru. It appeared long before the word came into use in the 1950s in the work of Richard Outcault, Rose O'Neill, Hal Roach, and Walt Disney, who taught us to enjoy the naughty but nice boy and the spunky angelic girl. Permissive child-rearing practices were anticipated by two generations in the incessant flow of advertising images and slogans glorifying wondrous children and all those goods that gave them delight. But this was hardly a conspiracy by some cabal of commercial manipulators. Americans literally bought wondrous innocence because it met their needs. Across the spectrum of the cute, from the primitive, rebellious, and coquettish to the dependent, domesticated, and unassuming, Americans experimented with new meanings of childhood. Parents became more tolerant of the diverse needs, desires, and imaginations of their offspring. The cute child offered an appealing alternative to the unrealistic romantic image of the angelic babe or the harsh doctrine that the young needed to have original sin beaten out of them. This new interest in the complexity of the child's emotions, motivations, and behaviors, of course, did not mean that wondrous innocence displaced the doctrines of the child development experts and their efforts to shape the child by controlling his or her emotions and eliminating jealousy and anger.[71] It did provide a very attractive way of understanding and relating to children. This more tolerant understanding of children's desires may be a product of improved child's life expectancy, but it also met adult needs for more expressive, less controlling ways of relating to their offspring. More playful images of children let adults be more playful, too.

None of this is to say that wondrous innocence was not shaped by commercialism. A new consumer culture ran through its very warp and weft. Cute children invited adults to spend. They evoked in adults a longing to care for, protect, and possess, as well as to sacrifice. These are some of the reasons people paid good money for Kewpie and Shirley Temple dolls, teddy bears, and Mickey Mouse T-shirts for themselves and their New Kid children. Still, the cute was not simply a good sales technique. Wondrous innocence and consumerism shared a common appeal—saying yes to desire. New Kid images by their very playfulness and "naughtiness" gave permission to adults to explore new possibilities, new ways of thinking about and acting out gender roles especially.

These images told men that they should let down their inhibitions, their instilled need to accumulate, to control, to deny, and to become the boys' chum (or the boy himself) in spending on playful things. Men could let loose if they embraced the perspective of the boy and thus freed themselves of old expectations of achievement and power that, for many, were no longer practical possibilities. As historian Woody Register notes, "Toys obviously destabilized the time-honored moral boundary between manhood and boyhood, an effect that appealed to an increasing number of middle-class men who were unsure of their manhood in a corporate consumer society and who envied the energetic and fun-loving zest of boys."[72] Even more, embracing the philosophy of the naughty but nice boy vindicated male spending not for family or business success but for fun and self. This ultimately was expressed in the "Playboy philosophy" of Hugh Hefner and the Peter Pan syndrome of adult American men who never want to grow up, assume responsibility, or make commitments. The female version of the New Kid may have been a less radical break with the past, but it became the model for the woman's quest for eternal youth in cosmetics, diets, and fashion, a rationale for a narcissism that had become natural and innocent in the cute little girl.[73]

For so many reasons, modern Americans needed the New Kid, even as consumerism sold it and expanded its meaning. Is it any surprise that wonder so often prevailed over protection, delight over development?

# Holidays and New Rituals of Innocence

4

T he anticipation of Christmas morning, the excitement of dashing
down that dark and cool street trick-or-treating, of being the birthday girl seated at a table surrounded by family with mounds of presents and a candlelit cake, and of sharing an afternoon with Dad at Disney's
Magic Kingdom—these are fond memories shared by many modern American children. They are also rituals invented by adults to evoke in their offspring the wonder of innocence. The images of the cute child were realized
in these rituals, very often expressed in gift giving. Without too much exag-
geration, we could say that holidays and pilgrimages, once expressions of
deep communal needs, were metamorphosed into celebrations of the wondrous child. This transformation coincided both with new attitudes toward
the young and with the rise of consumerism. Christmas, Halloween, and birthdays became the quintessential festivals of wondrous innocence, while vacations and tourist sites increasingly were changed into children's times and
places. To make sense of these subtle and ambiguous changes, we need to re-
consider briefly the traditional meanings of festival rites and why they have
survived the revolutionary changes of modern capitalism.

Most Americans today work and play in seemingly rational cycles, seeking personally to maximize the efficiency of both. They happily embrace
three-day weekends by shifting holidays to Mondays and have forgotten ethnic festival traditions for new and personal vacation experiences. Still, like
their ancestors, modern Americans try to break the routine through the an-

nual ritual of collective holidays and quasi-religious pilgrimages. Modernity has radically transformed but not eliminated religious and folk customs. Americans have discarded or altered some local traditions and saint's days, while they have created new holidays around patriotism, sports, and even sentimentalized commercialism. Yet holidays and pilgrimages remain central to the modern psyche.

Americans inherited the basic holiday cycle long practiced in Europe. Most of these work-free days were tied to the religious calendar, but they were also spaced in the relative ebbs of the rural work year—All Souls' Day (and Halloween) and Christmas to Shrove Tuesday (or Mardi Gras), for example. Additional short holiday periods, including May Day, Midsummer or Saint John's Eve (June 23–24), and a variable and local summer wakes week, also broke the daily grind of rural life. Holiday periods often extended for days, effectively jumbling religious, communal, and commercial motives and activities.[1]

While these characteristics survive today in the blending of shopping and celebration at Christmas and the periodic quest for community in public fireworks displays on the Fourth of July, many themes of the "traditional" holiday have not survived as well. The special appeal of the extraordinary, even supernatural, in encounters with the bizarre or unusual, which had been for so long featured in fairs and later in circuses and carnival midways, has disappeared. Wax figures of the famous and notorious and human curiosities like dwarfs and pig-faced ladies were commonplace in traditional annual fairs, but today they are mostly disdained.[2]

The traditional quest for supernormal wonder combined with the principle of saturnalia. Like participants in the ancient Roman festival in early December from which this term gets its name, preindustrial Europeans binged on food and drink with unrestrained indulgence. Saturnalia served as a psychological release for people who knew scarcity all too well. Even more, traditional holidays let people break with social and psychological rules by indulging in chaotic village ball games, cockfights, or races up greased poles. In annual holidays like Mardi Gras and May Day, people enjoyed a variety of games, masked plays and parades, and songs that expressed many subtle forms of protest against the rich and powerful. Adults threw flour or even eggs or rotten fruit at one another. Roles were reversed when men wore women's clothes, women dressed as men, and boys assumed the status of bishops for the day.[3]

Festivals also established bonds between unequals through shared rituals and feasts, as well as an exchange of gifts. Giving to inferiors was a display of power, while presenting tribute to the superior person was a concession of subordination but also a promise of protection. Gift exchanges reinforced dependency and power but also harmony between unequals. These transactions were usually peaceful, but in mumming rites meandering youths and laborers apparently forced the rich into "gifts" of food and drink on holidays. "Christmas boxes" of candy, fruit, or money had long been an obligation of superiors to subordinates (servants, apprentices, and, which is to say the same thing, children).[4]

The history of the modern holiday is, in large part, the history of the challenge to and decline of these classic elements of the traditional festival: wonder in the bizarre, the social inversions and disorder of saturnalia, and giving between unequals in the community. Key to this challenge has been the displacement of wonder onto the child and, with it, the domestication of celebration and gift giving. All this was certainly a middle-class invention even though it shaped the values and practices of working people and immigrants. The best example of this transformation is in the modern history of Christmas.

## Christmas: From Community to Children

American colonists were sharply divided over Christmas. For many colonists in the South and middle regions, where Puritans did not dominate, Christmas was a postharvest season of eating, drinking, and frolicking, often lasting from mid-December until the first Monday after New Year's Day. Festivities included mumming (or, in its Christmas form, wassailing) as groups of youth "begged" door-to-door for food and drink and sang and toasted their benefactors. Even slaves were allowed to mum in North Carolina and elsewhere. The ex-slave Frederick Douglass reported that in the 1850s "it was deemed a disgrace not to get drunk at Christmas. . . . These holidays serve as conductors, or safety-values, to carry off the rebellious spirit of enslaved humanity. . . . [T]he slaveholders like to have their slaves spend those days in such a manner [of drunkenness] as to make them as glad of their ending as of their beginning." Into the 1820s, motley bands of youths and lower-class New Yorkers calling themselves callithumpians gathered on the streets New Year's Eve to boisterously serenade guests at fashionable balls, throw eggs and trash at the homes of the rich, attack night watchmen, and break windows. The powerful and wealthy were expected to share in their bounty and they recognized the drinking and even temporary assaults on authority were necessary "safety valves." Christmas was, as historian Elizabeth Pleck notes, "a masculine, outdoor holiday rather than a feminine, domestic one." It was unmistakably a holiday for adults, not children.[5]

Puritan colonists were suspicious of these pagan (and unbiblical) celebrations and thus took a second, largely negative, approach to Christmas.
Leaders of the Massachusetts Bay Colony celebrated no holidays except the
weekly Sabbath as proscribed in the Old Testament. They even banned
Christmas celebrations in 1659, viewing the holiday as a pagan Catholic
holdover. Although their attitude became more accommodating in the eighteenth century, tolerating feasting and even singing some Christmas hymns,
the story of the Nativity was not taught in most New England Sunday schools
until the 1850s. It was only between 1837 and 1890 that individual states
recognized Christmas as a legal holiday in the United States.[6]

In the end, neither the traditional festival nor Puritan restraint prevailed. As historians Stephen Nissenbaum and Penne Restad argue, in the
early nineteenth century, Christmas revelries became more confrontational
and disruptive when youth and the poor became alien to and alienated from
the rich in the large towns. In response, elites called for a new holiday tradition that unified classes and the nation. Over the nineteenth century, the
austerity of Puritan/Protestant Biblicism was pushed aside, and Christmas
was transformed from a saturnalian public festival to a sentimental celebration of family and childhood innocence. Protestants (and others) accepted
this "compromise" possibly because family became a substitute for the religious community. As historian John Gillis notes, "Middle-class Victorians
turned the family into an object of worshipful contemplation. As a result of
the crisis of faith that had caused so many to have serious doubts about the
existence of God and his transcendent order, the family became proof of the
existence of the divine."[7] In new rites centering on family and especially on
the wonder of childhood, a benevolent deity could be experienced.

In the early nineteenth century, John Pintard, Washington Irving, and
members of the New-York Historical Society looked for an alternative to
both the Puritan/Protestant rejection of holidays and the boisterous Christmas mummers. One idea was the restoration of the "traditional" English
country Christmas in the vision of "Bracebridge Hall" stories by Irving.[8] The
more abiding solution, however, was to build a sentimental Christmas holiday around the celebration of family rather than community, ultimately shifting "patron-client exchange" to a parent-child bond.[9] This transformation is
often seen in the contrast between Dickens's *Pickwick Papers* (1837), with its
scene of a rural wedding on Christmas Eve (with no children in attendance),
and Dickens's celebration of family and the redeeming influence of innocent
childhood in *A Christmas Carol* six years later (1843). Ebenezer Scrooge may
have lost the traditional fellowship of his youth, fellow workers bonding with
the benevolent old master Fezziwig at Christmas. But he found again a lov-

**4.1**

A popular late nineteenth-century image of the grateful Crachit family gathering around the annual Christmas feast. *Harper's Weekly*, 31 Dec. 1881, 897.

ing community in old age in the scene of the Crachit family's joyous celebration centered around the innocent delight of "Tiny Tim."[10]

Often spread by popular middle-class magazines, new family-focused rituals included German Christmas trees in the 1830s, English Christmas cards in the 1840s, Dutch cookies and new carols published in the 1870s, and especially the exchange of gifts between family members.[11] The old themes of saturnalia and social reconciliation were replaced by a new festival aesthetic—the delight and intimacy of family. The Nativity story played a key role in this transformation. The manger scene symbolized personal renewal without the New Year's ribaldry. Most important, it centered on Christ's birth, a story that gained a new and renewed meaning in the nineteenth century. Birth was not a sacrament in traditional Christianity, and baptism was a simple rite that delivered the child to the protection of the church, not a celebration of the infant. Instead, the "churching" rite, which reintroduced the mother and baby into the community church, was the central celebration, and the focus was on the mother's relationship with the community, not the infant. In the nineteenth century, however, all that changed when Christmas became a rite around the "venerated Jesus and honored Children," and carols like "Away in a Manger" glorified the innocent baby Jesus.[12]

Americans and many Europeans turned Christmas into a family holiday, centered on the divine infant, surrounded by loving parents. This image of the holy family was not new, but it reflected real middle-class domestic ideas as it had never done before. Children were no longer seen as servants upon whom Christmas boxes were obligingly bestowed but as unique individuals, upon whom parents happily showered presents. The offspring represented the family and helped confirm it as a harmonious unit set apart from the public world of class differences. In contrast to the old holiday time spent mumming, throwing snowballs, or attending cheap theater, Christmas became by the 1830s ideally a time for subdued family activities in the parlor, especially playing moralistic board games—at least in the homes of middle-class northerners. Similarly, Christmas presents of books symbolically rejected the disorderly alternative of popular theater. These domestic pleasures of Christmas directly challenged and ultimately prevailed over the old rites of mumming and revelry.[13]

In the middle classes, the "family" and its celebration challenged the boisterous and bizarre festival and became an effective alternative to the seemingly impossible dream of restored community. As rituals were domesticated, so also the "gift economy," anthropologist Dan Miller notes, shifted from building communal to reinforcing family ties. Gifts were "tamed" as they became expressions of love and personal relationships rather than of power and wealth. The refocus on family and children helped to eliminate godless ribaldry, but it did not lead to sublime solemnity. Spending on gifts within the home and family suggested a new kind of "liberality," no longer a joyful protest against scarcity but a domestic inversion of the pinched calculation and competition of the business culture that Victorian Anglo-Saxon industrialism had created.[14] This process also eliminated the giving across social classes and replaced it with a "potlatch of magnification," when exchanges between family members and indulgence toward children concentrated, rather than spread, bounty. So dominant did this trend become that after World War I, many American Jews made the minor religious festival of Hanukkah into a week of family events centering on giving gifts to children.[15] Still, the sort of carefree spending that had characterized the old saturnalia continued to be suspect in the calm and prudent domestic Christmas festival. Especially problematic were the questions: Did Christmas giving

**4.2**
Victorian parents take delight in the delight of their children dashing to the Christmas tree. *Harper's Weekly*, 1 Jan. 1870, 5.

threaten the spiritual and moral development of children? How could manufactured gifts, the products of the impersonal world of machines and commerce, express love between unique family members?[16]

Of course, early nineteenth-century Americans avoided these tensions by presenting gifts of devotion (especially Bibles) or edification (parlor board games, for example). Some families exchanged homemade gifts. Even when the advantages of commercial presents became obvious (saving time and offering better quality), gift givers sought to add personal touches (complementary craft work, fancy wrapping, or, by the twentieth century, the time and care of extra hours of shopping for that special gift).[17]

Perhaps the greatest filter or decontaminator, shielding the gifting process from "materialism" and commercialism, was Santa Claus himself. This figure

Holidays and New Rituals of Innocence

evolved in the nineteenth century into the "stand-in" for the parental gift giver. Santa, in effect, disguised the indulgence of parents from children and to some extent from the parents themselves. It was Santa, after all, not the parents, who heaped box upon box under the tree. He also removed the ambivalence parents felt about the connection between the worlds of home and market by disguising the commercial origins of Christmas toys, masking them in the mystery and magic of their North Pole origins in the old-fashioned workshop of the master toy maker, Santa himself. In the twentieth century, Santa went modern and managerial, but only by employing happy elves in his toy production, not the immigrants or poor women who actually worked in the factories. Parents who encouraged children to write to Santa obtained vital information about what the children themselves wanted. This was a concession to children's choice without inviting a child to badger or beg the parent. Even more, the child's imaginative relationship with Santa made his or her longing and even greed seem charming.[18]

## Santa and the Wondrous Child

Repeatedly, commentators have complained that the "spirit" of Christmas has been corrupted by the materialistic appeal of Santa. Yet, as Russell Belk notes, modern Christmas and commercialization appeared simultaneously. Never was there a pure Christmas of charity and simple family traditions. Spending has always been a part of the modern sentimental holiday, and yesterday's tawdry commercialization of Christmas eventually became today's venerated traditions. Showy department store windows, the Coca-Cola Santa, ornate Christmas cards, Bing Crosby's "White Christmas," once crass commercial exploitations of Christmas, were transformed into the hallow tradition of nostalgia. As Belk puts the point, "With the secularization of society, we have relegated the sacred to the material world. In so doing, the control of transcendence has shifted from the central authority of the church to the diffuse authority of the media and merchant."[19] Involuntarily, the child became the priest of this transcendence through rituals of wondrous innocence that almost seamlessly were wed to the "diffuse authority" of the market. This can be seen in a number of contexts, beginning with the transformation of Santa.

As often told, the modern Santa is a nineteenth-century invention. He is borrowed from three major traditions: (1) England's Father Christmas, the jolly image of the twelve days of Christmas, long associated with old age, not children; (2) the Christ child, the German Christkindl, or Kriss Kringle, central Europe's giver of gifts to children on Christmas Day; and (3) Saint Nicholas, or Sinterklaas (hence Santa Claus), the Dutch incarnation of the fourth-century bishop from Myra (in modern Turkey) who on December 6 visits children to judge their behavior. Still, none of these precedents were immediately recognizable in the elf portrayed in Clement Moore's famous poem of 1822, "A Visit from St. Nicholas."[20]

Despite Moore's efforts to shift Santa's work to Christmas Eve and to transform his image from saintly bishop to jolly elf, Santa's role and appearance remained ambivalent in nineteenth-century America. For some, he remained the bishop, for others a peddler; he was even portrayed as a woman or a black man and appeared alternatively on Saint Nicholas Day, Christmas, or even New Year's. The traditional image of Santa as a judge rather than an unqualified bestower of beneficence upon children long remained. A 1821 poem in a book called *The Children's Friend* tells of a "Santaclaus" arriving on Christmas Eve in a sleigh but dressed still as a bishop. He gave good girls and boys "an apple or a tart, or wooden gun, or painted cart," but he said:

Where I found the children naughty
In manners rude, in temper naughty
. . . I left a long, black, birchen rod,
Such, as the dread command of God
Directs a Parent's hand to use
When Virtue's path his sons refuse.[21]

Christmas morning was like the Judgment Day. This image of Santa survived in the twentieth century, when parents warned children to be good or Santa would pass up their house on Christmas Eve or even leave coal in their Christmas stocking instead of sweets and toys. But beginning with Moore's poem, the emphasis gradually shifted to the concept of Santa as all-forgiving benefactor. The commercialization of this image, firmly established by the 1840s, certainly contributed to the emergence of an all-forgiving Santa. There is no sale in punishment. A kind and gentle Santa was firmly rooted in the American psyche only with Thomas Nast's illustration of 1879 showing the familiar jolly fat man surrounded by happy and playful children. Nast went on to produce a number of images of children in wondrous awe at Santa's arrival. These included toddlers asleep at the fireplace hoping to catch a glimpse of the elf, older children sneaking onto the roof to see Santa with his sleigh, and even a child praying to Santa beside a stocking hung on the fireplace mantle.[22]

The new Santa represented abundance, from his bottomless bag of gifts to his cheery cheeks and plump belly. As Belk observes, he recalled the an-

4·3

The whimsical image of children facing the judgment of Santa
Claus in the form of a frightening jack-in-the-box with a
punishment switch. This drawing of 1870 by Thomas Nast still
reflected the old idea of Saint Nicholas as a disciplinarian of
naughty children, not the unalloyed provider of wonder. *Harper's
Weekly*, 31 Dec. 1870, 865. Courtesy of the Allison-Shelley
Collection, Special Collections, Pattee Library, Pennsylvania
State University.

MERRY CHRISTMAS.

**4·4**

Drawing by Thomas Nast from 1879, fully revealing the "new
Santa," the grandfatherly friend of all children who, after
showering them with gifts, is lovingly and playfully surrounded by
them. Courtesy of the Allison-Shelley Collection, Special
Collections, Pattee Library, Pennsylvania State University.

cient god of pleasure, Bacchus, not a Christian saint. Santa became a secular god, all-knowing and prayed to, a miracle worker on Christmas Eve, filling stockings with sweets and trinkets and bringing heaps of toys for which no one had to sacrifice or pay for. Santa's largesse, it seems, was merely symbolic of God's love and, for parents, God's gift of delight seen in the eyes of their children.[23] In Victorian times, the miracle of Christmas Eve became the very essence of childlike faith. Adults encouraged it because Santa worship seemed to combat the cold, calculating world of secularity and science. And, as Ella Benson wrote in 1876, there was still another reason: "we shall still cling to, and cherish this custom of our childhood and youth, [so] that our children may be happy even as we have been."[24]

This shift of the gift from the community to the family and ultimately to Santa romanticized materialism and thus contributed to individualistic and market society,[25] but the appeal of Santa went further. It was a delight in the naive, innocent desire of the child, who, in Moore's words, had visions of "sugar plums dancing in their heads" and, whose fantasy of a "sleigh with eight tiny reindeer" could be relived by adults' "wondrous eyes." It is, Leigh Schmidt notes, "the romantic longing for enchantment in the face of the disenchanting forces of the Enlightenment and a market economy" that was realized through consumption, especially for children.[26]

Thus, it should not be surprising that Santa and commercialism grew together. In 1875, the New York toy store F. A. O. Schwarz used a dressed-up Santa to promote seasonal sales, and Santa surrounded by toys for sale in his own "grotto" became a regular holiday feature of other big-city stores in the mid-1890s. Santa had become part of the pageantry of the department store in its heyday. As toys and other children's gifts gradually decreased in price and as incomes rose, Santa gave more and more. No longer content with filling stocking or tying gifts on Christmas tree branches, he piled mounds of colorfully wrapped presents around the tree.[27]

Late Victorians were, of course, still capable of feeling guilt about this shift of Christmas from an affirmation of community to an indulgence of their own offspring. Louisa May Alcott's characters in Little Women bring Christmas presents to the poor in the neighborhood after receiving their gifts at home. This gesture was in harmony with the training of middle-class girls for personalized charity. It was also the adults' shield against the spoiled child whom they were in danger of engendering. Moreover, as Nissenbaum explains,

> Some members of the American bourgeoisie were facing a real Christmas dilemma. Their own children had become jaded with presents.

On the other hand, the actual poor—who were unlikely to be surfeited with gifts—were a sea of anonymous proletarian faces, and, in any event, were as likely to respond to acts of token generosity with embarrassment or hostility as with the requisite display of hearty gratitude. Giving to the *children* of the needy would solve the dilemma.[28]

Wonder and delight would appear in the unsullied eyes of poor children, for like their own *once*-unsuspecting child, they were not yet jaded! The contrast between the longing for and possession of the gift was always key to the meaning of wondrous innocence. Victorian Americans were moved by the pathos in the picture of a lighted window displaying "small Santa Clauses laden with tempting gifts" while orphans stared longingly on the cold dark street. Is it any surprise that the middle-class women who had also showered their children with "surprises" hoped to do the same with the virgin innocents of the poor?[29] Santa could not take away all the ambiguity of adult longings for wonder.

## Christmas as Rituals of Childhood Wonder in the Twentieth Century

In a typical story in the *Ladies' Home Journal* (October 1904), a mother describes how she succeeded in reawakening delight in her children, for whom "some of the novelty and surprise" of seeing the adorned Christmas tree had worn off, "for they know just what to expect." Thus, one Christmas she presented them with a surprise. While there still were stuffed stockings to greet them, they found no tree on Christmas morning. The eight-year-old fretted that "perhaps Santa Claus thinks we are too big for a tree"; then, after a leisurely breakfast, the father suggested that the family go on a "Christmas tree hunt." After a thorough search downstairs, they were led by Baby Nell to the door of the attic. When it was opened, the children were "dumb at first with delight and surprise" as they found a "Topsy Turvy Land." In a room with bright green walls, they found shelves full of "many collections of arrowheads, stamps, buttons," and those other treasures dear to children that would have been dreadful downstairs." They discovered also a dollhouse and toy carpenter sets. Venturing further, they found still more, a "forest" of Christmas trees with toys tied to the branches, and a hamper full of gifts from "distant friends and relatives."[30]

Few parents would have had the time, money, or even desire to create such a magnificent deception, but many related to this need to create fantasy worlds to evoke delight in children. Early twentieth-century women's magazines regularly offered Christmas season party ideas that featured brief plays or "tableaux." In *The Snowman*, a two-act children's play, tots meet an animated snowman the night after Christmas. The snowman takes them to the North Pole, where the children play storybook characters in a series of skits.[31] Women went to sometimes extreme measures "in planning surprises and festivals," as a *Ladies' Home Journal* editorial admitted in 1905, in order to "play at being a child, with the irresponsibility that it brings." The "coming back of the child-spirit to us older ones is the real blessing of Christmas time, after all." This echoes the famous words of journalist Frank Church in response to "Virginia's" question about the existence of Santa: Without drawing children (and through them, adults) to the shrine of Santa, "there would be no childlike faith . . . , no poetry, no romance to make tolerable this existence."[32]

But parents did not need to build their own "Topsy Turvy Lands" or even direct skits or organize costumed parties to evoke wonder in children at Christmastime. They had only to take them to view department store and Main Street window displays. Although strolling New Yorkers in the 1830s may have admired gaslight shop windows decorated in greens on Christmas Eve, it was only in the 1880s that elaborate Christmas scenes were displayed in department store windows. Often dramatically unveiled at Thanksgiving, window displays used mechanically animated dolls to evoke delight at the modern magic of making goods and storybook characters come "alive." Department stores competed with each other, offering elaborate tableaux of Niagara Falls or scenes from *Uncle Tom's Cabin*. Village scenes romantically recalling Dickens's *Christmas Carol* were a common theme. But the increasingly stylized scene of Santa and his workshop or sleigh soon were worked into the display. The child could imagine being in the window scene, especially in the darkness of early evening. In the 1890s, lucky children received their own miniature mechanical tableaux, romantic scenes of windmills and Italian organ-grinders, powered by tiny steam engines. By the first decade of the twentieth century, many department stores used train sets (often advertising Lionel electric models) to draw the viewer through the display. The glass barrier both lured and excluded, exciting the imagination and desire of children of affluence and harshly reminding the poor of their inability to join the consumer fantasy beyond the longing look through the window. Displays also drew adults into nostalgia for their own or imagined childhoods. But the Christmas display was more often an occasion for the grandparent or parent to evoke wonder in the child who had been brought on a special trip downtown to see and be dazzled.[33]

The pinnacle years of the Christmas display may have been in the first three decades of the twentieth century. By 1900, toy department Santalands or grottos provided stirring scenery to frame Santa's "throne." And by 1910, at Christmas the Gimbel's and Bloomingdale's toy departments abandoned their "majestic dignity" that gave them the aura of a museum for more child-friendly place. As historian Woody Register notes, "The 'toy department spirit,' as it was often described and proposed, aimed even more completely to transform merchandising, disarming its adult and child customers by creating an anti-patriarchal atmosphere of parentless freedom, intergenerational equality, and wish fulfillment." In the 1920s, Gimbel's of Philadelphia and Macy's of New York presented processionals for Santa's arrival at their toy departments (with accompanying circus acts) to draw a family crowd. By 1927, in Macy's parade, the miniature figures in the window display were transformed into giant balloon-puppets, kicking off what *Playthings* magazine called in 1930 the "buying season" for Christmas toys. Twenty-five-foot-high dachshunds and cartoon figures have awed children ever since. Even later, the post-Thanksgiving transformation of amusement parks like Pennsylvania's Hershey Park into romantic Christmas villages attracted families with young children.[34]

By the 1930s, the old pleasure of women organizing children's Christmas skits and tableaux may have faded, but the same quest for entering the child's "secret garden" of delight survived. Meridel Le Sueur offered the view that children had a natural dislike for rational and scientific distinctions that "cut you off from the universe and make you full of fear." Children would, she claims, "fill the world with wonder" if they could. And, by providing the scene, the fantasy, and the occasion of Christmas, she gave her two children the "fuel" so that she could "warm" herself "at their fires." Le Sueur let her children tell her about Mary and about Jesus' birth, without concern for accuracy, letting them "live in the story." When she listened to them, she exclaimed, "I felt I was newly born."[35]

Writers had no difficulty in associating the religious and spiritual with the sensuous and material when it came to gifting children. "Christmas is the face of the child," gushed another writer in 1941, the picture of "wonder, faith, joy, and expectancy." Thus, "at the first sight of the Christmas room, the child expresses, unreservedly, the innate longing of all humanity. . . . Christmas is immortal because it brings into the realms of possibility, even for a fleeting moment, life as one wishes it to be." This is truly an amazing claim for the delight in the child's first seeing the Christmas loot. This sensuousness hardly changed over the twentieth century: in 1964, an article in *American Home* still claimed that children on Christmas morning experience "with senses still fully alive to fresh beauties—music, the tree, packages like none ever seen before, . . . paper to tear, . . . boxes to open, toy upon toy—all reacted to simply with feelings uncomplicated by expectation, unhampered by responsibility." In 1967, despite the changes of that turbulent decade, one can still find this sentiment: "The eyes of children reflect the depthless mystery, their ears are tuned to music never heard." Christmas is the occasion for them to strut the stage to teach "grizzled veterans of lost innocence" and to give succor to "the thirsty wanderers in the deserts of self-interest."[36]

Old concerns about overindulging the child were forgotten when a *Look* magazine article in 1964 assured parents, "that for every child, Christmas is a still soaring moment of pure delight," and for them "the only thing better than getting a gift [they] wanted is getting one [they] wished for, but never told anybody about." For children, the "anticipation," the "mystery of hidden gifts," and the fact that their "senses tingle" make all the gift giving almost a religious act.[37] What made indulging the young an innocent act was the belief that children were "masters of sincerity and simplicity." Adults could understand the child's sensual encounter with the new and bountiful fruits of modern commerce as charming, even spiritual, because the child saw these thing with "fresh eyes," without the jaded and obsessed lenses of experienced adult consumers. The child's ecstasy of materialism on Christmas morning expressed the parents' longing to witness wonder in its Edenic state before the Fall into the disappointments of modern consumerism.[38]

To be sure, older traditions of community charity survived. Early twentieth-century children's magazines regularly offered stories of privileged youngsters forgoing gifts to offer succor to disadvantaged children, and women's magazine advised that children host Christmas parties so that they would learn to be generous and welcoming to guests.[39] And, of course, the old sentimentality about village and rural Christmases of the past survived in the modern media, appealing to nostalgic city dwellers.[40]

Moreover, the child-centered Christmas formula hardly pleased all. In the 1930s, a veteran San Diego Santa lamented, "You find more who are 'wise' at a younger age."[41] And even more relaxed and permissive mid-twentieth-century parents asked the question, How should they deal with children's unbounded imagination when kids begin to pray to Santa? From the late 1950s on, women's magazines frequently featured articles with titles like "Are You Doing Too Much for Your Children?" expressing the frustrations of parents who let "Santa" wear them out and overstimulate children.[42]

While, in 1969, the greatest proponent of permissive child rearing, the popular psychologist Haim Ginott, insisted that the "gimme kid" should be praised for "good taste" and that the unbridled desires of such children were only "fantasy wishes" that could be ignored, American parents were hardly convinced. In an 1980 article, *Redbook* advocated that the excess of the holiday could be diluted if parents spread activities out over a longer period and made special time for people (as opposed to things), such as holding a "Grandma's Day." Another article advised that children be obliged to select a limited number of requests from their wish lists to Santa. All this suggests that Santa had become the agent not only of wonder but also of unbridled desires and ultimately of jaded souls. Santa surely had become central to the child's fantasy world: In 1985, 87 percent of three- to ten-year-olds in an American survey believed in Santa.[43] Even more revealing was the fact that whereas only 20 percent of children felt "sorry" when they discovered that Santa was a myth in 1896, the percentage had risen to almost 40 percent by 1977.[44]

The problem with the child's "faith" in a Santa who gives and gives went deeper than equating the spiritual with stuff. In the modern child-centered family, the suspension of restraint common in all festivals took on a new meaning. In sharp contrast to the excesses of the traditional saturnalia, the child was not a temporary "king for a day" but the enduring center of family attention. Thus, the "innocent" child became the indulged child, in which Christmas was not the exception but the rule. Parents' delight in their children's youthful wonder turned into their disgust with their offsprings' greed and superficiality. The simple fact was that the Christmas ritual of wondrous innocence accelerated the loss of innocence and wonder.[45]

Unease at the frustrating contradictions of this ritual continues. As Karal Ann Marling notes, the TV special "How the Grinch Stole Christmas" (first appearing in 1966) appealed to a continuous concern of affluent white Americans who, "though they longed to deck themselves in the red and green trappings of the good life," yet have the "fervent wish . . . that there might be 'a little bit more' to the American Christmas" than delightful things. Americans identified with the childlike people of Whoville, who, despite the fact that the bitter and envious Grinch has stolen all their presents and decorations on Christmas Eve, could still celebrate the spirit of Christmas. Even if Dr. Seuss provides no definition of the "more" that the Whos honored, it was clearly embodied in the openheartedness of the principal child character, Cindy-Lou Who. When the Grinch realizes that there was something "more," not only does his heart grow bigger, but he becomes as childlike and joyous as the Whos. Wonder, it seems, was more than gifts and decorations. But at the end of the story, the Grinch still returns the stuff. The gloss of sentiment, it seems, simply spiritualized the materialism of this rite of wondrous innocence.[46]

## Infantalizing Other Holidays

Christmas was only the most prominent holiday to shift from communal saturnalia to wondrous innocence. Easter was, of course, the central celebration of the Christian calendar, or at least it was supposed to be. But the religious message of Christ's death and Resurrection, as powerful as it was to many believers, would not remain unaffected by the broader sentimentalization of the family. After the Civil War, Americans reinvented Easter as a day commemorating youth and family. They borrowed from the child-focused customs of German immigrants, including egg dying, the hunting for and hanging of eggs from a tree, and the legend of the Easter hare, which, like the early Saint Nicholas, plays the role of judge. The German hare was softened into the American Easter bunny, which no longer punished "bad" children and instead brought them delight when they discovered the hidden Easter basket. During the late nineteenth century, Easter became associated with women's fashion and display in church-sponsored Easter parades. Still, as early as the 1880s, Easter greeting cards began to feature images of angelic young girls representing the resurrected Christ. Even Sunday school souvenirs portrayed images of toddlers surrounded by Easter eggs and chasing butterflies. By 1900, with the development of milk chocolate and a profusion of new kinds of confection, Easter became as much a holiday of the child's sweet tooth as it had already become a day of women's fashion.[47]

This transformation of Easter was only part of a trend across the holiday calendar. By the end of the nineteenth century, American educators advocated passing "ancient" holiday traditions on to children. For example, the San Jose Normal School organized May Day games in 1902 for local schoolchildren, complete with chariot races, Grecian floral games, and dances. The custom of girls making cardboard baskets containing flowers to be hung on playmates' doors became an endearing tradition. In the 1920s, elite women's college students participated in strange retrogressive May Day celebrations involving hoop rolling, wearing little girl dresses (and boys' clothes), and electing May queens. A survey of elementary schools in the early 1930s found that teachers introduced pupils to crafts and pageants around the themes of Christmas and Thanksgiving, as well as Washington's and Lincoln's Birthdays. These might have been considered noble and educational activities, but teachers also taught children to celebrate the seemingly frivolous Valentine's Day. Numerous books published around 1910 offered teachers advice on how to undertake school plays, craft projects, and the like in the hopes of preserving "traditional" celebrations that were disappearing from an increasingly urbanized and mobile society. Thus emerged school customs like making Thanksgiving turkeys out of pine cones and exchanging valentines. Dorothy Spicer's *Parties for Young Americans* (1940) turned Valentine's Day, a minor holiday celebrating love between adult sweethearts, into a child's "bridge luncheon," with Jack Horner pie centerpieces and a game involving the selection of hearts on a tree that innocently matched boys and girls. This latter bit of romantic silliness was certain to embarrass the children, especially the boys, but it was one of many examples of infantalizing customs abandoned by adults early in the twentieth century. Adults found children charming when they dressed them in archaic clothes to act out old May Day or Valentine's Day rituals. In effect, the magic of lost beliefs and customs was preserved in the delight of the innocent.[48]

The passing of Halloween customs to children took this trend to an extreme. This dark holiday had unique features that separated it from the Christian and civil commemorations of other festivals. Halloween had distant roots in the Celtic New Year's, Samhain. October 31 was the day when Druids propitiated and warded off the hostile ghosts of the recently dead. Celebrants opened their doors, offering bonfires and even gifts of food to these returning ghosts, and later dressed as spirits to shield themselves from ghostly mischief. Ancient symbols survived, including black cats (once believed to be animal forms of witches). In medieval times, despite the nominal Christianization of the British Isles, black cats were burned alive, some suggest as a substitute for human sacrifice. Jack-o'-lanterns were originally hollowed-out turnips containing a lit piece of coal that had, according to legend, led Jack, an Irish sinner, safely through hell. The jack-o'-lantern was associated with the souls of dead and goblins. In A.D. 834, the church attempted to co-opt this ancient festival of harvest and darkening days of autumn by declaring November 1 All Saints' Day. Nevertheless, Samhain traditions survived through medieval times as All Hallows' Eve or Halloween.[49]

In the 1840s, these and other Celtic customs were imported to the United States by Irish immigrants, becoming part of a loose complex of Halloween celebrations. These practices and the fears behind them were certainly tamed by the nineteenth century, but they still had little to do with small children. One set of Halloween customs was female and domestic: Parties of mostly young women featured costumes, apple bobbing, nut roasting, and divination games that had once assuaged fears of death and the future. In a lighthearted spirit, teenage girls ate apples in front of mirrors, presumably to "see" their future husbands. If a nut designated as a girl's sweetheart was thrown into a fire and burned quietly beside the girl's nut, this signified lasting love, but woe to the girl whose boyfriend's nut burst.[50] Women enjoyed creating scenes of pumpkins and lanterns. They dressed up in "quaint" peasant costumes more often than as goblins and witches. The mood was nostalgic and playful, and no one took the pagan and magical origins of Halloween seriously.

A second set of Halloween customs centered around pranks and mumming committed by older boys. City revelers paraded through town, demanding money of passersby or "dusting" them with bags of flour. A few derailed streetcars and set fires. Masquerading as goblins and witches, male youth removed gates, broke, waxed, or soaped windows, tied shut doors, and even put buggies on roofs and tipped over outhouses. In sum, these pranks represented attacks on the domestic order. Sometimes householders avoided these "supernatural" assaults with gifts of food and drink. While some lamented this rowdyism, within limits, adults accepted these acts of petty vandalism because they were customary (something that now-respectable fathers and husbands had done not so many years before). Youth were simply letting off steam in acts that ritualistically "protested" the constraints of family life. Mostly, householders tolerated Halloween vandalism because they knew the youth involved and realized these that pranksters were just "boys being boys." As late as 1941, an article in *Life* magazine could defend Halloween tricksters as kids having "the kind of fun that makes Huck Finn, Tom Sawyer, and Penrod childhood immortals." Boys might put pins in doorbells and soap windows, but few were ever arrested, and "most men will tell stories of it for years afterward." This second group of Halloween customs was part of a broad tradition of disorderly festivities: ridiculing tradition and authority as well as masquerading and begging for treats as practiced on New Year's and even Thanksgiving in nineteenth-century America.[51]

What is especially interesting about these nineteenth-century and early twentieth-century Halloween customs is the absence of young children. Occasionally, a "Jolly Aunt" held a Halloween party for children. But in the first two decades of the twentieth century, these festivities were tame affairs, with games of blindman's bluff and apple dunking and party decor of pumpkins and corn stalks. Magazines suggested that the children could be fed "black cat sandwiches of date nut bread or doughnuts." There was no mention of candy. There was no attempt to slavishly follow ancient custom, certainly not to revive pagan beliefs, and the old mixed freely with the new. A 1913 issue of the *Ladies' Home Journal* actually suggested that in hopes of reviving the old tradition of symbolically "giving the departed their share" of the harvest, schoolchildren be provided with a "Brownie Night," at which mischievous boy elves (popularized by Palmer Cox) could be matched with girl "fairies" in an evening of apple dunking, nut divination, and line dancing.

These parties were part of a female-dominated process of infantilizing older communal customs. They remained distinct, however, from the mask and mumming traditions of male youth that later became trick-or-treating.[52]

Drawing on a thorough review of sources, folklorist Tad Tuleja argues that children became central to Halloween only in the 1930s and 1940s. The path followed in the transformation was very similar to what happened earlier to Christmas. Increasing urbanization and the social tensions caused by the Great Depression ultimately made the traditional rowdyism of Halloween unacceptable. This confirmed Margaret Mead's speculation in 1975 that, while in rural society "children were granted license to take mild revenge on adults," in cities or larger towns, the same actions became "angry destructiveness," especially when neighborhood social ties seemed to have broken down. To be sure, window soaping and other pranks survived throughout the twentieth century and even degenerated into urban violence (such as the arson waves on Devil's Night in Detroit in the 1980s and 1990s).[53] Still, in the main, these traditions gradually were bowdlerized when adults passed them on to young children in gentle, "cute" forms. Beginning in 1920 in Minnesota, and expanding in the 1930s, voluntary organizations like the

4.5
This Halloween snapshot from the heyday
of the trick-or-treat holiday in Milwaukee,
1958. Elaine Miller, photographer.

American Legion, the Rotary Club, and the Lions Club and municipal recreation departments sought to cajole pranksters to join in Halloween fairs and parades. Some even sponsored window art (with washable paint) on store display windows. The result, notes Tuleja, was a holiday that "has become simultaneously commercialized and infantilized."[54]

Trick-or-treating may have, as folklorists claim, distant origins in the rowdy mumming rituals of Saint Columba's feast day or the rite of giving soul cakes in memory of the departed on All Souls' Day (November 2), but the modern idea of small children shuffling door-to-door in oversized witch and ghost costumes became common no earlier than the 1930s. In a 1939 article in *American Home*, Doris Moss wrote of an "age-old" greeting, "Trick-or-Treat," and advised readers to redirect the energies of potential window soapers by inviting them indoors for doughnuts. The next year, *American Home* noted an alternative to hooliganism: costumed children going from house to house for short parties where they were served hamburgers and participated in apple dunking. But this was hardly an old tradition: Tuleja finds no dictionary reference to trick-or-treat until 1941, when it was the title of a poem in the *Saturday Evening Post*, even though an article in *Life* that year on Halloween festivities fails to mention this "tradition."[55] Only in 1947 does an *American Home* article offer proper etiquette for this emerging "tradition," informing householders that they must have "something" for the "paper bags" of the little witches and ghosts who will ring their doorbells on October 31. At this late date, the preferred treats still were still "traditional"—apples and popcorn balls (long served at private Halloween parties). Adults were supposed to engage the children by guessing who was behind the mask when they first appeared at the door. Only in the 1950s and 1960s did trick-or-treating evolve into its contemporary ritual form—the neighborhood door-to-door tour of costumed children with their open sacks acquiring as much candy as possible. Tuleja stresses how trick-or-treating became bowdlerized. In the 1940s and early 1950s, Halloween costumes often took the form of spiritual or social outcasts (ghosts and witches as well as hobos and pirates), reminding householders both of traditional fears of the unknown and recent social upheavals during the Great Depression. However, these gave way to costumes of Disney and other characters of popular media by the mid-1950s. The tradition of inviting trick-or-treaters into the home was replaced by the quick delivery of goodies at the door with practically no exchange between adult and child. Perhaps more mobile communities meant that adults no longer knew the kids well enough to play "guessing games" or that children just wanted to fill up their bags as fast as possible with candy. With its manufactured costumes and wrapped candy, Halloween had lost its power. Tuleja and others argue that this festival that once served to mollify deep-seated fears and social tensions has been reduced to turning the child into a "budding entrepreneur, whose packaging and legwork have produced personal income."[56]

There is much truth in this characterization, but it misses why Halloween was passed on to children in the first place. What was the appeal to parents in dressing their children in costumes that seemed to be anything but innocent and encouraging them to do the normally unacceptable—knock on neighbors' doors and beg for far more candy than they would be given in a year of pestering parents at the grocery store checkout line? Candy was a reward not for good behavior but, on the surface at least, for "naughtiness," for being a little devil or witch. The old social inversion of the mumming rite had been redefined as a holiday from responsible parental authority, but done in an innocent, harmless, and, of course, cute way. Trick-or-treating was a classic case of the ritual's "descent" from an ancient tradition of magical propitiation to mock fear and violence, ending in complete domestication in the delightful look of the charming child at the doorstep. As important, it was also a way of letting children toy with the scary and with power within a safe and playful context. Children had their way in selecting costumes and masks, in imposing themselves on neighbors, and even in stuffing their faces with tasty but unhealthy sweets. In 1941, *Life* magazine argued that Halloween might have Druid origins, but it had no religious significance to children. While many evangelical Christians today believe that Halloween teaches paganism, even Satanism, Anderson Rearick of the conservative *Christianity Today* noted in 2000: Halloween let kids dress up "as what they might grow up to be, what they wished they could be, or even what they secretly feared." Samhain had no hold on this modern holiday that let adults joke about what ancestors feared in the form of "cute Caspers, laughing pumpkin heads, and goofy ghouls."[57] Halloween became part of the cult of the cute, the naughty but nice, the infantilization of saturnalia.

## Birthdays and Vacations Memorialize Childhood

B irthdays became another occasion for celebrating wondrous innocence. In Europe, birthdays were never noted, except for some nobility, before the sixteenth century, and the medieval church condemned the celebration as an unchristian emphasis on the individual rather than God. In some Christian countries, especially in Latin America, the child's saint's day rather than her own day of birth was celebrated. In Japan, everyone shared a birthday on New Year's Day, when all became one year older. The modern Western birthday emerged from a new stress on the individual and a rising sense of the significance of calendar age, especially of the child. Writer Linda Lewis suggested: "A birthday gives a child a curtain raiser for his personal drama. . . . [B]y licensing egocentric behavior, a birthday suggests the suspension of limits . . . It is a time for dreams and a time for measuring dreams.[58]

The modern birthday was fairly long in coming. Historian Elizabeth Pleck found a reference to a birthday party for a twelve-year-old daughter of a wealthy Boston family in 1772; in the 1790s, another rich family gave a birthday party for a five-year-old but obliged him to present a gift to each servant. The German *Kinderfeste* was important in shaping the modern American birthday, celebrated in the form of a dinner party with family friends and children. The event sometimes including the "Birthday Man," who like the traditional Saint Nicholas (and Easter hare) punished the bad as well as rewarded the good. In imitation of Christmas gift giving, publishers were offering birthday books as early as 1837. By 1870, *Harpers' Weekly* noted a "pretty little ceremony" of cutting up a birthday cake into seventeen pieces, one for every year of a birthday girl's age, each with a lighted "taper" on it. Beginning with the middle classes, the birthday cake gradually entered the party with improvements in stoves, eggbeaters, and baking powder. Ice cream, bags of candy for guests, and storytellers embellished birthday celebrations still further by the end of the nineteenth century. Following the Christmas card's appearance in the United States, Louis Prang introduced birthday cards in the 1870s, and Joyce Clyde Hall of Hallmark made the birthday card a tradition four decades later.[59]

As children increasingly survived infancy, life became understood as a progression toward maturity, each year having special significance. Parents endowed the early years in particular with special hope and even the power of regeneration. The celebration of the child's birth certainly signified the growing respect and attention given to the individual (note, by contrast, that birthdays of slave children were not recognized by their owners). Still, in 1900, the party itself was often more about the pride and social goals of parents, especially the mother, than the individuality of the birthday boy or girl. Like Christmas and even Halloween parties, the birthday celebrations were primarily occasions for the display of women's taste and artistry, focusing on dressing up, decorations, gift buying, and display. A *Harper's Bazaar* article in 1906 called for a flower party, with the girls dressed as roses, lilies, and poppies. They "look so pretty . . . that they cannot help having a good time." Boys were spared the indignity of such costuming and were allowed to wear regular party clothes, but they were still expected to offer a flower and a paper wand to a girl at the party. This surely appealed to the sentiment of middle-class mothers, but it is hard to imagine small children really enjoying this rite.[60]

Gradually, children's desires became central to the party. The song "Happy Birthday to You" was introduced in 1893 by Mildred Hill, with words later added by Patty Smith Hill, her sister and a well-known kindergarten educator. Slowly this song became the anthem of the child's party, focusing attention on the birthday boy or girl just before the rite of making a wish and blowing out the candles. Published only in 1934, the "Happy Birthday" song filled a void in the emerging child's culture of the birthday party. It spread throughout the United States with little encouragement at first from schools or commerce. Nevertheless, it was adapted to languages throughout Europe and Asia. With its simple and repetitive lyrics almost always sung by a group to a single and special individual, "Happy Birthday" fully expresses the new celebration of the unique child and, as symbolized by the candles and (traditionally by spankings), how old the child is. Everyone except the birthday child must sing the song just when the birthday cake is fully lighted, a ritual that places all the attention on the birthday boy or girl. When adults sing the song to other adults, it is usually done in a childlike spirit.[61]

All this signaled a shift in the meaning of the child's birthday away from a display of maternal taste and accomplishment and toward a celebration of the child for simply being him- or herself. Already in the 1920s, department stores featured announcements of children's birthdays on store-run radio programs. By the 1930s, party planning books instructed parents to invite not their own friends but their children's pals to kids' birthday parties. By 1935, *Parents* magazine suggested that six- to nine-year-old boys should have a "pirate party," each participant given a red sash, greasepaint for his face, and an eye patch, along with the chance to win in a treasure hunt. By 1948, popular magazines had gone still further, stressing that even preschoolers had their own ideas about birthday parties, and warning that boys should not be "forced" into wearing crepe and other feminine forms of decoration. Even psychologists got into the act, advising parents to have enough toys and games to spare any guest from boredom. Child development guru Arnold Gesell and his institute at Yale inspired a party planning book published in 1956 that provided guidelines on birthday parties for every age from three to fifteen, detailing what behaviors to expect and how to plan games and rituals appropriate for the specific ages of the children.[62] All this certainly was in tune with the growing belief that children were to be the focus of their own celebrations, but, even more, that the delight of children was central to the birthday itself.

The annual family vacation followed a similar historical path. Vacations were rare for most Americans until well into the twentieth century, and only at midcentury did they begin to be organized around children. This is no surprise because few couples with children could afford an extended holiday. Even the affluent usually sought "diversions" for the children rather than time with them on vacations. Ideals of gentility—especially the quest for quiet socializing and contemplation of nature—continued to shape middle- and upper-class thinking about holidays. And these goals had little room for the boisterous child.[63]

A *Ladies' Home Journal* article titled "The Best 2-Week Vacation for a Family" (1904) focused on the needs of adults but finally, almost as an after- thought, noted, "Nor were the children forgotten," with the promise of di- versions such as exploring caves, fishing, and wading. At that time, many af- fluent parents sent their offspring away to summer camp. Even when families went on a holiday together, popular opinion makers warned that the vaca- tion was an opportunity for the young to "learn to play" and to get away from overdirecting parents. Indeed, the vacation was supposed to be a release from all roles (women's domesticity, men's work). On a holiday in the Rockies in 1916, the children would learn to play together at the stream and, in un- hurried days, develop a "natural" harmony with other members of the fam- ily. In this setting, even the busy father could have "time to enjoy them," es- pecially older children who normally were drawn to their friends rather than to their parents or siblings. Still, vacations were not about nostalgia for youth or centered on youth.[64]

By the 1930s, things began to change when the vacation became avail- able to wage-earning families. In 1930, only 10 percent of American blue- collar workers enjoyed a paid vacation, whereas 85 percent of white-collar workers and their children benefited from it. Paid vacation plans emerged in the 1930s and 1940s as part of the explosion of union membership (in- cluded in 93 percent of union contracts by 1949), letting at least relatively privileged union members take their kids to the seashore or camping. While the traditional pattern for wage-earning couples was to abandon holiday making once children had arrived, paid vacations and increased family in- come made it possible for millions of these couples to bring their offspring on vacations.[65]

At about the same time, across class lines, the holiday took on new meanings. *Parents* magazine signaled a shift in 1935 when it insisted that va- cations should focus on the child. But even here, the stress was educational rather than the emotional bond across generations: Vacations should teach the young about the varieties of life (work in a fishing village, the grandeur of the Rocky Mountains, or the historical legacy of New England). Children should be encouraged to observe nature, society, and history and to ask questions. The ideal holiday shifted still further after the war, with an emphasis on the adult's pleasure in the child's response to new experiences. An article in *Parents* in 1949 claimed that a long holiday by train with the children would be a delight because what children see is "lovelier" than what jaded adults notice; in 1956, *Look* featured an illustrated story, "Emily in Wonderland," which describes a five-year-old city girl's encounter with cows and horses and shows her surrounded by sunlit ferns, with a wondrous look on her face. The image of the child on vacation had begun to imitate that of the child on Christmas morning.[66]

The 1950s saw the widespread use of the station wagon for inexpensive and informal tours of national parks and heritage sites. The increasingly roomy family car provided family togetherness on long automobile trips to the Grand Canyon or Old Faithful. In 1954, *Look* helped lead the trend with a feature on Barbara Hale and her husband, Bill Williams (who played TV western hero Kit Carson), loading their two children into a station wagon for a "natural" holiday in the Sierra Nevadas. Their son, dressed in cowboy trappings, is pictured sliding down a snowy hill as Mom looks on with pride. The family car vacation also transformed the holiday site. The Civil War battlefield of Gettysburg, formerly a place for serious contemplation and memory of war (and alternatively a site for boisterous crowds on railroad excursions), became an obligatory destination for families in the 1950s. From the car, Mom, Dad, and the kids could read plaques and later hear taped guided tours about the glorious past, after which they could drive into the parking lots of their motels to wade and swim in the pool and visit child-oriented amusement parks nearby. In 1971, a magazine feature stressed the joy of spontaneously piling kids and equipment into a station wagon for a family campout in the woods.[67] The automobile tour, of course, had the advantage of containing the kids, but troubles abounded, enough for Benjamin Spock to offer his sage advice in a 1961 article: Keep drives short, do not try to do too much in one day, and make sure that children have in-car activities and a say in the trip's itinerary. Again, the focus was on keeping the children happy, perhaps even full of wonder.[68]

By the end of the 1970s, a new trend emerged, reflecting rising divorce rates. The family vacations could be for "just the two of us," as a single mother meets her "new friend," her five-year-old daughter, on a trip to New England. There the mother discovers how independent and wise her daughter has be-

**4.6**
A family celebrates the summer vacation through the "achievement" of the little brother. Kodak ad, *Saturday Evening Post*, 6 June 1959, 64. Reprinted courtesy of Eastman Kodak Company.

come as she visits "fisherpeople" and learns to spend the dimes and quarters given her by relatives. Proudly, the mother notes that the girl even offers to buy her a cup of coffee.[69]

Americans, of course, could be skeptical about the joys of the family vacation. Recall the 1962 movie *Mr. Hobbes Takes a Vacation*, in which James Stewart plays a frustrated family man stuck in a beat-up summer cottage with a son who wants to do nothing but watch westerns on TV and a teenage daughter who is unable to get a date to the local dance. Still, so central had children become to the annual vacation that an article in 1972 could make fun of a couple trying to enjoy a romantic holiday without the kids; they find themselves patting other people's kids on the head and watching *Captain Kangaroo* for days into their vacation "escape." Adding to the irony, upon their return to pick up the kids at Grandma's, they were told that the children "didn't mention you once."[70] The holiday increasingly was meant for the family, for bonding, for renewal and celebrations of children's desire (at least, as adults understood it).

## Disney Defines Innocence

When Americans reflect on how the rituals and meanings of vacations have shifted to childhood wonder, they probably think of Disneyland. But there certainly was nothing inevitable about an amusement park becoming a center of wondrous innocence. The amusement park, as Americans knew it in 1900, was a descendant of the medieval commercial fair, with its motley offerings of freaks, acrobats, and games of chance.[71] While children may have attended these parks, by the 1950s they were dirty, often unruly, and crime-ridden. The respectable alternative that also shaped the modern amusement park was the late seventeenth- and eighteenth-century pleasure grounds of Vauxhall and Ranelagh Gardens in London. These refuges from urban disorder attracted the aristocracy and solid middle classes with their well-kept greenery, open-air concerts and theater, fireworks, and fine dining. Notable, however, was the fact that children were hardly to be seen, much less heard, in these settings of adult escape and display of fashion. Another source of the amusement park was the international exhibition (first appearing in London in 1851). With its high-minded displays of artistic heritage and technological progress, it brought along with it a larger and more exciting version of the old fair entertainments. By the time of the 1893 Columbia Exhibition in Chicago, the "midway," with its newly introduced Ferris wheel, drew more crowds and more money than did the uplifting exhibits in the "White City." Still, even on the rides, children were rare.[72]

The modern American amusement park was most directly modeled after the midway. Beginning with the enclosed parks at Coney Island (Steeplechase, Luna, Dreamland) built between 1897 and 1904, these new sites of public pleasure were designed to attract a respectable working-class and middle-class audience. These parks reassured the crowd, wary of the disreputable past of Coney Island, where gamblers, prostitutes, and hard drinking had prevailed, with well-maintained grounds, courteous staff, the banning of drink, and the exclusion of unruly (and poor) with an admission charge to enter the gates. Luna Park and Dreamland created exotic environments romantically reminiscent of Venice and Delhi along with inventive rides like "The Trip to the Moon." One contemporary wrote that a "great surging mass of men and women with little children" was attracted to the early amusement parks. But many of the featured rides were often too rough and certainly too titillating for small children or families. And the vast majority who were attracted to Coney Island in the 1900s (which in addition to the amusement parks included beaches, bars, racetracks, and freak show attractions on a street appropriately nicknamed "The Bowery") were young adults. Far from seeking to share wonder with children, these crowds of teens and young adults were escaping the constraints of family life in their New York City apartments. By the 1920s, with cheaper subway access and reduced ticket prices, Coney Island drew poorer and younger crowds, but the amusement parks there hardly catered to the family. In fact, the new crowd drove out what respectable family trade had previously visited the resort.[73]

To be sure, the classic rides of amusement parks were passed down to children, but this was a very long, slow process. The carousel, today the classic kiddie ride, originated in the twelfth century as an Arab war game. It was transformed by French aristocrats into the sport of riding live horses while competing at the skill of tossing a lance through a ring. In the seventeenth century, wooden horses mounted on spokes radiating from a central post provided young competitors with an opportunity to practice their sport. Gradually, animal power and later steam power were used to turn the carousel, transforming a machine for military training and serious sport into a novel amusement. By the 1870s, the steam carousel equipped with a musical organ was a commonplace in fairs and urban pleasure grounds. Even then, many of the riders remained adults, and only slowly did the carousel pass to the charm of childhood. The same was true of the roller coaster, which in its earliest form was a snow-covered wooden trough in eighteenth-century Russia, patronized by young adults. The modern mechanical roller coaster on tracks emerged in 1884, but it was still too daring for any but older teens and young adults.[74] Before the 1920s, the amusement park had no special association with children. Only then did park owners begin to offer kiddie rides, most of which were simply miniatures of adult thrills or even playground swings and slides located in a supervised area that allowed parents to drop off their children while they enjoyed the thrills of the new roller coasters.[75]

The full infantilization of the amusement park came only in 1955 with the opening of Disneyland. Still, Walt Disney had not intended to commercialize innocence, much less transform the vacation, when he entered the entertainment business in the mid-1920s. His focus was on his Mickey Mouse cartoons that first appeared in 1928. Only because his movie income was insufficient to finance his expensive animation did Disney license the images of his cartoon characters to toy companies, book publishers, and others to make ends meet. When, in April 1954, he began to build his Disneyland amusement park, only ABC television was willing to buy into the idea. This was no surprise, since the traditional amusement parks had been in decline since the 1930s—rooted as they were in the streetcar traffic of the urban working classes and to a declining aesthetic of the sideshow. In 1946, Luna Park, one of the pioneers in turn-of-the-century amusement parks, burned down at Coney Island and never was rebuilt. New York planning czar Robert Moses had long awaited the demise of Coney Island—in his view, a tawdry, dirty eyesore that attracted only unsophisticated working-class and immigrant crowds. Since the mid-1920s, he had worked to build highways and services to other more family-oriented and middle-class state parks and beaches on Long Island. Though Steeplechase Park limped along until 1964, the reputation of Coney Island and other amusement resorts had long suffered because they attracted crowds of teenage kids and hoodlums and had become centers of racial conflict. Thus, when Disney suggested building a new amusement park in Los Angeles, investors thought he was mad.[76]

Disney had in mind a very different sort of amusement park—built not on the patronage of poor working-class youths but on that of middle-class families with lots of children, who had their own cars and could get to his park via a freeway in suburban Los Angeles. Disney bought a land parcel large enough to accommodate car parking (insufficient in Coney Island, a resort built in the rail age). Instead of building Disneyland around the familiar thrill rides of the old amusement parks and carnival freak shows that had dominated at Coney Island, Disney's vision sprang from his own experience in filmmaking and fascination with miniature railroads and nostalgic scenes. Since at least the early 1940s, he had contemplated building a small park across from his Burbank movie studios for tourists and their children who wanted to see "where Mickey Mouse lived." After the war, he had a ridable model railroad built at his home and, inspired by an older tradition of shadowbox miniatures, had his designers produce scale models of idealized American farm and small-town scenes. He even had a barbershop miniature fit with a singing mechanical barbershop quartet. Briefly, he thought about putting these curiosities on trains and charging a quarter to run them. Soon he abandoned this project and instead blew up these adult play sets into five-eighths scale buildings encircled by a railroad. In effect, he created a fantasy park through which adults and especially children, could walk about like the toy figures in the old miniatures. While this vision was not as unique as Disney and his propagandists later claimed, it deviated sharply from the contemporary carnival and amusement park. So revolutionary was it that Disney was obliged to set up a separate company and even borrow on his own life insurance to make his dream come true.[77]

Success for his California site came only after Disney decided to enter television, still anathema to other moviemakers. Although he was rejected by both NBC and CBS, he finally won financing from the fledgling ABC in exchange for producing a weekly show for the network. From its premiere in October 1954, Disney used the program to hype the opening of his new attraction for July 1955. He gained additional publicity for Disneyland with the success of a children's western, *Davy Crockett*, and a children's afternoon TV show, *The Mickey Mouse Club*, that appeared about the same time.[78]

In 1971, five years after its founder's death, Walt Disney World opened near Orlando, Florida. It was the culmination of a long-planned effort to capitalize on Disney's success on the West Coast with a much larger park on the East Coast—situated on 27,400 acres of wasteland in central Florida and eighty times larger than the original. The Disney company not only updated the California theme park (called the Magic Kingdom) but also added three comparably sized parks (Epcot in 1982, MGM-Disney Studios in 1989, and Animal Kingdom in 1998), along with three water parks, twenty-seven hotels, seven nightclubs, and much else. Walt Disney World became more than an attraction. It became a destination that eventually would consume a week or more of vacation time. Disneylands were also built in Tokyo (1983) and near Paris (1992), making the Disney phenomenon global.[79]

Many writers have attacked Disneyland and Disney World for sentimentalizing history and nature, for substituting "entertainment" for learning, and for being, in the words of historian Paul Fussel, "gravely sub-adult." But these critics often miss what really draws million across the world to these attractions. Each of the Disney theme parks is an anti–Coney Island, resistant to rowdyism, cacophony, and dirt. They reflect a middle-class longing for order, cleanliness, and unchallenged fantasy. Their rides are mild, hardly provoking the kind of thrill that is common at Six Flags and other modern amusement parks, or that once existed in the old amusement parks. And their prices (always high) keep out the poor or casual gangs of teens. One does not see many blacks or Hispanics, and then almost always in family groups. But these facts cannot reduce the parks to mere middle-class escape. They are environments designed to evoke wondrous innocence. Despite its appeal to families with children, commentaries often stress that Disneyland has attracted adults more than youngsters (with ratios of up to four to one), and especially since the 1990s, advertising and new features have been directed toward seniors hoping to relive their youth, rather than looking to children to evoke memories of youth.[80] There is much truth in this.

But the question remains: Why would adults want to go to such a childish place? Part of the answer can be found in the fact that Disneyland and Disney World became focal points for modern nostalgia. After all, the often cited plaque in Disneyland's town square says, "Here age relives fond memories of the past . . . and here youth may savor the challenge and promise and the future." At Disneyland the old fantasize, not just the young. The central role of "Main Street, U.S.A.," the "tunnel" through which all visitors must pass to get to the four "Lands" of Disneyland and the Magic Kingdom, certainly highlights nostalgia. As many have noted, "Main Street" is a highly romanticized replica of Disney's own childhood memories of small-town America (in his case, Marceline, Missouri). In his widely distributed park guides published in the 1960s, Disney himself noted, "Many of us fondly remember our 'small home town' and its friendly way of life at the turn of the century." While Disney stressed that this was a time when "the discoveries of the late nineteenth century were beginning to affect our way of life," it was really the intimacy of the Candy Palace, Penny Arcade, Swift Market House, and Puffin Bake Shop that appealed both to visitors and to Disney, a place where no one worked in factories or impersonal offices. Even though it was hardly a memory to suburban children in the 1950s, much less today, young people had to first pass through Disney's nostalgia before they could enjoy walking through the dreamworlds of Disney movies that they had experienced. As Disney lectured, "When you visit the apothecary, . . . we hope you'll visualize, as I often do, your own home town Main Street, or the one your parents and grandparents have told you about."[81] Adults enjoyed a nostalgia that recalled youth, even if it was not their own, and children were expected to play their parts in the "timeless" wonder of the scene. In this way, Disney perpetuated not only a sentimentalized view of his turn-of-the-century childhood but also the adult's understanding of the child as a repository of a wondrous past. In effect, adults like Disney invented the role of the wondrous child and expected real children to play it in the nostalgic setting of Main Street.

Despite the fact that visitors arrived by plane and car, they traveled within the park by "train" and by foot, as Disney did in his childhood. Main Street, U.S.A. re-created the nineteenth century's strolling town. It promised relief from the lonely crowds on city streets or in cars caught in freeway traffic on their way to the mall or suburban house. Disney's Main Street represents a kind of protest against the formless aesthetic and loneliness of the modern suburb and the disorder and alienation of the modern downtown. The wonder of the first generation of light and neon that brought millions to New York's Times Square (and Coney Island) in the 1890s and 1900s had become obsolete and shabby long before the opening of the first Disneyland in the 1950s. The ever-improving spectacle of modern life excited, but it also was emotionally insufficient for most Americans, and so Disney offered "the deep nostalgia for the kind of collectivities that used to be."[82] Disney architecture surely "reassures," as cultural historian Karal Ann Marling so well notes, with its "forced perspective" of buildings and castles that appear higher than they are (because they are progressively scaled down as the structure rises). Moreover, as Disney himself realized, Main Street, with its five-eighths scale to a "real" town, was also a "toy" to be played with rather than a monument to be awed, allowing one to relive a childlike past in whimsy, even if it was not one's own.[83]

Nostalgia, as Peter Fritzsche and Jean Starobinski note, has a distinctly modern appeal. It is not merely tradition (that would apply to rejected entertainments like freak shows) but a desire to "return home." This was especially craved in the America of the 1950s, a culture where one family in four moved each year, but where (in contrast to many European countries) there was no "home" village or neighborhood to return to because change in the United States had been so rapid. Going home in such a setting meant "returning" to an artifice—a Main Street, U.S.A. But, even more, it meant returning to an idealized childhood in an idealized time and place. As Starobinski put it, nostalgia is "the return toward a state in which desire did not have to take account of external obstacles and was not condemned to defer gratification"—in other words, a permissive childhood. Seen in this light, the seeming anomaly of a "kiddie land" that attracts a majority of adults vanishes.[84] The whole of Disneyland could be said to be an evocation of childlike wonder, with or without kids. Disney himself claimed, "The worst of us is not without innocence, although buried deeply it might be. In my work, I try to reach and speak to that innocence."[85]

None of this is to suggest that Disneyland as a vacation destination is not about children. For Disney, children were best equipped to appreciate his childlike vision. Entrance into Disneyland, he insisted, was "like Alice [in Wonderland] stepping through the looking glass," and as in Alice's Wonderland, things are not as they seem to be. As Beth Dunlop notes, Disney manipulated "size, shape, color and sound" to produce a wondrous effect. Just like the trade cards and mysterious comic strips of Nemo in Slumberland, Disney invited adults to share in the delight of children (or what adults think delights children). And, of course, the best way to do that is bring along your very own "Alice."

In a visit to Walt Disney World, I noticed that some fathers and sons seemed to blend in age, or both seemed to regress. The vacation site may be especially suited for cross-generational male bonding in a culture that still makes communication between fathers and sons in normal life more difficult than that between mothers and daughters. Forty-something dads seemed to revert to their youthful years of parenting, while sixteen-year-old sons regressed to six-year-olds. The message was clear: Fathers can get their little boys back again, and sons can get back their special relationship with dads, without holding hands. Contemporary ads continuously stress the magic of childhood across the generations. A TV commercial in 2001 commemorating Disney's one hundredth birthday featured a grandfather with his young grandson at Disneyland in front of the famous statue of Disney hand in hand with Mickey Mouse. The grandfather tells the boy that Disney was a man who "created magic," to which the boy replies, "Kind of like you, Grandpa." As a final touch, the boy and old man walk off hand in hand just like Disney and Mickey.

If the Disney parks were not erotic and the rides were tame, the result was not merely banal and saccharine. The thrill came from interacting with the childish stories embedded in the rides and the sheer sensual intensity of the place. The Mad Hatter's Tea Party is really "only" a whirl-a-gig ride, but with the critical addition of the people-sized tea cups in which families ride and are reminded of the movie *Alice in Wonderland*. The Dumbo ride is equally conventional except for the pleasure of riding on the back of a cute baby elephant, "proving" that in the miracle land of Disney, elephants really do fly. In Fantasyland, Disney stressed you could "wish upon a star," as did Pinocchio in the 1940 movie cartoon, and dreams actually could "come true." Disney rides are not so much about physical jolts and rushes as about encouraging children and adults to live out Disney stories. Many are like "riding a tracking shot" of the camera person on a movie set. Visitors can fly with Peter Pan across the nighttime London sky (where riders "see everything that Peter Pan saw" on his ship). They can travel on a Dutch canal boat through Storybook Land to see the homes of the Three Little Pigs or the village of Pinocchio in miniature, or race with Mr. Toad as he is chased by cops. Indeed, the thrill does not have to come in a ride at all. The boat rides through the jungle and submarine journeys in Tomorrowland were boring without robotic elephants and mermaids. Disney's Enchanted Tiki Room, a later addition to Adventureland, offered a cabaret-style show involving an elaborate setting of mechanical parrots and other cutsified animals passing songs and jokes back and forth. From his 1940s experiments in miniatures and automata through his elaborate 1960s mechanical figures, Disneyland was a link to the tradition of the Christmas tableaux in the department store windows of the 1880s. He wanted adults to recall their childhood delight at these automata and invited children to share in it.[86]

The lands beyond Fantasyland had their didactic overtones: Frontierland was supposed to evoke the "pioneer spirit of our forefathers"; Adventureland taught the pleasures of "traveling to mysterious far-off places"; and Tomorrowland was a place where we can "step into the future atomic age" and the "challenges of outer space and the hope for a peaceful and united world." Still, these lands were hardly museums to American history, geography, and science. They were to be fantasy adventures, not sites of learning: Their simulations of the rivers of America, Tom Sawyer's island, a jungle boat safari, and a trip to the moon appealed to the adult's view of the child's imagination. Of course, they defied the complexity of real history, nature, and technology, but they were intended to be like reading a child's storybook and to be accessible to all members of the family, despite conflicting interests and differing attention spans. When critics condemned Epcot's World Showcase at Walt Disney World as nothing more than cliché-ridden stage sets and even as "elaborately decorated entrances to restrooms," they neglected the real purpose of this attraction. It was designed not to present the real facts and figures of Morocco or France but to provide a wondrous feeling— tourism from the street with all the boring bits removed. Disney would say, perhaps, that Tinker Bell had sprinkled "pixie dust" on it all.[87]

Still, Disney represents more than the sentimental side of the cute. Shows over and over let in glimmers of the smart aleck (as in the comments by Ellen DeGeneris, the wisecracking "dumb girl" who leads us through the Animal Kingdom's Dinosaur feature to "learn" about the origins of fossil fuels). Here the child can be naughty if nice.

Everyone comes to a Disney park with his or her own agenda, which doubtless changes from visit to visit. The reason, in part, is the sheer aesthetic complexity and intensity of the place. It is an overload of delightfulness that makes for a cross-generational attraction. And it surely brings people back. The key is not that the Disney park is controlling and sentimental but that its wonder is so intense, within, of course, the confines of the sensibilities of the middle-class family. In this way, it really is an elaboration of the parlor on Christmas morning or treat-or-treating on Halloween. But Disney delight, like the Christmas morning potlatch, leads inevitably to satiation and sensual fatigue, often midway through a week at Disneyland or Walt Disney World. I saw a father try to talk his five-year-old into buying a sword at the Moroccan village store, only to be presented with a face so bored it seemed to say, "I already have one."

Through the ubiquitous viewings of Disney movie cartoons, the endless cross-marketing of Disney images on clothes and toys, Disneyland and Disney World have become sites of modern pilgrimage. They do more than take the visitor into a counterworld where miracles happen (as was the expectation of medieval pilgrims). They also deepen the meaning of Disney icons by, in effect, really letting people go where Mickey Mouse lives. Disney storybooks come alive, and children's "dreams" come true. Adults, whose childhoods have been marked by Disney "events" since the 1930s, share with their children or grandchildren the same awakening of "dreams." It is no surprise that an old man (even without the added benefit of grandchildren present) can be seen strolling down Main Street, U.S.A. wearing an orange-billed Donald Duck hat. Adults who two hundred years ago had worn masks and costumes to ward off evil spirits or to reverse social roles in saturnalian festivals today fend off old age and "reverse" age roles at the festival of Disney.

Walt Disney's achievement was to package, combine, and intensify a half century of images of wondrous innocence. This is not to say that he "co-opted" all these images (there were a few that were too big even for Disney, like Santa). He and his company filled a cultural need that the traditional amusement park, national park, and museum have failed to satisfy. So effective has Disney been in meeting this need that "to be a child means going to Disney films and theme parks." It seems that every American must make a "double pilgrimage" to a Disney theme park, "first as a child, [then] later as an adult with his own children." In many ways, Disney has captured the meaning of innocence, and to deprive one's child of a Disney pilgrimage is to be a bad parent.[88]

Rituals of wondrous innocence at Christmas, Easter, and Halloween and on vacations had origins in the middle-class desire for the magic of belonging and belief in an age when community and the supernatural could no longer be so easily embraced. Rites of giving presents, festivals, and experiences to children created what adults needed and had lost from the decline of the old holiday culture. But, in the end, it was the commercialism of Disney, Halloween, and Christmas that sustained this need for wonder.

# Gremlin Child *How the Cute Became the Cool*

In the 1984 film *Gremlins*, we see wondrous innocence gone astray. Set in Kingston Falls at Christmastime, it invites us to recall George Bailey's ideal small-town life of Bedford Falls in *It's a Wonderful Life*. The story presents a wonderful "all-American" family, the Peltzers, including a befuddled father, naively trying to invent a better mousetrap, a tolerant and wise mother, and a boyishly creative teenage son, Billy. Looking for the ideal present for his son, the father happens on a Chinese curio shop, where he is enchanted by a cute and cuddly pet "moguai," a live version of everyone's favorite stuffed animal. The wise and mysterious shop owner will not sell it, not trusting the brash father to follow the rules for its special care (no bright lights, no water, no feeding past midnight). Still, the father secretly buys it from the owner's Americanized (and thus money-mad) grandson. The creature is the perfect image of the cute—about the size of a small dog, with droopy ears and big, sad eyes that make a person want to cuddle and care for it.

But the boy is careless. When the moguai (cutely renamed Gizmo) gets wet, it multiplies, and when the new and far less lovable moguai offspring trick Billy into giving them food after midnight, they transform into Gremlins, the very opposite of the cute Gizmo. With their claws, narrow slits for eyes, and sharp-toothed grins, they look and act like homicidal aliens as they multiply in the hundreds. The film shifts into a horror mode when the Gremlins viciously attack Billy's science teacher and an old woman. The mother goes on to stab one of the beasties with a butcher knife and spatters another in the microwave. Slowly, however, it dawns on the viewer that the Gremlins are not just vicious monsters. They are really naughty children, bullying the still sweet Gizmo, causing mayhem as they mischievously disrupt traffic signals, wildly indulging themselves at the local bar, and finally occupying the local theater to watch *Snow White and the Seven Dwarfs*.

In the end, Billy (aided by Gizmo) succeeds in killing them all with fire and daylight, bringing peace back to Kingston Falls on Christmas morning. Just then the Chinese curio shop owner returns to reclaim Gizmo and scolds the Peltzers for their irresponsibility. They obviously lacked the "depth" of the Eastern mystic to handle the mysterious but delicate delight of the moguai. This story, however, is more than a modern update of the "The Sorcerer's Apprentice" or even merely a condemnation of Western disrespect for the mysteries of nature. It is also a cautionary tale of wondrous innocence. The adorable Gizmos on which we lavish love and attention in our typical middle-class homes can become the bratty Gremlins almost without our seeing why. Though the Gremlins remain children in their curiosity and taste, they are out of control and become our enemies that we symbolically would love to annihilate.[1]

In real life the transformation of the Gizmo into the Gremlin is, of course, not so obvious and simple as in the movie. Still, most parents today will admit when pushed that they think this change has to do with their "breaking the rules" like the Peltzer family did. Figuring out the rules is not easy in a culture that insists that parents raise the "enchanting child." Famous etiquette authority Emily Post expressed the dilemma when she asked parents to "cross the rainbow bridge of memory to the enchanted garden" of childhood even as she admonished them to "cultivate" their offspring like a well-tended garden.[2] This contradictory image reflects a persistent ambiguity about childhood innocence: Is it a wild and wonderful place of imagination and desire or a delicate and threatened setting where caring adults must cultivate character and reason? The quest for the "enchanting child" does not necessarily lead to the cultivated child; instead, many fear, it may produce brats.

Adding to the dilemma, the modern child often needs to become a rebel, if not a Gremlin, to break away from the stultifying demands of "enchantment" and become free of babyhood. Thus, as anthropologist Donna Lanclos notes, children tell "dirty" jokes to liberate themselves from their parents' view that childhood is a sanctuary from "obscenity." This was and still is difficult for parents to recognize. Even the renowned children's folklorists Peter Opie and Iona Opie refused to catalog scatological and sex games and language in their exhaustive studies of children's games in the 1960s because only "ogre" children used them. For generations, child development experts have had to warn parents to be circumspect in reacting negatively to their children's defiance of cultural standards.[3]

Until recently, middle-class adults could see such deviations as manageable in a childhood that seemed to move smoothly from the naughty-but-nice toddler to the robust boyhood of a Tom Sawyer and on to a responsible and caring adult. Generations of rite-of-passage fiction have affirmed the normalcy of occasional childhood defiance. In the first half of the twentieth century, adults offered children a number of literary outlets for freedom that hardly challenged grown-up authority and offered a gentle transition from innocence to mature responsibility. St. Nicholas, a magazine for middle-class children, featured a predictable array of "goody-two-shoes" fare ranging from illustrated poems, animal stories, and folk songs for young children to the latest trends in sports and science and heroic current events for youth. One issue in the 1920s took readers from adventures in the Everglades to places described in articles such as "The Smallest Republic in the World" and "The Romance of Metal Mining." Stories favored boys, but girls' serial fiction about adventure and relationships was not ignored. St. Nicholas was supposed to help raise men and women of energy and responsibility. Stories often featured achievers—inventors, discoverers, sports heroes, and statesmen—and invited youthful readers to identify with them. An ad for St. Nicholas's Stamp Club insisted that stamp collecting offered not only an education in history and geography but also a chance to share an activity beloved by "kings and presidents." Like its rival, Youth's Companion, St. Nicolas met the standards of middle-class respectability and showed the path to entry into adult life. It was the sort of magazine that the young George Bailey of It's a Wonderful Life would have read as he dreamed of becoming an engineer and traveling across the globe. Although St. Nicholas ceased publication in 1943, the weekly TV program Disneyland of the 1950s and 1960s carried on the same mix of themes of adventure abroad, pioneer life, and scientific progress. For Walt Disney and many Americans of midcentury, the passage from wondrous innocence to the young-at-heart adult was a straight, unencumbered path.[4]

## How Gizmos Became Gremlins

This formula was not to go unchallenged, as the history of modern children's culture makes clear. The fantasy life of the middle-class child did not necessarily follow the story line of St. Nicholas. Manufacturers of darker

CHEMCRAFT opens the door into the fascinating wonderland of Chemical Magic and Industrial Chemistry. It is much more than a toy. Not only will it furnish hours of amusement for the fortunate owner, but it also teaches in an intensely interesting way the relation of chemistry to our daily life, its application to the industries and its importance to our nation. There are no dangerous explosives or poisons, and the experiments may be repeated as often as desired.

**5.1**

This promise of "Wonderland" is a very different place than the fantasy world of Alice or later children's fictional world of the cool. Rather, it is the delight that the middle-class child is to experience by entering the exciting world of "industrial chemistry" and the dream of future success and achievement. Chemcraft ad, *Youth's Companion*, 21 Oct. 1920, 651.

images of crime, science fiction, and even sexuality often captured this fantasy and wondrous innocence slipped out of the control of parents. This was no simple theft. Parents, merchandisers, and children themselves contributed to this change.

Ironically, the ways that adults have shared the image of wondrous innocence with their children explains part of the shift from the cute to the cool. As we have seen, adults met deep-seated needs by giving their children unexpected excitement and relief from today's reality and tomorrow's uncertainty. By their very nature, these gifts of fun connected children neither to a live heritage nor to a responsible future. The cute provided no cues for growing up, even though maturing is precisely what adults expected children to do. And, because the culture of wondrous innocence required parents' acceptance of children's self-expressiveness, even a measure of naughtiness, children quite naturally transformed adult-imposed fantasies into dreamworlds of their own. It is no surprise, then, that by the 1930s these gifts of fantasy began to mirror the actual aspirations of children and not those of parents, especially when the young borrowed the stories of street culture for their own. The young took up their parents' offer of freedom in a world that was distinct both from adults' childhoods and their own futures. Aiding in and accelerating this transformation, media and toy fantasy makers began to market directly to children. Although signs of this trend appeared as early as 1900 in children's magazines and toy catalogs, in the 1930s, with the coming of children's radio, Saturday film matinees, and the comic book, this drift from parental values was vastly extended.

What had been the cute, ultimately controlled by parents, became the cool—the opposite of the cuddly and delightful to parents, but to kids, an expression of freedom from adults' possessive needs. Merchandisers first approached older boys in the 1930s and 1940s with the hard mechanical visions of Buck Rogers and Dick Tracy and in the 1950s with dark, violent worlds of horror and crime comics. In the 1960s and 1970s, they extended rebellious fantasy to girls and small children with the cool, even cold, look of Barbie and grimacing action figure toys that partially displaced Tiny Tears baby dolls and electric trains. Often this culture of the cool seemed to defy the bond between parent and child. The cool even helped to erode traditional paths to maturity with its mockery of adult responsibility and denial of the need to "grow up," contributing to the childishness of adult pleasure and desire today.

## Passing the Cute to the Cute

A dult fascination with the image of the cute child—the naughty-but-nice boy and the sweet and coquettish girl—redefined adult understanding of childhood in the rituals of family life in the early twentieth century. Even more important, parents passed that fascination on to the children themselves. New Kid images, from Kewpie to Mickey Mouse, were popular because they appealed to adults trying to get "back" to childhood through their children. During the teddy bear craze of 1906–7, not only did adults buy bears as accessories but women's fashion magazines offered patterns for making teddy bear clothes. Teddy bears were a fad in the fashionable quarters of major cities in the United States and Europe, where women carried them on walks and to the theater as if they were pets. Toy makers even marketed the character as a good-luck charm in the form of a "laughing Teddy," which helped adults "bear it" through "tight money, hard times, and pessimists" in the recession of 1907. Men bought Kewpie dolls for their office desks and women for their dressing tables.[5] They succeeded as "charms," however, not because they had supernatural power but because they were fads and a fantasy, playfully embraced. As such, they represented the wonder of childhood, a dreamworld that adults, if not children, knew to be mere dream, but that was nevertheless enchanted because it enchanted children.

Thus, for these modern talismans to be "charmed," adults had to share them with children, the source of their "power." The adult not only imagined children as cute and invited the young to participate in rituals of wonder but also encouraged them to identify with the adult's playful fantasy. The teddy bear closely held by its owner, immortalized in millions of photos since 1906, "charmed" the child. The world of the marvelous that science and capitalism had taken from the world of adults was regained in and by the child. As in the ritual of the surprised child on Christmas morning, the little ones had to play their parts by acting cute.

Another example of passing the cute on to the cute child was the introduction of commercially made masks to the repertoire of children's play. After 1900, department stores began selling these props of traditional carnival to parents to give to their children. As in the ancient saturnalia, medieval Mardi Gras, and traditional Christmas mumming, these masks featured the faces of the marginal and even fearful (to the white middle class): Indians, Irishmen, devils, clowns, and blacks. Significantly, to this array of traditional stereotypes were added the images of new and largely ephemeral comic strip characters. Like the image of the African American, the comic strip character stood outside the "norm" of white middle-class culture. In effect, adults were passing Mardi Gras on to their children, letting them take on the role of the rebel and the outsider who sometimes mocked authority in rites of social inversion. By 1907, the anarchy implied in the carnival mask, however, had become domesticated in the child's "innocent" fantasy, just as would Halloween a generation later. The devils and Indians masking the child's face were no longer threats but, like the boy hugging the teddy bear, amusing, reassuring, and "wonderful."[6]

On a wider scale, parents delighted in the peculiar "magic" of the New Kid look and invited their children to imitate and interact with these images. This was, of course, a gesture at giving the young a "secret garden" of their own, but a garden whose gates adults immediately crashed. The New Kid dolls were distinguished by their use of soft, "can't break 'em" materials that encouraged active play (in contrast to the fragile fashion or shelf dolls of the past). No longer did adults insist that the dolls look and dress like adults. The Patsy and Campbell Kid dolls featured up-to-date informal fashions: overalls and sun dresses, not the fussy adult-pleasing dress-up costumes of Little Lord Fauntleroy. Most important, these New Kid images exuded "personality" that children were expected to imitate and role-play with.[7]

A curious penchant for the "exotic" appeared early in gifts of dolls and figures for children. Paired sets of boy and girl dolls (e.g., the Indian Kickapoo and Pocahontas and the black Cotton Joe and Topsy) were commonly

**5.2**

Early examples of dolls adapted from the Campbell Kid icon of the Campbell's Soup Company, selling the advertiser's image of the New Kid cute as playthings for children. *Playthings*, Oct. 1912, 2.

sold through mail-order catalogs around 1910. This appeal to cross-racial play was derived from a nineteenth-century folk doll that had a white face but that, when turned over, had a black head under her dress. Children doubtless enjoyed role-playing with these personality dolls. In a general way, this perpetuated an old tradition of recognizing children as universal innocents with ethnic and national variations (seen in late nineteenth century trade cards and later in Disney's "It's a Small World" ride). Yet, as with masks, these playthings invited children to cross ethnic and cultural boundaries.[8]

These dolls introduced kids to a new fantasy land, full of topical characters from the comics, that had little to do with parents' nostalgia for their own childhoods and much more to do with initiating children to novelty and even anarchic popular culture. In 1912, for example, Sears sold dolls and shaking-head figures of Foxy Grandpa, Little Nemo, and Happy Hooligan, popular comic strip characters of the time. In effect, these toys introduced children in play to the comical world of the cute—incompetent adults and childlike but seemingly parentless animal crazies and characters, broadly sharing spunky but decent personalities. Although the comical setting made these figures unthreatening to most adults who gave their children these tokens of anarchy, this was no longer the world of *St. Nicholas* or even the Brownies with their goody-two-shoes moralisms.[9]

Parents never completely controlled or were responsible for "passing" the cute to the cute, of course. From an early date, merchandisers recognized that they could sell to the parent through the child. In 1913, *Toys and Novelties*, a major trade journal, noted that "an advertisement to a child has no barriers to climb, no scruples to overcome." The child had not yet learned to discriminate, and the youthful imagination was not constrained by tradition.[10] A common sales gimmick in children's magazines until the 1950s was to invite children to show toy ads to parents. Some manufacturers even encouraged children to place toy ads in their fathers' newspapers or under the milk bottle just delivered on the front porch to "trick" their elders into "discovering" that their offspring were ready for a BB gun or an electric train.[11] An advertising culture that encouraged adults to think of children's desires as natural and good helped merchandisers use children to sell playful products to their practical parents.

It is no surprise, then, that the entertainment industry appealed directly to children, in effect, accelerating the parents' penchant for passing the cute to the cute. Through ads and store window displays, they encouraged the young to want objects that made them feel connected to imaginative stories introduced by their parents. As early as the first decade of the twentieth century, merchandisers passed on adult fads quickly to the kids (novelty figures like the Billiken, for example). This process went further when the childlike image of Mary Pickford in the film *Little Annie Rooney* was reproduced in a doll. Kids' celebrities like Hal Roach's "Our Gang" characters were also made into children's play figures almost as soon as they became movie idols in the mid-1920s. The age of the child star emerged only in the 1920s and took off in the 1930s. Youthful celebrities like Jackie Coogan, Shirley Temple, and indeed Mickey Mouse appealed to adults, but they also attracted children. In fact, these stars belonged to the kids.[12]

Kids won entry into a special community of the initiated and of fantasy when celebrity images of children like themselves were made into dolls and toys. By possessing a celebrity doll or figure, the child assumed a bit of the charm, courage, or power of the character. And such toys were new, not part of the parent's folk culture but products of an ephemeral world of the commercial fad, made just for the younger generation.

The culminating celebrity image of the cute child was, of course, the Shirley Temple doll in the 1930s. Adults bought the doll to share with their daughters Shirley's charm and fame (despite the fact that it cost twice as much as an ordinary companion doll).[13] The attraction was the accuracy of the doll's likeness to the live Shirley. Her mother, Gertrude, insisted that children on the street recognize Shirley in the doll before she allowed it to be sold. This association was reinforced when the doll became a special souvenir released with the movie *The Littlest Rebel* on Shirley's birthday in April 1936. The Shirley Temple craze brought together adults and children in a collective fantasy of sharing in the aura of the ur-cute. Magically, it seems that the "charm" of Shirley rubbed off on little girls who owned her. The doll was not merely a companion, like the New Kid dolls of the past; it gave girls, in their dreams, access to Shirley's world in the movies. In so doing, it freed them temporarily from the confines of home and the demands of mothers (which Shirley in the movies, if not in real life, never had to face).[14]

The first step in the passing of the cute to the cute was that parents shared a fantasy with their offspring, though the appeal was often different for each party. This phenomenon has been central to the success of the Disney company since the 1930s. Early Disney cartoons shared much with slapstick comedy and even the vaudeville skit. Yet, as noted earlier, Disney quickly discovered a new formula: Mickey became "at heart, an unselfish little guy," as Walt Disney would later say, and, even more, the ideal boy—complete with dog and pals. The cartoon behavior of the mouse became more constrained, less anarchistic, and thus more appealing to parents. By contrast, children admired Mickey because he had adventures in a charmed and secure world of small-town America and yet, unlike them, was free of big brothers, big sisters, and parents. While Disney replaced the anarchic side of the early Mickey with Donald Duck in 1934. Donald's "crazy" behavior differed from the anarchy of early animal comic strips (like Krazy Kat) or later cartoons (like Warner Brothers' Bugs Bunny or Daffy Duck). Donald's stories often updated the appeal of the Katzenjammer Kids, when he played the "Captain" to his nephews' role as the "Kids." As in the Katzenjammer strip, the "adult" Donald was bested by his nephews, with whom children could safely identify without antagonizing parents. In the 1930s, children wrote Donald, asking him why he had such a bad temper. Children could feel superior to Donald, knowing that they had more self-control than he did. Still, all this amused rather than threatened "real" adults because they knew they were not really like Donald, nor were their children really like the nephews. Disney understood that with the right mix in his characters' images and stories, he could keep the generations together in a shared fantasy of family entertainment.[15]

In 1930, the Disney company, in an attempt to build children's loyalty to its cartoons (and licensed merchandise), set up 150 Mickey Mouse Clubs across the country. Unlike the later TV version, these were actual Saturday-morning gatherings of children, opportunities for the young to have the theater to themselves, to see their favorite cartoon character, and to choose

Mickey Mouse goods with the aid of premiums. This was part of a widespread marketing strategy that turned children's desire for group identity and personal freedom into profits. Yet the blatant commercialism was buried in goody-two-shoe rituals that reassured parents. A meeting of officers, the chanting of a moral creed, news about the club's sponsorship of sports teams, and even musical performances by local child talent preceded the cartoons. Here again, Disney combined appeals to both generations, offering the assurances of the cute to parents and promising autonomy and respect to children, and in the process selling Disney products.[16]

## Origins of the Cool

The problem came when the parent's vision of the cute was subverted by the child's vision of the cool fed by makers of children's commercial culture. The cool has many components and origins. It may mean simply a kind of cutting-edge fashionability or more subtly emotional restraint. Here, though, I want to focus on the cool as the opposite of the parent's cute. Cultural critic Daniel Harris argues that the cool is the "aesthetic of the streets, a style of deportment specifically designed to alert potential predators that one is impregnable to assault." What began on violent city streets is imitated by white middle-class kids. "The menacing nonchalance of coolness" became the "aesthetic plaything" of suburban youth, "mimicking gestures and facial expressions designed as deterrents to attack." It offers disaffected bourgeois youth "an enticing fantasy, that of going downscale, of descending into abysmal yet liberating poverty." Even more important here, "coolness represents a denial of innocence on the part of youth culture." Ironically, Harris notes, "the romantic movement's cult of the child has created a foul-mouthed enfant terrible who has turned the playground into a necropolis." Signs of it are the child's "emphatic rejection of the smile" and of "rosy-cheeked good looks" for the "cult of the grotesque."[17] Today, we may recognize all this in the grungy look of ten-year-olds, in teens' tattoos and pierced body parts, and in the continuing popularity among ten- or twelve-year-olds of horror movies and violent video games. But where did all this come from?

With Harris, I argue that the cool ultimately comes from the adult's romantic idea of the cute, the wondrous child, and the child's simultaneous embrace of and reaction to it, all of which merchandisers fed and flamed. The key to understanding this transition is the child's need for distance from parents.

Very early in the history of consumer culture, children found ways of becoming independent of adults. About 1900, the psychologist G. Stanley Hall and his students noticed that youngsters seemed to have a "universal" desire to collect objects. This "collecting instinct" began with the six-year-old and peaked by the age of ten. Hall's group found that the child collector was motivated by the desire to imitate peers and gain status and esteem by possessing a whole set of things. In a study of children living in Santa Barbara, California, in 1900, Hall's researchers found that ten-year-olds had an average of 4.4 collections and that children gathered both natural objects and adults' castoffs: While 60 percent of the boys and 39 percent of the girls collected bird's eggs, 64 percent of boys and 24 percent of girls also collected cigar tags. Parents might have provided guidance for and even additions to these collections, but collections were the child's obsession and achievement. They introduced the young to a peer culture of collectors and gave them a sense of power and accomplishment apart from their elders.[18]

While these collections came from nature and discarded *adult* goods, merchandisers also learned how to create a special world of children's own consumption that pulled the young much further from their parents' culture and experience. As early as the 1870s, magazine publishers offered children "prizes" for signing up adults to subscriptions. For decades, this remained a way for children to get access to their own stuff without having to wait for their birthdays or Christmas. Manufacturers of brand-name goods offered colorful trading cards in their packages that children hoarded. Ivory Soap promised collectible stamps for product wrappers, and Post Toasties offered picture cards of birds or presidents for kids, who cut them out of the back of the cereal box.[19] In many subtle ways, children got their own fantasy stuff.

In the late 1920s, new outlets for a unique children's commercial culture emerged that not only gave the young autonomy but also challenged middle-class sensibilities by drawing on the "cool" culture of the street. After movie houses were widely wired for sound in 1927, movie attendance rose 55 percent in three years, with a disproportionate number consisting of children and youths. At the same time, certain forms of movies became juvenilized. One was the movie serial. With roots in cheap working-class magazines, these short "chapter" movies appeared first in 1913 in the thriller *What Happened to Mary?* A run of "cliffhanger" serials followed, built around beautiful women pursued by bad guys. Each episode ended with the heroine hanging on to a cliff for dear life or in some other seemingly impossible situation, to be rescued or saved at the beginning of the next "chapter," only to endure the process once again. Early serials sometimes featured veiled sadistic sexuality (as women were tortured by depraved men) and relied on futuristic and supernatural fantasy ("death rays" and devil worshipers, for example). It is no surprise that respectable middle-class critics attacked these chapter movies as unsuitable for children. In fact, most were really created for adults, as was most entertainment of the era. Though they became less sensational over time (shifting toward Western and detective themes), movie serials resembled adult pulp magazines rather than children's fiction. However, by 1930, with the coming of the talkies and more sophisticated adult audiences, movie makers more or less "passed on" the serials to the young and their Saturday afternoon matinees. The first sound serial—*The Indians Are Coming*—appeared in 1930. Repeated musical themes, often accentuated with rhythmic pulsations, introduced a new intensity in storytelling. Universal, Columbia, Mascot, and especially Republic Pictures borrowed from the comic strips, pulp magazines, and radio programs to produce "chapter plays" of ten or more episodes shown successively on Saturday afternoons. Their cheap production (often using the same sets and music over and over, and even recycling silent film footage) may have put off the sophisticate, but the kids loved them.[20]

When network radio emerged in 1926 with the founding of NBC, another children's venue appeared. NBC pioneered national programming of popular entertainment that split audiences not by region or ethnicity but by sex and especially age. At first, radio networks offered children's programs as a public service without commercials, and radio producers were reluctant to annoy parents with violent programming designed to attract the attention of the young and impressionable. By 1930, however, advertisers had learned that children were extremely attentive and loyal listeners. Thus, they were excellent targets for commercial messages, especially for breakfast foods. Just as homemakers had their serialized soap operas in the early afternoon, children could tune in at four o'clock to hear fifteen-minute episodes of their favorite heroes beating seemingly impossible odds. These programs used repetition in musical themes and script lines to create an aura of familiarity, thus making children feel like they possessed the sounds and words they heard. Premiums reinforced their identification with the program, its stars, and especially its advertiser. Merchandisers encouraged children to mail in the tops of cereal boxes and cap liners of coffee jars to obtain Sergeant Preston's "Yukon dog cards" and Little Orphan Annie "decoder" rings. Advertisers hyped these trinkets as essential to becoming a "friend" of the star and associated them with the story line, giving listeners a sense of being part of the adventure.[21]

Only a few years after the introduction of sound movies and network radio, the child's comic book appeared, providing the young a third site of autonomy. The older newspaper comic strip had appealed first to adults, though family themes were common, and children in the stories often got the better of adults. While the strips had been reprinted in cheap books from the first decade of the twentieth century, they still reflected adult humor, experiences, and frustrations. In the early 1930s, comic strips were bundled in cheap booklets and given away as advertising promotions. So popular were these strips that their printer, Eastern Color, decided to sell them as *Famous Funnies* in 1934.[22] Soon publishers began to target the children's market. Comic books were cheap enough for even a child to purchase directly, without necessarily obtaining permission from parents. Mickey Mouse cartoon strips appeared in cheap comic book form in 1935, and in 1940 the Dell Publishing Company won the contract to publish all of Disney's characters in comic books. Soon thereafter, comic books featured Warner Brothers' Bugs Bunny and Walter Lantz's Woody Woodpecker. These new cartoon characters were far more independent and willful than the gentle Mickey, and they frequently outwitted their adultlike adversaries. The cute character of Little Lulu, originally appearing in the *Saturday Evening Post* in 1936, was turned over to the kids in a comic book in 1944. No longer was she mischievous, the naughty-but-nice kid whom adults found adorable. She had been transformed into the single-minded independent girl who ignored adults and always got the better of the neighborhood boy, Tubby, and his friends. The picture book form with balloon texts reached children with limited reading skills or patience even more effectively than did the earlier illustrated storybooks. Some adults applauded when new publications like *Education Comics* and *Illustrated Classics* presented Bible stories and pictorial versions of famous novels in comic book form. Still, in the 1940s, the comic book had become a distinct form of children's culture over which parents had little control.[23]

This becomes even more apparent when we consider still another side of the shift from the comic strip to comic book. From the start, the people who manufactured cheap detective and adventure magazines for adults also published comic books. Malcolm Wheeler-Nicholson, writer of formulaic adventure stories for *Adventure* and *Argosy*, in 1934 started a group that later became Detective Comics (DC) and publishers of Superman. Even the founder of Dell, George Delacorte, published detective and true-confession magazines. These publishers were simply looking for what sold. And, what would sell was not necessarily comical. A key ingredient was the cool, the appeal of the world of the rough and tough adult in the crime, superhero, jungle, and eventually horror comic book.[24] By the end of the 1930s, comic books were becoming the reading of material of choice among children and youths. Monthly sales rose from 3.7 million copies (1940) to 28.7 million (1944), peaking at 59.8 million in 1952. A survey conducted in 1944 found that 95 percent of boys and 91 percent of girls between six and eleven years of age regularly read comic books. The percentage for older children, twelve to seventeen years of age, hardly dropped (87 percent of boys and 81 percent of girls).[25]

Children's stories and stars were now available on the child's schedule. The parent's invitation to dream and desire things, so long confined to the holiday calendar of Christmas, birthdays, or a summer week at the beach, was now offered every Saturday matinee at the Orpheum, every weekday afternoon on the radio, and anytime a kid could curl up with a comic book. The child's desire to connect to his or her fantasy world could now happen with scarcely any adult involvement.

## Literary Genre and the Transition to the Cool

Children's new media fantasy, of course, did not appear out of nothing. In movie, radio, and comic book form, that fantasy had roots in youth fiction that was not all threatening to parents. Still, merchandisers gradually colonized children's stories with new themes and challenged middle-class parents' perception of appropriate paths to adulthood. Let us briefly consider four genres—the growing-up adventure, the Western, the detective and crime thriller, and science fiction combat—each, in turn, more distant from white middle-class parental values.

Parents who gave their children the standard juvenile fiction of the early twentieth century expected stories similar to their own Victorian tales of maturation. Continuing the tradition of Horatio Alger's *Ragged Dick* (1867), boys still enjoyed stories of youths born to poverty who, through luck and pluck, climbed the ladder of success. These tales were long reprinted as exemplary reading for aspiring children of the middle class. They may have stressed the perils of the climb (cheating peers, confidence men, and temptations), but they seldom suggested direct conflict with parents. The bad adult was usually an outsider or a stepfather. Edward Stratemeyer was Alger's protégé and an experienced writer of travel, adventure, and Wild West stories who built a business in publishing juvenile fiction. His stories were built on character-forming challenges that led to responsible and happy adulthood. To maximize his output, in 1905 he created a "syndicate," assigning book outlines to be fleshed out by professional writers in assembly-line production. His shop produced some of the most famous children's fiction series of the early twentieth century: the Rover Boys (first appearing in 1899), the Bobbsey Twins (1903), Tom Swift (1910), the Hardy Boys (1927), and Nancy Drew mysteries (1930). Many continued to be published by Stratemeyer's daughter long after her father's death in 1930. Tom Swift was typical: This energetic teenage son of an inventor from upstate New York delighted in exploring the modern world of technology and travel. Stories were constructed around his motorcycles, motorboats, airships, and other new devices. Swift even built his own glider, which he used to recover rare plutonium from Siberia. He went off to war in 1918 (*Tom Swift and His War Tank: or, Doing His Bit for Uncle Sam*) and in the 1930s dabbled in electronics (*Tom Swift and His Television Detector*). Tom Swift, along with his contemporaries, the Rover Boys, fulfilled youths' fantasy of freedom from the constraints and boredom of small-town family life and school, but their extraordinary adventures were grounded in reality and prepared them for future success. In the end, they remained close to the support of parents or uncles. Moreover, they grew up to be like their parents: Tom Swift married Mary Nestor, his longtime girlfriend, and had a son, Tom Swift Jr., who continued the series into the 1960s.[26]

The Hardy Boys mystery series also appealed to the juvenile fantasy of escape from small-town America. Realizing their readers' dreams, Frank and Joe Hardy used cars, boats, and motorcycles to escape the narrow realm of home life. In the *Shore Road Mystery*, they even bested their dad, Fenton Hardy, in solving a case. In fact, the Hardy Boys' parents gave them extraordinary freedom. According to literary critic Gary Westfahl, their father was "a friendly but distant older brother," and their mother was "an acquiescent and nurturing older sister." Although the Hardy Boys were seventeen to eighteen years old in the series, they had the sexual and emotional lives of their nine-year-old readers. They desired nothing more than adventure and good food, and at the end of each book they always returned home. The Hardy Boys stepped into but also out of their heroic roles. All this reassured middle-class parents. Like the young George Bailey in *It's a Wonderful Life*, the Hardy Boys and their readers would grow up to be responsible family men, maybe even, as George did, work for their dads and take over the family business.[27]

These themes were repeated through the 1930s and 1940s on radio and movie serials. Frank Merriwell, a character from a dime novel series of the 1890s, was updated in a 1936 movie serial as a college sports star who made friends easily and hunted criminals. Other serials followed the formula, including *Jack Armstrong, the All American Boy*, which ran on the radio from 1933 to 1951. Like the Rover Boys, Jack was a high school student, in fact, a sports star. But, more important, he was also perpetually on adventures in South America or Asia fighting criminal gangs. Though independent, Jack often was helped by adults (especially his "uncle," really the father of sidekicks Billy and Betty Fairfield). General Mills hoped Jack's wholesomeness would rub off on its Wheaties cereal, whose advertising slogan was "Jack never tires of them and neither will you." Kids coveted mail-in premiums based on gadgets used in the program, including the Hike-o-Meter, which gauged distance when Jack pursued foes in tunnels. Armstrong followed a well-trod formula: a boy adventurer, backed up by parental guidance and small-town virtues, who grows into responsible adulthood.[28]

The theme took a comical twist in the hometown films about Andy Hardy. This wisecracking teen, always finding himself in a fix, was a lovable teenage version of the naughty-but-nice boy. Growing up in the intimate environs of the all-American small town, with his doting mother and advice-giving, white-haired judge of a father, Andy both amused and reassured adults. The fact that Andy, played by Mickey Rooney, was three inches shorter than his "girlfriend," Polly, made him all the more endearing and harmless. Yet children loved him, too, because he was, like them, trying to find his way and having fun doing it. Another variation was *Henry Aldrich*, a radio show made into a matinee movie in 1939. This teen goof-up failed to make the high school football team and always forgot his father's advice, but he still had his mother to watch out for him. There were, of course, more serious models of growing up: the series built around young aviators, especially *Ace Drummond* (1936) and *Captain Midnight* (1942), who had outgrown parental support. These heroes let boys fantasize about the freedom of flight, up-to-date technology, and the excitement of the fight, but within a parent-pleasing moralistic and often patriotic context.[29]

Most of these growing-up stories were about males. But the Nancy Drew books and movie serials in the 1930s offered girls a hero, too. In each episode this sixteen-year-old, supported by her lawyer father, stumbled into a mystery and used wit and courage to pursue and prevail over villains. All this, too, was a girl's fantasy—freedom from parents and having exciting adventures, including car chases in her blue "roadster." Nancy Drew not only had a car but also investigated cases deemed by all to be "too dangerous" for a girl. At the same time, Nancy was tactful with adults, even if she did not follow their advice to stay off the case. Her daring was always tempered by the safe middle-class setting of the stories. Most girls' fiction of the time was not about breaking with parents (*Anne of Green Gables*, for example) but of maturing into adult roles as mothers and homemakers.[30]

Although the growing-up story was especially designed for a youthful audience, the Western had cross-generational appeal. It reached a mostly male adult audiences, attracted to a nostalgic "return" to the simplicity, excitement, and virtue of an age before cities, factories, and offices. The genre reflected and reinforced myths about American character and destiny. But the Western also appealed to youth. Street and Smith, one of several publishers that manufactured formulaic Western "dime novels" from the 1860s, also specialized in adolescent Western adventure. These booklets featured heroic poses of boys and girls on their covers, offered prizes or money when readers convinced their friends to buy Street and Smith books, and included appealing ads for magic tricks and cheap gadgets. Often the stories were about the sons of ranchers, giving children a figure to identify with. Pulp magazines like *Wild West Weekly* (first appearing in 1902) offered stories of a fifteen-year-old orphan from the East who led a band of characters (an old scout, a Chinese cook, a black laborer, a younger western boy, and a girl friend) to catch crooks. This formula let children fantasize about freedom and power. And yet parents wholeheartedly embraced the juvenile Western genre. In the first three decades of the twentieth century, the Western became widely popular across the generations, extending far from the cheap dime novel tradition. It entered the imaginations of Americans of all ages through Wild West shows and silent movies. Mainstream Western writers like Zane Gray published in middle-class magazines such as *Collier's* and *Harper's Monthly*. Between 1930 and 1955, there were 2,772 Western movies made in Hollywood that attracted some of the best known stars and directors.[31]

By 1910, parents associated the Western with their own youth and nostalgically passed this genre on to their own children in the form of cowboy suits and toy "six-shooters." The adventurer and Western movie star Tom Mix, who had delighted adults for two decades with his stories about his days as a sheriff in Oklahoma, his friendship with Teddy Roosevelt, and his skills with gun and horse in movies, became the hero of a children's radio show, *Tom Mix and His Ralston Straight Shooters*, in the 1930s. With their central theme of "testing" character against adversity and primitiveness, Westerns were easily assimilated into the maturation motif of boys' fiction. Adults often associated the young boy with the "Indian." From about 1910, parents gave masks and Indian costumes to kids, encouraging their young to play the role of the primitive "savage" like the "lost boys" in Disney's movie version of *Peter Pan* thirty years later. But adults also admired the Indian's natural resourcefulness and independence. In this context, adults happily let kids read and watch Westerns, encouraging them to identify with their "noble savage" stage of development. Still, parents knew in the end, the victor would be the cowboy and sheriff, who embraced Gene Autry's code of the Wild West: Never take unfair advantage of an enemy; be kind to small children, the old, and animals; be clean in word and deed; respect womanhood and parents; and be patriotic. That code was embodied by William Boyd, an aging leading man from the silent movie era, who transformed himself in 1935 into Hopalong Cassidy of the Bar 20 Ranch. He made a fortune starring in a series of sixty-six cheap "Hoppy" Westerns. Boyd, with his trademark white hat, never smoked, rarely kissed a girl, and let the bad guy draw his gun first or even simply lassoed him instead.[32] The Western was a perfect vehicle for the cross-generational (especially male) imagination and remained so until the end of the 1950s.

A much more challenging change in children's fantasy came when their stories adopted the coolness of the pulp detective and science fiction character. Direct descendants of the "dime novel" of the second half of the nineteenth century, pulp magazines were noted for their cheap woody paper, formula fiction, and working-class readers. Adventure magazines like *Argosy* and police fiction like *Dime Detective* and *Detective Fiction Weekly* competed for young male wage earners able to pay five to twenty-five cents for about 130 pages of stories. During their peak years between the late 1890s and 1950, they offered a sharp contrast to the middle-class, often female-oriented, "slick" magazines. Beginning with *Munsey's* magazine of 1893 and quickly followed by *Ladies' Home Journal, Saturday Evening Post, McClure's,* and *Collier's,* the "slicks" not only attracted more affluent readers (and advertisers trying to reach them) but also supported a middlebrow culture largely hostile to the "escapism" of the pulps.[33]

As literary historian Erin Smith notes, pulp heroes were often "hardboiled" detectives who distrusted "higher-ups," worked in the seedy part of town, were suspicious of "uppity women," and tended to stereotype ethnic and minority groups. They worked hard and eschewed family life. They were tough talking, seldom showing emotion or even anger in the face of a foe or difficult situation. Smith argues that this persona appealed immensely to young male factory workers who identified with the hard-boiled detective's social resentments and dreamed of recovering the detective's autonomy and freedom from bosses. This story line, however, also appealed to middle-class children—despite, and maybe even because of, its roots in a genre despised by middle-class parents. The coolness of Marlow in *The Big Sleep* represented an escape both from the "cute" of early childhood and from parents' genteel aspirations for their offspring.[34]

Even here, however, there was room for accommodation because the cop theme often contained a conservative parent-pleasing message. Chester Gould's comic strip, "Dick Tracy" (1929), was in the pulp tradition. Even if Gould used many pulp themes (surprise endings, the supernatural, and futuristic gadgetry like radio watches, X rays, and "Flying Wings"), his stories were based on police investigative procedure and glorified law and order. They pleased the FBI's director, J. Edgar Hoover, with their portrayals of vicious and utterly unattractive criminals and their rejection of the romantic journalistic treatment of gangsters like John Dillinger. Like the Western, Tracy transferred easily from an adult comic strip to a radio program in 1933. Following this success was a movie serial in 1939 and comic books, both of which were directed toward children. Tracy, with his trademark strong jaw and curt speech, stirred the imaginations of kids. Reprints of the strip were offered in cheap book form in 1936 that were labeled "suitable for coloring."[35]

The fourth genre, science and superhero fiction, was the most radical departure from the growing-up myth inherited from the Victorians. These works most unequivocally affirmed the cool. Like the jungle theme of Tarzan, adults passed down science fiction to children in the 1930s. Yet the story of space wars removed the child entirely from the world of parents, the past, the realistic future, and the duty to grow up. The best example, perhaps, is the science fiction hero Buck Rogers. When this tale, which first appeared in the adult pulp magazine *Amazing Stories*, was turned into a comic strip in 1929, space fantasy became available to children. In 1932, Buck Rogers spoke daily to the young on an afternoon radio program, and in 1939 he appeared before children on Saturday afternoons in a movie serial. His background story set the stage for an accessible fantasy: Rogers, an Air Corps officer, was transported from the twentieth to the twenty-fifth century thanks to an accident that preserved him for five centuries in a "radioactive coma." Revived by forest dwellers, Rogers finds a world ruled by the tyrant Killer Kane. Led to a "Hidden City" inhabited by rebels, Buck joins Dr. Bill Huer, an older inventor of many space gadgets, and his lovely assistant, Wilma Deering, in an ongoing struggle against Killer Kane and the female co-villain, Ardala. This formulaic time travel adventure appealed to the escapist moods of working-class Americans and became cool to youth of all classes. When this adventure was passed on to children on radio and Saturday serial movies, Buck gained a boy "sidekick," Buddy Wade.[36]

The series thrived on technological fantasy and heroic individualism. Buck's story tapped into the same romance with gadgetry that earlier had made electric train sets appealing to boys. But Rogers's technology was pure make-believe. Dr. Huer obligingly provided antigravity belts, invisibility rays, and disintegrator guns to help Buck, Buddy, and Wilma in their struggles again the Robot Battalions and many others. This technology had nothing to do with the world of work and unemployment during the Depression of the 1930s. It was worlds removed from the real technology that took away jobs from real dads and had betrayed the dreams of exciting careers as engineers and tycoons that had once inspired boys as they played with electric trains and Erector sets. These fantasies of interplanetary combat replaced aspirations of business success encouraged by the traditional construction toys and uplifting boys magazines like *St. Nicholas*. With his origins in pulp fiction, Buck Rogers offered a child's version of working-class escapism rather than bourgeois aspiration.[37]

The Buck Rogers model of boys' fantasy was imitated many times—Flash Gordon in the 1930s and 1940s, Captain Video in the 1950s, and, of course, Star Wars since the late 1970s. Only the names have changed. Flash, a blond Yale polo player, and his girlfriend, Dale Arden, join scientist Hans Zarkov on a rocket ship to stop a comet from hitting the earth, only to land on the planet Mongo and pool talents to fight the wicked and oppressive Emperor Ming. Like later children's fantasies, Flash Gordon's movie serials (starting in 1934) drew freely on Roman and Chinese references, as well as then popular ideas about the age of the dinosaurs. Time and place were mingled in a fantasy that denied all reality except the thrill of the struggle and the miracle of escapes from danger.[38]

Superman inevitably followed. Dreamed up by two teenagers, Joe Shuster and Jerry Siegel, in 1932, this wonder of a man was deemed by newspaper men too unbelievable to be published as a comic strip. Shuster and Siegel found success, however, in the new child's media of the comic book in 1938. The first issue's cover showed the costumed Superman in a crude drawing, holding a car over his head. His earliest stories featured a tough wise guy. Superman seemed more like a hard-boiled detective than the moralistic figure created by actor George Reeves, whose 1950s TV program *Superman* opened with an image of the statuesque Reeves, with the American flag waving in the background. Nevertheless, by 1940, up to 1.35 million *Superman* comic books were sold per issue, and Superman had a radio series three days a week. He started a wave of imitation, beginning with *Batman* in 1939 and followed immediately by *The Flame, The Green Hornet, The Human Torch, Sandman,* and *Captain America*. The comic book rose in circulation with the wave of superheroes. These characters shared many features: They usually fought enemies almost as powerful as they, had a second identity as an ordinary mortal, and often had a young sidekick. Unlike the growing-up characters in the Jack Armstrong and Nancy Drew stories, most of the superheroes were young adults, not teens still under the distant authority of parents and adults. The older adults were the villains or the humorous and kindly scientists, never the authorities. In these fantasy worlds of coolness, there were no parents.[39]

Captain Marvel, a popular superhero of the 1940s, was even more blatantly marketed to children seeking the cool. According to the story line, Marvel was, in reality, an orphaned newsboy, Billy Batson. This "Ragged Dick" of the mid–twentieth century did not gain fame and success by inner character and hard work. Instead, in a strange encounter with a lone figure,

**5·3**
Captain Marvel, a competitor of Superman, is an appealing
superhero for young children with his magical story and superhuman
powers. Cover of *Whiz Comics* 1940. "Whiz Comics" © 1940 DC
Comics, all rights reserved. Used with permission.

Billy was led into a passage in the subway past the "Seven Enemies of Man"
to meet a magician who taught him the mysterious word "shazam." By utter-
ing this word, Billy magically drew upon the powers and virtues of six ancient
gods and heroes and, with a bolt of lightning, became Captain Marvel. Aided
by a charming talking tiger friend, Tawky Tawny (curiously dressed like a sophisticated suburbanite in a sports jacket), the all-powerful Captain Marvel
fought Dr. Sivana, "the Greatest enemy of civilization," in the dark town of
Nastyville.[40]

For all their variety, these heroes were really the ultimate child's dream "self," a powerful figure underneath the bored, bossed-about kid. Their stories were surely liberating, and in ways inconceivable in the earlier genre of the growing-up story or Western. They freed children from the constraints of memorializing the past and allowed the child's imagination free rein in dreaming of the future. In the new world of the comic book, movie serial, and radio program, the child could choose his (or her) own forms of fantasy, not merely accept the parents' nostalgic vision of play. Even the stress on individual combat that these superhero stories so often showcased was geared to the child's imagination and expression. It vented aggression and prized ingenuity rather than valued adult interests in military tactics and team play. It was an exciting childlike dreamworld, not diligent or didactic.

As important, perhaps, as the new fantasy world of fiction for children was a new form of collecting. While gathering bits of nature and castaway consumer articles had long empowered children, until the 1930s collecting store-bought novelties and knickknacks remained within the orbit of grown-ups. During the Depression, toy and novelty companies realized that they had to appeal to the wishes and wealth of children if they wanted to stay in business. Rather than sell expensive sets of toy cars and military figures to adults (who, in turn, gave them to children on special occasions), these manufacturers learned to market single vehicles or military figures, often made of new cheaper materials. Toy soldiers, long sold in complete sets and constructed in lead, appeared in the mid-1930s made of cheap rubber and metal and packaged individually at prices cheap enough for even a nine-year-old boy to buy.[41] The key to the success of this sales strategy was adapting these commercial "collectibles" to children's new media heroes. For Christmas 1934, Daisy, long the producer of relatively expensive air rifles, offered a Buck Rogers Space Pistol at twenty-five cents, a price within the reach of many kids.[42] Soon a vast array of cheap figures and toy weapons based on radio and comic book characters appeared in dime-store sales bins. These collectible toys and figures only accelerated the trend of taking the fantasy story away from the parents or doting uncles.[43]

To be sure, superheroes were hardly isolated from the wider society: Captain America and the Green Hornet pursued Nazi spies during World War II, and fears of communist expansion and the atomic bomb permeated the comic books in the decade after World War II.[44] But the characters also heralded a children's counterculture against the world of the responsible adult. Science fiction and superhero stories became especially problematic to adults because they reflected the influence of the subterranean culture of the cool, a parentless world of exciting but otherwise emotionless violence. As historian Peter Stearns notes, the heroes of boy fiction and radio programs by the 1930s were "tough-guys" who encountered endless danger but coolly showed neither fear nor doubts and anxiety: "Rather than grappling with fear, or even considering fear in retrospect, the new breed of Tarzans and, later, Supermen, had no emotions to deal with one way or another. Their coolness was as remarkable as their ability to fly or withstand bullets or communicate with apes." In contrast to the fiction of an earlier generation, the stories were not about growth and character-building so much as about pure adventure in a child's world of the cool where there was no adult-imposed past or future. Parents' role in play and imagination faded, replaced by Dick Tracy and Buck Rogers.[45]

## Boys and Girls Back and Forth across the Line

The cool culture of children in the 1930s, created by merchandisers to expand "street" commercial culture to willing youth, was the beginning of the challenge to the cute, goody-two-shoes ideal of the Brownies, Mickey Mouse, and Andy Hardy. By the late 1940s, that culture seemed even more strange and threatening to adults. Comic books, cheap, easy to find in any drugstore or on any newsstand, and fun to trade and collect, were the perfect expressions of children's cultural autonomy and the flight from the cute. This cheap and often garish medium not only had roots in the world of working-class pulp fiction but also increasingly displaced pulp magazines and attracted older readers, especially young soldiers during the war and in the military afterward. In fact, 44 percent of draftees in 1949 regularly read them. This meant a radical change in the content of comic books that had originally been designed for eight-year-olds. Publishers shifted their story lines to accommodate this growing audience of young adults. In the mid-1940s, Captain America lost his boy sidekick and won the chance to rescue sexy women from compromising positions, even situations of bondage. In the late 1930s, "jungle comics" had offered children's stories featuring Clyde Beatty, the animal trainer, and Tarzan with his pet chimpanzee, Cheta. By the end of the war, the jungle genre shifted to stories of virile men and sexy, buxom women rescuing the opposite sex from wild animals.[46]

Even more dramatic was the shift in the detective comics. In 1942, *Crime Does Not Pay* introduced realistic, graphic, and even glamorized stories of real murderers, rapists, and bandits. Justice was served only in the last frame or two. Garish covers of half-dressed busty women, terrified at the approach of a ghoul or a maniacal criminal, the stock-in-trade of adult pulp magazines, invaded the comics. In 1948, 57 percent of the readers of *Crime Does Not Pay* were over twenty-one years of age. That still left many young people exposed to its violent contents. Similarly, romance pulp stories, long the mainstay of working-class women's culture, also shifted to the comics (though with less notice). In 1949, William Gaines, the son of a pioneer in the comic book business, introduced a series of horror comics. His *Vault of Horrors*, *Weird Science*, and *Shock SuspenStories* today are praised for their inventive plots, surprise endings, and sensitivity to issues of race and social equality. But in the early 1950s, they were a radical break from the accustomed fare of children. A summary of one issue will illustrate how: The overweight people of an ordinary town, after taking pills provided by a Dr. Perdo, find that they not only lose weight but all waste away and die after the doctor departs. When later the relatives of the dead spot the doctor in town, he is chased into the town cemetery. There, out of curiosity, he opens an aboveground coffin, only to be discovered in the next frame eaten by a monster tapeworm that he had placed in the pills given to his victims. Older children delighted in these stories in part because they were so horrifying and therefore tested their stamina, but also because they defied the so-called innocence of children.[47]

The comic book industry had crossed "the line," encouraging cute kids to become cool kids and even, in the eyes of some, Gremlins. Government pressure and much public criticism led publishers to pull back sharply from this obvious excess in the mid-1950s. Still, the child's quest for the cool hardly diminished. At first, Gaines attempted to carry on with his horror magazines, but he shifted his efforts to *Mad Magazine*. Although not as offensive to adults as his horror magazine, Gaines's satirical newsstand magazine mocked TV shows, movies, advertising, and even the cold war. With its knowing cynicism, *Mad* became a mark of liberation from childhood for preteen-agers who often surreptitiously bought it on their way home from school. Moreover, the comic book made a comeback in the 1960s with a science fiction and horror formula based on exotic monsters and more sophisticated stories of alienated and fallible heroes (like Marvel's Incredible Hulk, Daredevil, and Spider-Man).[48]

The male-dominated comic book had a female equivalent, but it was far more constrained, less likely to cross the line. In the 1940s, *Parents* magazine published several girls' magazines, including *Calling All Girls* and, for the "kid sister," *Polly Pigtails*. In an attempt to update the tradition of *St. Nicholas*, these illustrated magazines provided girls with uplifting stories about role models like Louisa May Alcott, along with fashion tips, comics, and stories

about movie stars. Occasionally, they featured tales of girl newspaper re-
porters, one possible profession for females in the 1940s. MLJ Publications, a
minor maker of superhero comics, in 1941 created a new subgenre in the
comic book *Archie*. This humorous comic book featured a teenage boy with
his friend Jughead and competing girlfriends, Veronica, the rich snob, and
Betty, the sweet blonde. Although told from the male perspective, *Archie* and
its imitators were bought mostly by preadolescent girls. The image of the fun-
loving high school student had already become a fixture in American popular culture with the movies of Mickey Rooney, Judy Garland, and Deanna
Durbin. *Archie*, with its gentle gags and youthful humor, certainly was no
threat to the protective parent. From the mid-1940s to the mid-1950s, career
comics for girls (*Tessie the Typist* and *Nellie the Nurse*, for example) attracted
large audiences of girls, though most also featured rivalries for men. While
more sexy comics emerged by the end of the 1940s (one featuring Torchy,
with her deep cleavage and six-inch spikes), the lead character of one of the
most popular, *Katy Keene*, was no bimbo and had a job (as a movie star). Her
comics also offered activities that were attractive to the preteen (paper dolls,
puzzles, and other opportunities for interactive fantasy, including a fan club).
For the somewhat older girl, there were romance comics, modeled after *True
Confessions*, *Personal Romances*, and other adult women's magazines from the
1920s. Still, these were tame, with no mention of sexual intercourse. The
"bad" girls had reputations for kissing too many men or for falling for the boy
who got in trouble with the law.[49]

Although not a comic book, *Seventeen Magazine* (appearing first in 1944)
epitomized this subdued approach to the cool girl. Although it promised to
provide girls with their own magazine, the editors' goals were commercial,
and therefore they presented teen girls as viable consumers to advertisers and
manufacturers. Recognizing the continuing influence of mothers, *Seventeen*
featured a "conservative, controlled sexuality" not only in stories and advice
columns but also in ads. Instead of lowering the distinction between children
and young adults, as did the male-oriented comic books of the era, *Seventeen*
promoted special "teena" cosmetics and flats, not sexy makeup and spike
heels. Although some girls wrote letters to the editor complaining about the
magazine's preaching against "necking," *Seventeen* continued to favor a parent-pleasing image of "good girls" in modest clothes using sensible beauty
products.[50]

Late in the twentieth century, girls rebelled against the constraints of the
magazines and comic books made for them. The age at which girls begin
reading *Seventeen* and similar magazines had dropped by the 1990s (with 53

**5·4**
Especially appealing to girls was the comic book *Archie*. This cover
shows Veronica getting the best of the amorous Archie. Cover of
*Archie Comics*, July–Aug. 1955. "Archie" comic book courtesy of
Archie Comic Publications, Inc., © 2003. The "Archie" property
© and ™ of Archie Comic Publications, Inc. All rights reserved.

percent of readers thirteen years of age or younger in one survey). Girls in
their teens "graduated" to women's magazines like *Glamour* and *Mademoiselle*.
This suggests that girls were beginning to cast off what once was designed for
teenagers and to stray closer to the line that *Seventeen* and other girls' magazines had respected. *Seventeen* also responded to this desire of girls to "grow

up" faster (as well as to the growing impact of feminism) by placing greater emphasis on the academic and professional accomplishments of women and girls. In the 1980s and 1990s, many girls who defied the mainstream media adopted the "Madonna look," dressing in thrift-shop clothing and accessories. In recent years, some young teenage females, especially in urban areas, have rejected traditional codes of beauty and instead chosen body piercing and tattoos. For many parents, they have crossed the line.[51]

But there were severe limits to the girls' version of the cool. The overarching emphasis on beauty, diet, and relationship has remained constant in girls' magazines for over half a century. Some feminist scholars may critique the simple formulation that "girl culture . . . starts and finishes in the bedroom," and that it is defined primarily by clothes, beauty, and popular music. But there certainly were far more controls on the cool in the commercial culture of girls than boys.[52] As Dawn Currie notes, girls' fashion magazines at the end of the century continued to propagate "traditional femininity" in spite of feminism. The beauty myth, based on individualistic preoccupation with dress, exercise, diet, skin care, and even plastic surgery, has trumped newer themes of women's independence, career, and life choice. There has been a trend toward more overt sexuality in ads and advice in "teenzines," but this too remains confined to the "getting a man" theme.[53]

Even more important, adults did not give girls the freedom to cross the line. In the late nineteenth century, while boys were portrayed as Tom Sawyer, girls were Pollyannas. Their literature made them saints, or at least far less rebellious and far more childlike than boys. The naughty-but-nice girl was a narrow theme with a much shorter history than was true for boys. Little Lulu may have bested adults and boys, but she never had to grow up. The same was true of Pippi Longstocking. But as real girls grew older, reaching the age of Peter Pan, the tomboy had to metamorphose back into a demure female.

The problem was what to do with the girl after her tomboy years, after her "cute," naughty-but-nice phase. The coquettish cool girl, the female Gremlin, was threatening and dangerous. The boy's fantasy of Superman was an escape from the normal path of development, a dream of accelerated maturation, but the girl's fantasy of being a sexy woman went beyond the acceptable, with its consequences in premature pregnancies and life-destroying reputations. Of course, there was a female equivalent of the boy Gremlin, but there was much less cultural opportunity for her to emerge. In the 1990s, feminist comic book writers wanted to make girls into tough but sensual "grrrls." Still, this was an option mostly for grown-up "grrrls" who were free of parents, husbands, and children. Girl children were and are not so free.[54]

## TV as a New Site of Coolness

E ven more than radio, movies, and comics, the new medium of television promised in the late 1940s and 1950s to give children a new setting for escape from parental values. Unlike the book, television required neither literacy nor pocket money. Even so, for years, both the public and broadcasters looked upon the TV as a vehicle of cross-generational culture or parent-approved children's programming. Westerns, family-friendly sitcoms, but also old movies and cartoons from the 1930s and 1940s were widely aired in the 1950s. The *Our Gang* movie shorts of the 1930s became TV's *Little Rascals* in 1954 for a new generation of children watching the antics of Alfalfa, Spanky, Buckwheat, and Darla. Beginning with *The Cisco Kid* in 1950, American TV was swamped by Westerns. In the early 1950s, hoping to win over family audiences (and to please regulators), the networks devoted almost thirty-three hours on weekdays and twenty-one hours on the weekend to children's programming. Especially striking were early evening children's programs (including *Lassie*, a sentimental dog drama, on Sunday evenings beginning in 1951). All of this assuaged parental fears of the influence of comic books and assured them that their kids were not growing up to be Gremlins.[55]

To reinforce this confidence, early children's programming featured adult hosts who introduced cartoons or Westerns. The assuring adult's presence was evident in the silly song and dance program *Pinky Lee*, which featured a former vaudevillian; *Ding Dong School*, hosted by the motherly Miss Frances; and Buffalo Bob Smith's puppets on the *Howdy Doody Show*. Most of these programs were intended for the young child. But there was also a science program, *Watch Mr. Wizard*, hosted by a teacher, Don Herbert. For fourteen years beginning in 1951, "Mr. Wizard" conducted simple experiments with nerdy middle-class preadolescents.[56]

Cross-generational entertainment and educational programming may have won parent approval. But advertisers quickly learned that they earned higher ratings with more adult fare. By the late 1950s, the networks not only began to shift their own children's programming to Saturday morning but also turned over the late afternoon slots to local TV stations that often aired reruns and old cartoons, drastically cutting back on quality children's shows. By 1970, there were only five hours of network children's programming on weekdays but twenty-four hours on weekends. Saturday morning programs became a child's TV ghetto, and kids' tastes (as understood by producers and advertisers) set the standard. There was a sharp reduction in soothing story-book reading programs for the young child (declining from 20 percent of children's programs in 1948 to 7 percent in 1958). Adventure shows of various kinds filled the gap. Adult hosts declined from 90 percent to 35 percent of children's programming in the decade after 1948. Increasingly, children were entertained without the interpretation (and often moralizing) of adult conveners. The cool gradually pushed the cute off the screen.[57]

The Mickey Mouse Club of 1955 led this trend by making kids the stars of a revue. Daily, children saw a team of other kids singing and dancing on-screen. Many viewers had a favorite with whom they identified as the Mouseketeers shouted their names one by one in the ritual of "roll call." Even the adults on the show, Jimmy and Roy, wore the same costume with the mouse-ear skull-cap. Jimmy, so energetic and fun, was more like a big kid than a parent, and even the gentle and grandfatherly Roy had a talent for cartoon drawing that made him childlike. Disney staff obviously focused on making this a program suited for children's imaginations, hardly of any interest to parents who were busy driving home or making dinner during the 5:00 to 6:00 P.M. time slot when the program was aired. The Mickey Mouse Club was no threat to adults. The mouse-ear caps worn by the Mouseketeers, from the teenage Bobby and Annette to the primary school–age Cubby and Karen, made them all uniformly cute to adults. But youngsters saw them as individual, independent, and cool kids. Disney remained cross-generational in his appeal, even as he opened the door onto a more autonomous child's commercial culture.[58]

Although a slow process, the trend was toward the cool in the 1960s. As late as the 1959–60 season, Saturday morning TV waited until 10:30 to show cartoons (Mighty Mouse and Heckle and Jeckle). More typical fare was Children's Theater, Roy Rogers, and Circus Boy, especially in the early morning hours when toddlers and early elementary school kids tended to monopolize the dial. By the end of the 1960s, however, Saturday morning was a "kidvid" ghetto, and the parent-free fantasy of the comic book era had returned. A revolution in animation made this transformation economically possible. In 1958, Hanna-Barbera introduced limited animation (greatly reducing the number of figure drawings necessary). A load of highly repetitive cartoons appeared (Ruff and Ready, Huckleberry Hound, Yogi Bear, Pixie and Dixie), capped by The Flintstones in 1960 and The Jetsons in 1962. Comic book characters, often written first for older children and teens, appeared as Saturday morning cartoons in 1966. Marvel's superheroes were sold first in syndication (bypassing the more fussy networks). Dark fantasy and violence had entered the scene with the resurrection of Captain America and also a TV cartoon version of the Incredible Hulk. The networks soon followed in 1967 with Spider-Man, Aquaman, and other superhero fantasy cartoons. The percentage of children's programming devoted to cartoons rose from 23 percent to 80 percent in the 1960s.[59]

Kids' TV may have been driven by the ghettoization of children's programming and cheap cartooning, but as important was the introduction of direct and specialized advertising to children on television. Kidvid not only offered children a world free of the guiding hand of parent substitutes but also presented toys, sugared cereals, junk food, soda pop, and candy to appeal to their desires. Ad makers no longer directed messages toward parents as in the early 1950s. While ads in magazines like *Parents* and *Ladies' Home Journal* continued to promote educational or toddler toys and wholesome full-grained cereals, kids' TV in the late 1950s began to sell cap guns and fad dolls on children's shows that few parents ever watched. Indeed, as communications scholar Ellen Seiter notes, the point of kids' cartoon programs and ads became the opposite of the tone and character of "improving" programming like *Mr. Rogers' Neighborhood*: "Children's commercials are everything educational shows typically are not: flashy, quick, energetic, pop, fantastic, humorous, catchy." By the 1980s, Brian Young argues that commercial television addressed the kid as a "blend of potential anarchist and hyperactive maniac."[60] Children's television, even more than the comic book, was the child's escape from the cute into the cool.

## The Kids' Culture of the Cool after 1960

During the 1960s, children's commercial culture lurched radically toward the cool, passing older boys' rebellious fantasies of the 1930s and 1940s on to young children and girls. This culture embraced elements of the wondrous child but took the fantasy away from the parent. In the 1960s, toy makers adopted the theory that children seek an excitement that is created only in unreality. How did toy companies know this? In that decade, leading manufacturers began to base new toy designs on children's fantasies, abandoning the playful gadget and traditional toys that imitated adult life. Toy company researchers asked kids to send "letters to Santa" to learn about their deepest desires. Even more revealing, they observed how children played away from their parents—seeking to find their spontaneous, undirected fantasies, which could be developed into new toys.[61]

The underlying assumption was that children had natural and autonomous desires that parents could not know or challenge. Ads featuring "cute" children since about 1910 had implied this romantic idea but never in such an unalloyed form. As toy developer Bernard Loomis noted in 1976, the key to a good toy was if "the child lights up when he gets it and plays with it over and over again."[62] The fantasy that had once been shared with parents no longer counted. Kids now had their own desires, and parents' only role was to be sure that they lit up when given a gift. But the trend toward the cool went beyond simply affirming the child's right to a world of excitement and unreality that had to be separate from adults. Children's culture became adult defying as once again it was invaded by the cynical world of marginal adults or teen males. The rebellious culture of the teens of the 1950s had trickled down to the children of the 1960s. The cute had transformed into the cool, Gizmo into the Gremlin.

Extreme, but illustrative, was the trend toward monster and smart-aleck model figures in the early 1960s. The manufacturers of such toys had emerged after World War II, offering a hobby that at first attracted both fathers and sons. In the 1950s, Revell, for example, offered model planes and cars as collectibles, but these toys still required skillful assembly with glue. Aurora Plastics specialized in unusual miniatures of historic figures (for example, D'Artagnan from *The Three Musketeers*); it even manufactured a series for girls called "Guys and Gals of All Nations." By the mid-1960s, however, these companies were promoting toys designed to separate parents from their children, advertising them in comic books and other children's magazines, usually far from the eyes (and disgust) of parents. Companies capitalized on children's attraction to the monster movies featured at drive-in theaters and on TV, patronized by young adults and older teenagers. In the early 1960s, the magazine *Famous Monsters of Filmland* published "insider" accounts of how the movies were made, tidbits about the stars, and personal accounts of favorite scenes, all told in a sardonic style with an endless string of bad puns ("Haunting for something to read?" "There's a frighteningly good treat for every boy and ghoul!"). This magazine looked for a readership similar to that for *Mad Magazine*: kids of about nine to twelve who were breaking from the "leading strings" of parents and home and who identified with the "forbidden" pleasures of teens. Aurora joined with *Famous Monsters of Filmland* in a contest that asked children to make miniature sets of monster characters and even used these submissions to design a new series of monster models in 1965. This was not the first time that a toy company invited kids to help in designing new products, but Aurora broke new ground by asking children to fantasize about horror and violence.[63]

Another particularly glaring example of this trend was a line of figures inspired by Ed "Big Daddy" Roth, a customizer of cars for drag racing. Roth cultivated a grunge persona and introduced a disgusting and nasty figure, "Rat Fink," on T-shirts (a deliberate mockery of Mickey Mouse) that appealed to a young adult culture of hot rod enthusiasts. In an attempt to reach a new market of "cool" children who rejected the goody-two-shoes character of model airplane collecting, Revell licensed Roth's idea for model race cars in 1962. "Big Daddy's" scruffy image on packaging promoted hot rod miniatures driven by tiny versions of Rat Fink, grotesque monsters, and Roth himself.[64]

Other manufacturers introduced children to the grotesque and horrifying. The "Born Losers" collection of model kits featured caricatures of Fidel Castro, Napoleon, and Adolf Hitler—sick humor that amused some adults, but a curious choice for a toy. During the French Revolution, toy guillotines were sold on the street, but in 1964, Aurora's introduction of a toy guillotine caused a great uproar, forcing the company to discontinue the toy within a few months. Even so, there was obviously a market for play fantasies of death and torture. A few years later, in 1971, Aurora returned to the theme with a series of models that included a "Hanging Cage" and "Pain Parlor" (including a half-dressed female torture victim). Aurora understood (as did William Gaines twenty years earlier) that children of nine or ten years of age were easily entranced by the horrifying, especially when their parents found their interest horrifying.[65] This was clearly the motive of children wanting Remco's "Horrible Hamilton" series of giant bugs or Mattel's Thingmaker, which let kids mold plastic images of insects and monsters. In 1967, besting them all, was the "Incredible Edibles" set, horrible insects in candy form that a child could dramatically eat in front of a horrified mom or little sister. Though these toys attracted only short-term attention, the principle kept reappearing. In 2002, Hasbro introduced the Queasy Bake Oven, a parody of its widely successful Easy Bake Oven dating from 1963. Instead of the conventional cakes and cookies baked in its pink predecessor, the Queasy Bake Oven, colored in garish purple and decorated with a yellow brain and a spider, let little boys mock their sisters while baking batter from Bugs 'n Worms Mix and Mud and Crud Cake.[66]

Horror and the grotesque, however, did not prevail in children's culture. In fact, soon after the appearance of Aurora's Pain Parlor in 1971, protests by women's groups against the obvious association of sex and violence led Aurora's new owners (Nabisco) to opt out of gore and instead to manufacture innocent race cars powered by balloons. Due to fear of parental backlash, the return of monster magazines in 1975 was free of the gore of the 1960s.[67]

The more appealing and ultimately more successful path was in the return to another strand of postwar "cool," the superhero. As early as 1960, DC Comics introduced the Justice League of America (a team of superheroes, many of whom dated from the late 1930s and 1940s, including Superman, Batman, Wonder Woman, Flash, Green Lantern, Aquaman, and Martian Manhunter). In 1961, Marvel Comics added its new and darker superheroes,

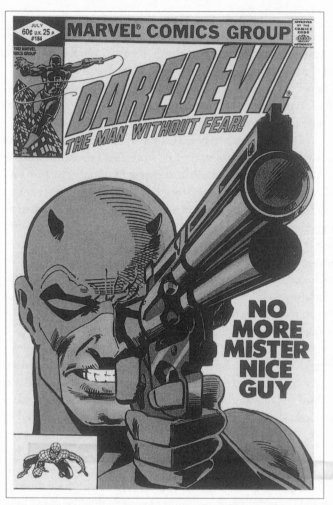

**5.5**
An example of the new, more "edgy" generation of comic books by
Marvel that appeared in the 1960s, drawing on the Clint Eastwood
line to appeal to a hard and utterly unsentimental vision of the
cool. Cover of *Daredevil* July 1982. Daredevil ™ & © 2004 Marvel
Characters, Inc. Used with permission.

the Incredible Hulk, Spider-Man, and Daredevil, whose irony and cynicism
appealed to the older child and teenager. Similarly, the movie and the TV
series *Batman*, an adult-oriented spoof on superheroes, were huge hits in 1966
and 1967. Again, these marginal manifestations of a cynical youth culture
were quickly shared with children as puppets and action figures.[68] This re-

mained mostly a boys' cultural phenomenon. While the superhero comics flourished, the girls' romance comics, in decline since the mid-1950s, disappeared. Although feminists published their own womyn's comix in the 1970s and "grrrl comix" in the 1990s, few were ever seen by children.[69]

The cowboys of the 1950s had long disappeared, and the makers of children's culture had come to understand the commercial power of the cool fantasy. Like its milder form in the science fiction radio and movie serials of the 1930s, the new cool of the 1960s was based on a world free of parental figures where conflict without emotion or regret in a story could evoke an intense audience excitement. In the past, adults had captured the imagination and the channeled rebellion of children in stories of college boys hunting bad guys, of smart teenage girls solving mysteries, or even of ordinary kids dreaming of becoming engineers or sports heroes. By contrast, merchandisers created and kids embraced the new excitement in the surprisingly unreal environment of monsters, superheroes, and science fiction.

By the 1960s, grown-ups seemed no longer to know how to make the future appear attractive to children. The TV show *Disneyland*, with its glorification of exploration and space, had mass appeal in the 1950s and early 1960s, and although it limped along under six different names until 1983, it had clearly lost its cultural impact many years earlier. The girl's story of romance or even mild adventure seemed very dated in light of 1960s feminism. In the meantime, experts and advertisers had told adults that childhood was a time for the child's exploration of play and fun. By the 1960s, these ideas were finally realized, despite frequent parental horror when the cute led to the abhorred cool.

As we have seen, that process was slower to emerge in girls' culture, but in 1959 it accelerated with the debut of Barbie. Since about 1900, baby dolls had encouraged companion and nurturing play to prepare girls for caring for their own children. These dolls mirrored adult fantasies about the ideal child, fresh-faced, healthy, and even a little impish—the cute. By the 1940s and 1950s, mothers could fondly recall their own Patsy and Shirley dolls and see their childhoods in their daughters' play with their Ginny dolls, still very much in the New Kid mold. Ginny had fashions, but she still had the chubby, short legs, round face, and bright eyes of the idealized cute child. How different was Barbie, with her cold stare and grown-up, self-assured posture. Ginny was cute; Barbie, cool.

Barbie's developer, Ruth Handler, responded to the modern girl's desire to identify with the pleasures and body of the adult woman and not having to be "cute," as their mothers wanted them to be.[70] For generations, being a mature female had meant being a mother and homemaker. By 1959, the ideal of being grown-up had begun to change, and Barbie embodied it in her image as the carefree, single, sensuous, and somehow forever young female. In fact, Barbie anticipated by a few years Helen Gurley Brown's magazine, *Cosmopolitan*, which preached a similar message. Barbie was about fashion, of course, but also about cars, dates, and popularity. She was the consummate consumer. In the context of the family of 1959, girls saw Barbie as free from their future responsibility of motherhood and from their present reality as dependent daughters. In a way, Barbie was an early rebel against the feminine mystique to be laid out in Betty Friedan's book four years later. But Mattel's doll was also a free and spontaneous teenager recalling *Archie* and other "teen" comic books from the 1940s. She reflected the teenage culture that had burst forth so strongly in 1954 with the coming of rock and roll and was sustained in an ongoing wave of teen exploitation films shown in drive-in theaters across America in the late 1950s. A large crop of teenagers was just emerging from the vanguard of the baby boom; these adolescent girls had more choices and were freer of adult control than were their parents, who had been teens in the Depression. To eight-year-old girls of 1959, Barbie represented this freedom; she was an escape from the nurturing play expected by their mothers.[71]

Barbie represented the cool girl in school, the one who was popular because she had all the in-style clothes and shoes. According to a recent profile of preteen girls' standards of popularity, Barbie was a perfect fit: She had access to money and status; she had beauty and clothes; and she was not "supervised." In her study of Barbie culture, Mary Rogers found that women remembered their childhood Barbie doll for her clothes and possessions and recalled that girls who had Barbie accessories had status. Barbie owned everything the middle-class lifestyle of the time demanded: a swimming pool, motor home, and fast car. In dress and appearance, she looked like the models in the 1959 *Vogue*. Barbie was a girl's ticket from the land of the cute to the land of the cool, and all it took was money to buy her.[72]

Instead of teaching girls how to diaper a baby doll, playing with Barbie was an education in the life of Helen Gurley Brown's sexy single girl. This doll seemed to rush girls into the sexually charged world of adolescence long before they and, more important, their mothers were ready. Parents at first were appalled by Barbie's adult female body (exaggerated as it was), especially when they saw their daughters dress her. Those bare breasts just seemed to threaten childhood innocence. Yet Mattel offered six- or eight-year-old girls what they wanted—an image of the grown-up female that had both breasts

**5.6**

A contrast of the cute (in Ginny, center left) and the cool (Barbie, center right). Ginny and her "older sister," Janet (left), recalled the childlike dolls of mothers who were children in the 1920s and early 1930s. Barbie challenged that cute image with her icy stare and grown-up clothes, softened only slightly by her younger sister, Skipper (right). Courtesy Kathy George, collector.

and the latest products and styles. Barbie divorced sexuality from motherhood and instead associated it with a carefree world of consumption. Not surprisingly, early market testing found mothers often disliked the Barbie look and concept. Still, Mattel knew that girls loved her, and through their pester power, they got adults to buy her. A real testament to the permissive revolution in child rearing is that parents conceded to their daughters' wishes.[73]

Hasbro's G.I. Joe miniature soldiers (first sold in 1964) represented a similar break from adults' expectations of children's play while offering the child a taste of the cool—although only in the long run. Like Barbie, G.I. Joe was originally a dress-up doll. Costumed in the uniforms of the four American military services, he taught boys to identify with the experience of fathers (mostly World War II veterans) and their older brothers or uncles (regularly drafted or enlisted into the U.S. armed services). G.I. Joe transformed the tradition of the miniature soldier sets. No longer was war play, as had been true for centuries, the reenactment of an aged general's role of deploying a set of soldiers like chess pieces on the board. Rather, war play became more appealing to children when it was turned into the fantasy of one-on-one fighting of young soldiers, ordinary G.I. Joes. Still, the early G.I. Joe did not challenge adults the way that Barbie did. G.I. Joe's success in the 1960s was based on the parent-pleasing reenactment of the adult male's world of heroic action aided by realistic military equipment and gadgetry. In its way, it was educational, and like the old pre-Barbie dolls of mothers, play that fathers could relate to.[74]

During the Vietnam War, however, G.I. Joe's popularity suffered as intergenerational bonding around male military heroism broke down. By 1967, Dr. Spock and other child-rearing authorities were attacking war toys, forcing Hasbro in 1970 to transform its line of "fighting" Joes into an "Adventure Team," which searched for sunken treasure and captured wild animals. Even after the Vietnam War ended in 1975, military toys were a hard sell. With the ending of the draft, military service was no longer a nearly automatic rite of passage in young men's lives, and the lingering anger and humiliation over Vietnam made parents reluctant purchasers of realistic war toys.[75]

Boys, however, still wanted to escape the cute and cuddly culture of their preschool days in the thrill of combat play set in an exciting world of their own. The problem with the G.I. Joe Adventure Team was that it was too adult-pleasing and denied these needs. If it was not exactly goody-two-shoes, it was too much like the Hardy Boys and therefore was not cool. Toy makers certainly understood this when they modernized the science fiction combat figure of the 1930s and 1940s. In 1976, G.I. Joe became Super Joe, a fantasy figure equipped with laser beams and rocket command vehicles who fought off space aliens. G.I. Joe turned into a toy line built around the clash of exotic science fiction enemies. Without reminding adults of real war, this new type of toy provided boys with a heroic escape from their dependence on adults.[76]

G.I. Joe's transformation was not isolated. In fact, he was overshadowed by the figures and fantasy of George Lucas's *Star Wars*, a three-part movie epic that captured a generation of American youths in the years between 1977 and 1983. Action figures and toy space vehicles provided boys with a full set of props to reenact the rivalry of Luke Skywalker and Darth Vader. Beyond its obvious commercial success, *Star Wars* helped to change the meaning of play. Media toys no longer simply invited children to identify with the screen hero by owning a relic like Davy Crockett's "coonskin cap." With *Star Wars* figures and play sets, the child was invited to stage scenes from the movies, to play a god orchestrating a miniature world of high-tech adventure. Adults had no role in the "setup" of the scene, as they had in the past. Their knowledge of electric trains and Erector sets was useless. The child was the convener, the creator, and the director.[77]

*Star Wars* shaped a generation of cool play in boys. There was a veritable avalanche of imitators on TV. *He-Man and the Masters of the Universe*, the *Transformers*, and *Thundercats* appeared in 1983, followed by *Captain Power* and the *Soldiers of the Future* and the *Sectaurs* in 1985. *The Dino-Riders* cartoon serial and toy line offered a story of survivors of a devastated planet in the distant future who were sent back in time to 65 million B.C., where they met dinosaurs and the evil Krulos. The good guys, the Dino-Riders, allied with kindly plant-eating dinosaurs, persuading them to serve as their mounts, while Krulos and his evil gang enslaved meat-eating dinosaurs, using "brain boxes" to control them. The science fiction serials of the 1930s had reached their extreme, if logical, conclusion.[78]

The gender divide remained as wide as ever in the 1980s. Despite some imitative clash fantasies with female heroes (the cartoon series *She Ra*, for example), girls' cartoons stood in sharp contrast to boys' action animation. Series like *My Little Pony* and *Care Bears* featured a "democracy" of heroes rather than the exceptional individual and celebrated nature over technology, emotions rather than coolness, and moral suasion instead of violence.[79]

These differences, however, were not as great as they seem at first glance. Female-oriented animation and toys were designed to appeal to younger girls than were the boys' action figure cartoons and movies. The Barbie doll was the female equivalent of the boys' action figure, and her hard look was made even cooler in the appearance of the doll line and cartoon series *Jem and the Holograms* (1986). This teenage lead singer in an "outrageous rock band," the Holograms, was really the alter ego of Jerrica Benton, a successful owner of a music agency and rival of Eric Raymond, manager of a still more punkish girl band called the Misfits. Here the cute image of the My Little Ponies had finally been supplanted by an adult world of competition and "outrageousness." Still, it is instructive to realize that *Jem* was not a great success, and while Barbie has had her punkish appearances in the 1980s, girls' cool was still largely defined as subdued sexuality, fashionable display, and unabashed consumerism.[80] For boys, the cool was purified, violence shorn of the old dross of reality, emotion, and moral message. It found its most successful venue in the video game.

## The Culmination: The Video Game and Parlor

The culture of the cool has been a long-developing phenomenon, sometimes popping up in unexpected places. That was certainly true with
computer-generated video games. The first, Space Wars, invented by Steven
Russell at the Massachusetts Institute of Technology in 1962, was merely a diversion from the serious business of computer engineering. The mainframe
computer, with its punch cards, was associated with the world of accounting,
corporate record keeping, and the military. But by 1972, Nolan Bushnell was
using new microprocessor technology to create Atari. Originally an arcade
game machine, in 1975 the Atari was introduced to the home TV with a computer console. The game of choice was the simple, tennislike Pong. While
video games became more violent with the introduction of Space Invaders
in 1978, the shooting was aimed at crude space ships, not people, and hardly
more offensive than classic carnival shooting galleries. In fact, the early computer and video games were less threatening to middle-class parents than were
the old pinball games because they were not associated, at first anyway, with
the shady bar and pool hall world of the pinball wizard. When Atari and other
companies introduced the arcade machines, entrepreneurs were quick to follow. Tico Bonomo placed his Time Out game parlors in malls throughout the
Northeast and made them parent-friendly by using orange lighting that created mystery for kids without the dark and dirty look of bars and lounges. In
1981, $5 billion in quarters was spent in video arcades. While some health ex-
perts and more parents believed that Pac Man and other video games were addictive, store owners were surprised to find that in 1977 and again in 1983,
bored kids passed by arcades and overflowing bins of home game cartridges,
resulting in major companies like Mattel and Magnavox abandoning the
video game industry and Atari going under. The Time Out chain shifted to
kiddie games (Shee Balls and crane machines that grasped for stuffed animals). The lesson was that the intensity of play and the graphic sophistication
and realism of the screen must be enhanced to hold customers. The Nintendo
Entertainment System (NES) of 1986 greatly improved the graphics, but
games remained within the rather gentle, even cute, culture of childhood.
Nintendo's Super Mario was hardly a threat to many parents: With the help
of the player at the controls, this cartoon image of an Italian carpenter evaded
barrels and other obstacles thrown at him by a gorilla on his way to rescue a
damsel in distress. In 1989, Nintendo introduced a much improved handheld
computer system, Game Boy, an expensive antisocial device that still pleased
many parents because it kept active boys occupied on long car trips.[81]

Subtly, however, the video game was changing. The NES quickly became the most popular toy in the United States with sales of $3.4 billion by 1990, pushing traditional toys and even action figures off the Christmas wish lists of many boys. In 1990, the arcade game Street Fighter II introduced a new level of graphic violence when the player used buttons to simulate the intense combat of Asian kung fu. The arrival of Sega as a serious competitor to Nintendo in 1990 raised pressure to increase the intensity and violence of game play. In 1992, Nintendo's Mortal Kombat offered children the shocking opportunity to electronically tear off the head or pull out the heart of a defeated opponent. Perhaps, however, the most important change was the simple fact that video games reached a very broad age-group. Although the games were targeted at eight- to thirteen-year-olds, 35 percent of Nintendo's consumers were over eighteen years of age, and 39 percent were between twelve and seventeen years old. Older children and young adults were no longer giving up their toys. This important shift toward older consumers seems to have begun with the comic books of the 1940s, and like the producers of comic books, the video game makers felt pressure to make their product more grown-up. The older child and young adult wanted to distance themselves from the cute and aspired to be cool—in this context, meaning playing video games that featured sex and violence. By accommodating the older player, the video game industry also introduced eight-year-olds, a group that adults thought should still be cute, to these cool games.[82]

Even more than with the comics and radio premiums of their grandparents, children today use their play culture to create a world of "secret knowledge," ranging from special users' magazines to computer sites that help them to find "training tips" or "cheat codes" for their computer games. That private world was vastly expanded with the Internet, when youths began to download games from FTP sites in 1993. Even more, video games have given children ways to project themselves into a fantasy world where they become Mario, Harry Potter, or Spider-Man and into a fantastic space and time free of parents and siblings. Despite cute heroes used to assuage adult anxieties in many video games, the cyberworld of gaming increasingly copied the harsh, emotionless, and even horrifying scenes of earlier comics and action figure cartoons. There, at the computer keyboard or game pad, the child learns to "take it" in continuous encounters with "enemies" and threats. The successful player quickly becomes cool and strives for a controlled but eager response to the mounting intensity of the game. This explains the popularity in the early 1990s of the game Doom, in which the player, stuck on Mars in a postapocalyptic universe, fights a continuous onslaught of grotesque enemies. This was an invitation to the exciting fantasy of facing the ultimate threat all alone, shorn of the old heroics, the unvarnished cool in all its cynicism. Even more problematic was Play Station's Grand Theft Auto–Vice City (2002), a game featuring a released convict's violent efforts to take over the underworld. Like the endless stream of *Terminator* and *RoboCop* movies of the 1990s, Doom and Grand Theft Auto spit in the eye of the cute and at the expectation of growing up to become a part of the rational world of work and bureaucracy.[83]

The origins of the modern Gremlin child are many: Children found freedom from the cute in the liberating danger of the street while parent's encouragement of the "innocent" urchin and coquette inadvertently led to the violence and sexuality of the cool. We see the change both in the cynical capitalist's quest for profits in the manufacture of "excitement" for kids and in the liberal's rejection of moral "hypocrisy" and blind faith that children can make the best choices for themselves without moral guidance. The glazed-over, intent look of the child at the controls of a video game remains a disturbing culmination of a childhood of fun and fantasy, a shocking realization that the child has left the parents' dreamworld and entered a new place that by no means leads to a world of achievement and maturity. The problem was that the cute unwittingly led kids to the cool. It is no surprise that the Peltzers had to kill all the Gremlins to save their Gizmo. But who made the Gremlins in the first place?

# Setting the Boundaries of Innocence

6

Commercial culture abhors a vacuum and thus never leaves unsatisfied a marketable desire. Because modern adults often see their children's longings as innocent and kids' satisfactions as measures of their own happiness, the family becomes commercialized. This is especially true in middle-class America and has spread with increasing affluence. But when children's desires get away from parents' control and understanding and when capitalism draws out those youthful longings in ways that meet the immediate, but not the long-term, needs of children, parents see red. They demand boundaries and reassert older meanings of innocence, seeking shelter rather than wonder.

Over the course of the twentieth century, entertainment entrepreneurs have learned to draw on the widest possible range of appeals and satisfactions, packaging them in the most extraordinary array of products. When adults conceded that their offspring have autonomous needs and desires, merchandisers learned to sell the cool to kids. Merchandisers introduced the marginality of adult street culture to teenagers and ultimately even to younger children. Their object, of course, was and is not to subvert but to expand markets. Teens and children respond to the sales pitch. Today they are attracted to the surge of excitement promised in the trailers of testosterone movies, the fantasy of freedom from home realized in violent video games, and even the smart-aleck dialogue and ever so slightly coded sexuality of cable TV. Certainly some of this appeal is natural and developmental, part of emerging sexuality and the need for detachment from parents. Yet modern frustration with commercialized childhood beyond the family is rooted in the culture of modern families. Young children learn from their parents that free-dom means reaching for the edge and that they have the right to be naughty, if they are also nice. Few parents see the connection between their longing for the cute and its consequence in the commercial tapping of the cool. In-evitably, parents object to this intrusion of the street into the home, even if they are partially responsible for it. They protest that they want their kids back and call for laws and regulations to protect the innocent. Wondrous and sheltered innocence have coexisted for more than a century. In fact, the modern penchant for associating childhood with wonder and the way that the cute becomes the cool have led inevitably to a renewed demand for the sheltered child.

The call to isolate the innocent has four separate but often blended goals, some relatively conservative, others more liberal. First, middle-class adults have endeavored to shelter their children from working-class and mi-nority culture, presuming that it is unrefined, often violent, and dangerously sensual and that it encourages immediate gratification. Second, conservative parents have sought to isolate their young to make them repositories of threatened religious, moral, or even political values. Third, by separating children from adults and only gradually introducing them to grown-up life and institutions, adults have tried to mold kids into self-disciplined decision makers. Fourth, adults (especially liberals) have believed that children are especially vulnerable to commercial pressures; by regulating youngsters' ac-cess to tobacco, alcohol, pornography, and even advertising in general, the influence of commercialism generally in American life could be reduced. These were efforts to contain the Gremlins (even if they also betrayed so-cial biases) and to shape the young into the responsible adults. More subtly, they were attempts to defend or restore cultural standards for the whole of society under the banner of sheltered innocence.

Over the course of the twentieth century, cultural critics on the left and right have challenged all four objectives. A more egalitarian nation made it taboo and elitist to say openly that minority and working-class Americans generally led illicit and unrestrained lives that threatened innocence in chil-dren. Modernists questioned the goal of preserving traditional music, litera-ture, and games by force-feeding them to children. Even a more permissive perspective on child rearing challenged the austere assumptions of the de-velopmentalist strategy, finding children's consumer culture expressive of kids' needs and legitimate wants. By the 1970s, free-market advocates were even disputing the rights of parents to protect their children from unwanted marketing, claiming that the young had natural needs and the right to pursue personal wants beyond the wishes of adults.

Just as childhood wonder served to open the valve of adult desire, childhood protection justified closing it. Sheltering the innocent expressed a standard for decency, taste, and restraint against a wide variety of longings— violence, sex, and even consumerism. The core response was outrage, but this emotion hid a complex and often inconsistent set of objectives. The results were halting and often ambiguous demands for setting boundaries around children's commercial culture. Not only did critics offer a conflicting range of rationales for regulation, but self-interested business groups found support among the ranks of civil libertarians and progressivists in rejecting censorship. This chapter will explore how adults have attempted to redefine the boundaries between the permissible and impermissible in children's commercial culture across the widest possible range—from regulating children's access to movies, radio, comic books, and TV to controlling the commercial pressures of advertisers, pornographers, and tobacco companies on children.

## Chasing Down the Gremlins: Attempts to Rein in Kids' Culture

Whenever moralists censored movies, they usually claimed that they were protecting children. In 1906, the architect Stanford White, who had once had an affair with the ex-showgirl wife of Harry Thaw, was murdered by her husband for violating her purity. This society scandal produced several lurid movies featuring Mrs. Thaw's erotic, mirrored boudoir, which had a swing suspended from the ceiling. When it was reported that schoolchildren were seen at one of these movies, *The Great Thaw Trial* (1909), the Children's Society of New York obtained a ban on its exhibition. The next year, the mayor of New York closed all movie theaters in the city, and the Chicago City Council set up a board of censorship to protect the young from this and similar attacks on their morals. Even after the courts reopened the movie houses, the city council temporarily banned children under sixteen from attendance. To forestall such radical measures, New York exhibitors created their own review board and pursued a mild form of self-censorship to deflect more extreme legal controls. They had good reason to worry: under pressure from women's clubs and the Ku Klux Klan, state legislatures attempted to censor movies through their own boards. Well-respected social reformers and scholars like social worker Jane Addams and psychologist Hugo Munsterberg did not go so far, but they argued that movies fostered an emotional and illusory view of the world that threatened youth with irrational and unrealistic expectations. William Healy's *Individual Delinquent* (1915) argued that children imitated the sexual and criminal acts seen in the movies. In 1926, there was even an effort to create a federal censorship office to protect children from sex and violence.[1]

To diffuse these attacks, the film industry imposed censorship on itself. Following a series of sex scandals, in 1922 the Motion Picture Producers and Distributors of America hired conservative politician Will Hays to clean up Hollywood's image. Hays not only imposed morals contracts on actors and banned the scandal-tarnished comic Roscoe "Fatty" Arbuckle but also, in 1927, published a list of warnings against use of profanity, misuse of the flag, and depiction of attempted rape, among other offenses.[2]

Still, the pressure did not let up. Between 1933 and 1935, a group of scholars published a series of studies, sponsored by the Payne Fund, which investigated the presumably negative impact of movies on American youth. Their well-supported research, including in-depth interviews about delinquent children's moviegoing habits and measurements of physical and emotional response of kids to movie scenes, yielded ambiguous results. But Henry James Forman's journalistic "summary" of the research in *Our Movie Made Children* (1933) unequivocally condemned the film industry, stressing the most sensationalist findings. Movies, one advertisement for the book claimed, were "a monster Pied Piper . . . playing tunes irresistibly alluring to the youth of the present day." Forman argued that children imitated the sexuality of films of Jean Harlow and Mae West and the criminal behavior glamorized in the gangster movies of Edward Robinson and James Cagney. When the Catholic Legion of Decency attempted to boycott morally suspect films, the film industry embraced the so-called Production Code of 1934, which not only prohibited graphic violence and sexual innuendo but also outlawed racial or radical political themes.[3] These efforts to protect children were sometimes ruses to impose moral or religious standards on the public. In any case, they set boundaries in the name of innocence.

The 1930s produced another concern about children's culture in the proliferation of toy weapons and war figures. With the rise of inexpensive war toys, especially cap guns and dime-store miniature soldiers, adults worried about their children purchasing their own aggressive fantasies, often without parental supervision. Adult concern was exacerbated in the 1930s by the rise in urban crime and the widespread perception that young people were attracted to the exciting lives of gangsters. At the same time, public disenchantment with America's past role in World War I and fears of future European conflicts made boys' war play a part of a serious debate about militarism.[4] In 1935, a mothers' group organized by Rose Simone gained national attention when it persuaded Chicago area children to throw their toy guns into a bonfire. Even earlier, in 1931, disarmament advocates weighed in against the "killers' thrill" that boys felt when playing with toy tanks and submarines. What produced the idea of the "normalcy of war," critics warned, was childhood experience with war toys. After all, hadn't Winston Churchill, British cabinet minister during World War I, boasted of owning fifteen hundred toy soldiers as a boy? War toys were an imposition of European militarism on American youth, subverting their long-standing preference for progressive construction toys like Erector sets, Lincoln Logs, and electric trains.[5]

Manufacturers naturally defended toy weapons. A *Toys and Novelties* editorial claimed that to blame toy weapons for crime or war is the "same as saying baby dolls promote illegitimacy." The makers of Daisy air rifles insisted that guns built "comradeship" between fathers and sons. This was predictable, but child-rearing experts also agreed that violent toys were harmless, even beneficial. The coming of war (and the perceived decline in urban criminal violence) reversed enlightened opinion by the end of the 1930s. Adele McKinnie, in *Woman's Home Companion* (1942), calmly noted that boys naturally imitated their elders going off to war. More important was her claim that war play would "get things out of their systems" and help "in relieving tensions."[6] A new theory challenged the old religious idea of concupiscence. No longer was a temptation (in this case the thrill of violence) character transforming (a first step to criminality). Instead, it displaced and vented aggression. Giving a child a toy gun prevented a fixation on violence rather than created an obsession with guns. This face-off would be repeated in the 1960s during the Vietnam War and again in the 1990s with widely publicized incidents of gun violence in schools.[7]

Through the 1930s, debates about where to draw the line in kids' culture became ever more contested. The rise of children's adventure programming drew the ire of some mothers' groups and cultural magazines (*Literary Digest* and *Amercan Mercury*, for example). The Federal Communications Commission (FCC) chair, Anning Prall, even attacked violent "blood and thunder" programming as frightening to young children and threatening to their fragile "emotions, attitudes and personalities." Although Prall recognized that mystery, science fiction, and detective shows were more appealing than the "written word," the "progressive solution" was for the networks to produce better children's radio with "real literary quality" like that heard in "Russia and Europe," an interesting response by a New Deal Democrat a decade before the onset of the cold war. By 1935, the radio network CBS agreed to a code that renounced glorifying violence in children's programs, a standard embraced in 1939 by the voluntary National Association of Broadcasters.

By the mid-1930s, however, a new psychology was already challenging this approach as cultural elitism. The director of the Child Study Association of America, Sidonie Greenberg, rejected the view that children should be repositories of high cultural values and criticized adults who expected ten-year-olds to be "angelic little girls and high brow boys." Because parents "want to do the best possible for the few children upon whom they can shower their anxieties," they frequently misread children's needs. Exciting, even violent, programs help children "live though their childhood and out-grow it." Children given only "the best" in art and literature often revert to "childish levels of enjoyment." The young want to be with their peers and believe that it is a right of growing up to have their own programs. In any case, "the new is always upon us. We can't stop it." This mixed brew of arguments essentially conceded that commercial culture met kids' unacknowledged needs, and that it was narrow, old-fashioned, and selfish for adults to challenge it. Greenberg's colleague Josette Frank added that radio offered the "adventure" that modern middle-class life denied children, and if the child could not "handle" it, he or she may be abnormally insecure. This, of course, psychologized the problem of violent radio but, most important, foisted it back onto the parents. While mothers' groups would still gather petitions against crime programs on children's radio as late as 1947, readers of *Better Homes and Garden* were reassured in 1945 that thriller shows let six-year-olds break from the emotional hold of their parents and gain psychological release through excitement. In any case, parents, not radio programmers, needed to monitor the listening habits of their offspring.[8]

Protected innocence had long been an article of faith of both religious conservatives and secular progressives. By the end of the 1930s, however, social scientists increasingly questioned the linkage between media violence and children's behavior that had been so central to the ideal of the sheltered child. Not only were youngsters not nearly so "vulnerable" as often claimed, but much of the motive to "protect" them was merely an excuse for blind conservatism and a denial of the natural right of the young to express their own needs. Of course, the fact that advocates of these new ideas like the editors of *Parents* magazine were also linked with manufacturers of new children's consumer goods and media somewhat undercut the legitimacy of these "scientific" views. Still, the young researchers involved in the Payne studies found little evidence that gangster movies had a direct influence on children, and the new, more permissive psychological argument was very much in tune with more "democratic" views of popular and children's culture, even if it was commercial and violated middle-class values. No longer was there a consensus that children were slates upon which "bad" as well as "good" characteristics could be written, much less that the young had a propensity to antisocial behavior that had to be channeled and subdued. Rather, through the doctrine of child developmental stages, children became "subjects" who naturally expressed new desires and longings as they shifted from one stage to another. All this suggested that children's desires were natural and yet very different from those of adults. This made many criticisms of children's infatuations with "blood and thunder" radio programming and much else highly suspect.[9]

This trend would not win on every front. Pinball, a new arcade game that emerged in 1933, quickly acquired an unsavory reputation because it raised the specter of gambling addiction at an early age. Based on the old bagatelle machines of nineteenth-century arcades, pinball games used a spring-powered plunger to drive a steel ball up an incline and onto a board full of holes, pins, and bumpers that impeded its slide to the bottom and out of play. Points were earned and registered electrically when the ball hit these obstacles. By 1935, there were an estimated half million of these games placed in candy stores, cafés, and arcades. For store owners and barkeepers in the Depression, pinball machines were effort-free moneymakers. At the same time, the low cost of play (five cents or even only a penny) made pinball accessible to teenagers and even children. Like the cheap war toy, pinball was a pleasure that parents found nearly impossible to monitor. The problem was compounded when pinball games offered payouts to high-scoring players. In arcades, attendants gave coupons to players with winning scores to be turned in for "prizes," like cooking utensils, rugs, radios, or even theater tickets and washing machines.[10] Soon money replaced these often practical and grown-up prizes, associating pinball with mechanical slot machines and thus gambling, organized crime, and tempting vulnerable children.

According to New York City police commissioner Louis Valentine, "pinball machines are a harmful influence because of their strong tendency to instill and develop a desire for gambling in immature young people." A court decision in 1935 declaring pinball to be gambling machines allowed Mayor Fiorello La Guardia of New York to order police raids to eradicate them. Over the next seven years, authorities threw confiscated pinball machines into the Long Island Sound, converted pinball table legs into billy clubs, and finally smashed the machines and sold the scrap for the war effort. The machines were even outlawed in Chicago, where most were manufactured, to be made legal again only in 1976. Despite promoters' arguments that pinball was a game of skill and not of chance, officials found it hard to believe that anyone would play pinball just for fun. The words of one frustrated judge in 1941 make the point: "Men and boys are not going to stand around sticking nickels in a wall without getting money back. In this day and generation, it may be that youth has so deteriorated that it has become a practice, but if so, some doctor should place them in an insane asylum."[11] Pinball was part of a lower-class gambling culture that American municipal and other governmental authorities had targeted in the 1930s. Viewing it as a threat to thrifty habits and as addictive to the vulnerable young, these officials inevitably tried to protect children from this menace. Few defended pinball outside the amusement industry, and none did so from the ranks of child-rearing experts. Probably because of its associations with the underclass, pinball was a boundary not to be crossed.

## The Comic Book Battle

The comic book produced a far more ambiguous response. These illustrated stories had only just appeared when a Boston educator attacked them as a threat to literature and children's cultural development. As early as 1938, the National Office of Decent Literature, backed by the Catholic Church, condemned comic books for glorifying crime, fostering disrespect for authority, and offering lewd and violent images to impressionable youth. A sensationalist article in the *Chicago Daily News* in May 1940 labeled the comic book craze a "national disgrace" and "a hypodermic injection of sex and murder [making] the child impatient with better though quieter stories." The equating of comic books with drugs was typical. Though the war years silenced critics (in part because of the patriotic appeals of the comic books), attacks returned with an article in *Time* magazine in October 1945 that went so far as to suggest that comic books encouraged "fascist" ideas. After all, *Superman* taught that only the superior man counts while humanity is a mere herd. Even *Superwoman* made allusions to Nazi-like pagan gods. The article quoted a Harvard psychologist who warned that American youth were drifting into an "Amazonian Matriarchy" when they read *Superwoman*. All this may have been silly, but it reflected an ongoing concern about the vulnerable child. Mary Mannes wrote in the *New Republic* that comics were simply "the greatest intellectual narcotic on the market," a mortal threat to "inner growth."[12] The old genteel critique of working-class popular culture was now directed toward children's entertainment. This was in part because the themes of the pulp magazine—crime, fantasy, and sexuality—had been adopted by the comic book. Critics insisted that the excitable and constantly changing popular culture sidetracked the development of young people's minds and imaginations.

Frederic Wertham best expressed these concerns in a *Saturday Review* essay of May 1948. This respected psychiatrist was a liberal Jew with a well-grounded concern for civil rights, including free speech. Yet so obsessed was he about the impact of crime comic books on children that he advocated their prohibition. Just as Nazi propaganda had led millions of Germans to violence, so comic books, with their graphic and often romantic treatment of vicious crime, were turning impressionable American children into criminals. The young, especially those who did poorly in school, were susceptible to copycat behavior. Wertham was not alone in this assessment. Judith Crist, for example, argued that five- to seven-year-olds, who had not "yet made full adjustment to family life, to school, and to society," were especially likely to imitate the violence read and seen in comic books. Wertham became the lightning rod in the debate over banning comic books when he published his *Seduction of the Innocent* in 1953. Adopting the view that children were like garden plants, susceptible to dangerous weeds, he insisted that adults be good gardeners and root out these threats to inherently innocent children. He focused on images of violence but avoided blanket condemnations of mere fantasy or even sexuality. Nevertheless, he insisted that violent crimes "once restricted to adults are increasingly committed by young people and children" who have seen the horrific tales of cruel murder and rape in comic books. Even when a crime comic concluded with a moral lesson, children remembered only that "a man puts a needle in a woman's eye."[13]

The comic book became a target because it traversed a wide range of taboos. In 1953, Cincinnati's Committee on Evaluation of Comic Books trained eighty-four reviewers to censor newsstand comic books. They targeted scenes that depicted women as gun molls, portrayed police as stupid, featured attacks by reptiles on humans and the kidnapping of women and children, and detailed black-magic practices. This broad opposition led the Canadian and French governments to ban crime comics in 1949.[14]

That was not, however, an American option. While the Supreme Court confirmed that pornography could be banned as obscenity in 1948, it rejected outlawing violent images, claiming that such restrictions were unconstitutionally vague. Instead, as with the movies (and similarly with radio), the American answer to the problem of comic books was self-censorship. For example, the Association of Comic Magazine Publishers demanded that members avoid the sympathetic portrayal of crime, the depiction of sadism, the display of female sexuality, the use of vulgar language, the mockery of religion, and the humorous treatment of divorce. The makers of *Superman* addressed the bad publicity by publishing episodes that promoted liberal calls for interracial tolerance and appeased conservatives with a campaign against juvenile delinquency. They appointed an oversight board that included prominent psychiatrist Lauretta Bender and educator Robert Thorndike. In a scholarly article from 1941, Bender had already defended comic books as a new form of folklore that provided a mental catharsis for the young. She insisted that the problem of comics was in the minds of adults, not kids. These positive takes on comics followed closely the new tolerance shown in the 1930s toward violent radio programs.[15]

*Parents* magazine supported this approach by trying to make good use of the visual appeal of comics without their violent content. In 1941, the magazine began publishing *True Comics*, which featured colorful, well-crafted illustrated stories of adventure and heroism, including realistic accounts of the lives of famous people like Winston Churchill. Presumably to obtain the perspective of their youthful readers, *True Comics* included Shirley Temple and Mickey Rooney on its board of advisers. In 1947, *Classics Illustrated* attempted to bridge the gap between kids' love of the graphic format and parents' desire for uplift with comic book versions of literary masterpieces. Some twenty thousand schools bought these publications to encourage kids to read "classics." While purists from the *Wilson Library Bulletin* condemned this strategy of "fighting comics with comics," these comic books were successful, at least compared with regular children's book sales.[16] Scholars, who had played prominent roles in a similar debate over movies nearly twenty years earlier, further blunted the impact of comic book critics. Payne Fund sociologists Herbert Blumer and Frederic Thrasher challenged Wertham's claim that comic book violence produced violent children. From their earlier studies, they had learned that media only reinforced a predisposition toward, rather than sparked, imitative violence and criminality.[17]

Although this debate may say more about the cultural wars of adults than the needs of children,[18] a U.S. Senate hearing on juvenile delinquency and comic books from 1954 makes it clear that the attack on comics was also a reaction to the commercialization of children's culture and outrage at its threat to innocence. Although witnesses and Senate investigators drew upon extreme cases to point out the dangers of comic books, no one even attempted to prove a linkage between youth crime and comic books. Evidence presented by the American Psychological Association claimed that there was no proof that comic books negatively influenced children's school performance. Instead, testimony focused on outrage at the inappropriate content of comics. For example, James Fitzpatrick, a New York state legislator, was horrified to see a picture of a sign for a "Sex and Sadism Department" in an issue of *Tiny Tots Comics*. Richard Clendenden of the U.S. Children's Bureau showed a comic book with a graphic image of two murdered men opposite a page featuring an ad for "dolls for little girls."[19]

The issue was essentially a moral one: Wasn't it outrageous that children were reading stories with graphic illustrations of husbands cutting up alcoholic spouses and putting their body parts into whiskey bottles? Even Wertham's testimony stressed the appalling images of men playing baseball with the head of a murder victim, using his intestines as baselines and organs as bases. The threat, Wertham argued, was that children would become "unconsciously delighted by horror" in the way that Saint Augustine became entranced by the gore of gladiator fights in Roman times. This could only brutalize the young, desensitizing even those from middle-class homes.[20]

Wertham's outrage was pitted against the young publisher of horror and crime comics, William Gaines. In his testimony, Gaines insisted that "pleasure is what we sell, entertainment, reading enjoyment," not violence. "Perverted little monsters," not comics, were to blame for crime, implying that violent children were "bad seed" (not, as Wertham argued, innocents led astray). Gaines insisted that normal children are too smart to be influenced by his fantasy stories. Far from encouraging violence, his tales promoted racial tolerance by sometimes "indirectly" denouncing bigotry. The senators had no difficulty in trapping Gaines by asking him how he could indirectly influence children to be more tolerant and not directly push violence in his stories of ghoulish murder. Gaines's response was merely that the violence was "fantasy." When asked what were his limits in portraying violence, he blurted out, "the bounds of good taste." Committee member Estes Kefauver then sprang his trap. He produced a cover of a recent Gaines comic showing a man holding a bloody ax and the head of a woman and asked if this picture was in "good taste." Gaines could only respond that it was in "good taste for a cover of a horror magazine." After all, he insisted, the cover art did not show the neck dripping in blood. Despite his spirited defense of free speech and warnings about the dangers of censorship, Gaines had crossed the line. He had made a preposterous claim in the context of childhood. His cover illustration had perhaps shown constraint, but not nearly enough to respect the sanctity of the innocent child. A child had to be shocked and brutalized by the cynicism and even banality of the horror portrayed on Gaines's comic book cover, and everyone in the room knew it.[21]

Still, all this sound and fury led neither to federal legislation nor even to a protracted condemnation of comics. Rather, in 1954, the Comic Magazine Association of America placated Senate investigators with an code of con-

**6.1**

The classic cover of William Gaines's crime comic that a Senate panel investigating the impact of comics on children found so difficult to believe was in "good taste," much less not harmful to children. *Crime SuspenStories*, 5 Apr. 1954, cover. Courtesy William Gaines Agency.

duct very much in line with the movie Production Code of 1934. It required members to show no sympathy for criminals and to leave explicit details of crimes out of their stories to prevent copycat juvenile crime. There was to be no disrespect for police, and the stories must show how good always prevails over evil. "Undue exposure" of female bodies was disallowed, as were the use of profanity and humorous discussion of divorce. Stories of cannibals or werewolves were banned, as well as ads for liquor, tobacco, gambling, knives, and concealed weapons. Although Wertham continued to call for legal action against crime comics, the code met most standards for protecting the innocent in the 1950s, however arbitrary and scattershot they may appear today. The comic book suffered a sharp decline shortly after the code was put into practice, but this was doubtless due more to the rise in TV viewing than to pressures against comics. The code was even relaxed in 1971 and again in 1989 as standards of "good taste" changed.[22] This relatively moderate response to the "threat" of comics illustrates the growing uncertainty about how to define and defend the boundaries of innocence.

## The Struggle over the Screen

In the 1950s and 1960s, the debate over the sheltering of children from television violence followed the deeply rutted tracks of radio and comics, but it became more intense because of the visual appeal of TV programs and eventually aggressive TV marketing of the cool. Typical was Eve Merriam, writing for the *New Republic* in 1960, who lamented the prevalence of crime programs and saccharine sitcoms. She called for children's programming to be modeled after the children's book industry, which had emerged in the 1950s with stories by authors such as Dr. Seuss and E. B. White. In 1958 Frederic Wertham, along with notable allies radio inventor Lee De Forest and cultural critic Gilbert Seldes, reported that increasingly graphic TV violence was threatening even well cared for, but still impressionable, children. Congressional hearings in 1952, 1954, and 1955 all featured concerns about violence in children's programming, and the 1952 code of the National Association of Broadcasters (NAB) warned of members' special "responsibility toward children."[23] On the other side, experts from *Parents* and noted psychologists such as Bruno Bettelheim assured parents that children did not imitate the violence of Westerns or crime shows, or even emulate the "eye-poking" humor of the Three Stooges. Rather, such fantasy helped them displace aggression, and, in any case, parents should help their offspring find "positive" alternatives like outdoor play rather than let them watch TV passively.[24]

In the 1960s, the debate intensified when TV programming seemed to become more violent, especially in shows that featured contemporary urban crime (as opposed to the distant and seemingly ennobling violence in Westerns). A 1964 study found that depictions of crime and violent themes on prime-time TV had risen sharply: In 1954, only about 20 percent of the programming featured violence, but that proportion had risen to 60 percent by 1962. Despite the often praised inventiveness of Hanna-Barbera's cartoon series (*Rocky and Bulwinkle*, for example), the mid-1960s saw an increase in the number of superhero cartoons. While the liberal *Christian Century* could praise the campy prime-time *Batman*, which mocked cultural platitudes, the magazine still worried that the program might well lead to more cynical children. Popular magazines began to warn parents of the "Saturday morning menace," those wall-to-wall cartoon shows their kids watched while their elders slept in.[25]

By 1969, the National Commission on the Causes and Prevention of Violence seemed to confirm the concerns of longtime advocates of sheltered childhood. The *Saturday Review* insisted that, "particularly among the poor and disorganized" children, TV violence contributed to real violence. Richard Tobin demanded that mayhem be limited to programming after children's bedtime (9:00 P.M.) and that the consequences of violence (pain to victims and punishment to perpetrators) be clearly presented. In 1969, Alberta Siegel, a Stanford University psychologist, warned mothers that "every civilization is only twenty years away from barbarism" and implied that children's TV warranted immediate reform or government action would be required.[26] As with radio and comics, the debate about violence turned on an unresolvable difference of opinion about childhood. Did stories of crime and aggression imprint on the impressionable child and ignite an unquenchable desire for destructive excitement, or were they a vehicle for defusing tensions and symbolically expressing needs for independence? The voluntary NAB code for TV, like the movie and comic book codes, provided a crude compromise in this unending debate about protecting childhood innocence.

Given the history of American "panics" over movies, radio, comics, and TV, it is no surprise that video games should produce a similar response. A flood of video game machines filled drugstores and pizza shops in 1980 and 1981. Like the comic book panic thirty years earlier, local opposition emerged fast and with force. In middle-class areas like Long Island in New York, the PTA and other parents' groups condemned the "addictive" influence of video games and their encouragement of aggressive behavior. Others denounced their "magnetic lure." Another issue was the "sleazy environment" of video game parlors (though games could be found even in Laundromats) and that these games seemed to attract "bad kids" who might corrupt innocent children. One upscale town prohibited any video game parlors within five hundred feet of a school and banned anyone under sixteen years of age from entering them. City councils from places as different as Mesquite, Texas, Indianapolis, and Washington, D.C., waged wars against video parlors. Famed psychologist Carl Rogers expressed concern that the popular video game Missile Command trivialized the threat of nuclear war, making it a "personal response" rather than a political responsibility. The appropriate reaction to the possibility of a nuclear exchange should be shock, not a feeling of excitement or the player's cool disinterest. And education scholar Eugene Provenzo argued in 1991 that video games not only limited creativity and fostered sexism but also provided "an almost perfect simulation of the actual condition of warfare" in the modern impersonal form of aerial combat. Like the comic book, video games drew fire across the ideological spectrum.[27]

At the same time, the games sparked a spirited defense. In 1983, early video game manufacturer Atari sponsored the Video Games and Human Development Conference. Attending scholars obligingly provided positive publicity by insisting that video play did not interfere with schoolwork but instead helped the autistic and social loners come out of their shells. Yet even unquestionably independent researchers found heavy video game use had no impact on stress, aggressiveness, or social isolation. Geoffrey Loftus noted that video games provided "training" for modern computer-based jobs and could easily be adapted to new, more effective types of learning. Psychologists observed that video play relieved anxiety and gave children a sense of control.[28] They traced addictive behavior to personal, family relations, not the impact of any product, and some argued that video games provided an "adaptive response" to "family stress." The video parlor even had its defenders who claimed that it provided insecure children with an autonomous and safe environment for the display of game skills. Communications scholars like Martha Kinder insisted that video games, though often celebrating violence and sexism, provided otherwise dependent children with a necessary opportunity to "play with power." Far from being passive, video games let children join in the story and interact with it in the innumerable choices the games allowed. More extreme, but certainly widely supported, was the view of J. C. Herz, self-proclaimed child of the video age, who insisted that even the most violent games like Doom were nothing more than an up-to-date expression of American values. Doom was only the "Lone Ranger transplanted to Mars."[29] Although the terminology had changed slightly, similar arguments had been presented in the 1930s and 1940s in the debates over radio and comic book violence. Video games, the latest form of aggressive children's entertainment, displaced tension and expressed children's need for freedom from adult control. Defenders of video games more or less balanced the critics, largely neutralizing the attack. The cool was cool to many even as it frightened others.

A Senate hearing on video games in 1993 practically mirrored the investigation of comic books almost four decades earlier. Senators Herbert Kohl and Joseph Lieberman, joined by veteran children's TV personality Bob Keeshan, insisted that video games were bringing a "plague" on children. This response was prompted by recent changes that had made video games much more violent. A Sega official admitted that games had become more graphic (due to faster, more powerful computer processors) in the late 1980s and early 1990s. He even acknowledged that his company had targeted older customers (estimated to be a mean age of twenty-two years old) and, to meet their expectations, had created more violent games. One result was Night Trap, a game featuring realistic males who seek out a sorority member and then try to "hang [her] on a hook" and drain her blood. Nintendo, maker of the cute Mario, felt the heat of Sega's competition and entered this new "adult" field with Mortal Kombat, a hand-to-hand fighting game that, as noted earlier, offered as a prize for the winner the opportunity to tear out the beating heart of the defeated opponent. Lieberman wished that the U.S. Constitution allowed Congress to ban these games, and even without that power, he was convinced that "parents want us to draw the line" at Mortal Kombat and other violent games. In a later House hearing, Congressman Tom Lantos expressed outrage when he saw his grandchildren, "otherwise marvelous little children, . . . relishing the degree of sadism and torture that they could engage in" when playing video games. Again, as with the horror comics of the early 1950s, these House members expressed concern about how graphic video violence was desensitizing children. Still, far from revealing a hysterical reaction, these congressional hearings had a moderate tone.[30]

Rather than calling for legislation, Congress conceded to the industry's efforts to establish a rating system. The Interactive Digital Software Association hired a former elementary school principal, Art Pober, to establish "premarket" ratings for each new video game. These ranged from EC (Early Childhood) to E (Everyone), Teen, and Mature, corresponding to progressively intense and realistic violence along with more explicit sexuality, profanity, and character use of tobacco and alcohol. Not surprisingly, these ratings corresponded closely to the movie ratings first imposed in 1967 (currently, G, PG, PG-13, R, and NC-17). What had changed since the 1960s was that the media no longer had to conform to the community's code of innocence (as the movies had done in 1934 and comics in 1954). Instead, video game makers had only to warn children (and their parents) that a Teen-rated game showed graphic violence against humans and that an E-rated game only had violence done to animals and fantasy figures.[31]

From organized protests against movies after the turn of the century to concerns about home video games in the 1990s, Americans have repeatedly experienced what historian James Gilbert calls "a cycle of outrage" against the commercialization of children's culture.[32] To be sure, these "moral panics" were often irrational and authoritarian, reflecting wider cultural and social insecurities projected onto the young. But they were also attempts to rescue the innocent child from an aggressive consumer market. The problem was sorting out the motives for drawing the line. When protesters attempted to protect the middle-class youngster from the sexuality, compulsiveness, and violence of the "street" and market, they evaded a central problem. Even moral, hardworking, and enlightened parents could not contain children's fantasies and desires in modern consumer culture. These futile efforts showed that Americans wanted to set boundaries, but not too close to home. Few were willing to acknowledge the origins of the Gremlin child in their adoration of wondrous innocence.

"Panics" often forced the entertainment and children's culture industry to back down: In response to the outcry against the sexual and violent themes of early 1930s movies, the entertainment industry offered Shirley Temple and Mickey Rooney. Reacting to the outrage over lurid comics and Elvis Presley in the 1950s, TV assuaged anxieties with *Father Knows Best* and other paternalistic sitcoms. Nevertheless, the effect was only short-lived. Ultimately, even Disney products strayed close to the line. And the outrage against each new, seemingly greater assault on childhood innocence grew weaker.

## Advertising and Containing the Cool Consumer

Despite a century of the creeping commercialization of childhood and repeated failure to erect walls between the young and the adult, many Americans remained outraged. This anger went beyond any specific taboo (sex, violence, or "addiction"), child development objective, or even efforts to reduce parents' anxiety at their children's rush to the "cool." This outrage had another cause—the still strong belief that children represented values and purposes beyond the market. Although underlying the politics of innocence is much hypocrisy and guilt, it continues to be a rationale for moral standards and the right to raise offspring according to those standards. Moreover, reformers found a rare means of constraining the market in sheltering the child.

In U.S. history, there have been few barriers to the expansion of commercialism. While Americans have a rich religious and moral tradition of self-control and protecting communities from perceived vice and corruption, they have also long equated freedom with unfettered markets. Compared with more homogeneous societies, informal controls of family and neighborhood have been unusually ineffective in moderating consumption in the United States. Thus, efforts to regulate children's markets have been especially important not only to protect the young but also as a way for restraining commercialism on a broader front.

Advocates of regulation cut across ideological lines. Both conservative proponents of Victorian family values and modern left-wing critics of manipulative consumerism embrace parents' right to be free from the pressures of Hollywood or tobacco companies. Most agree that children lack the ability to make consumer choices and thus that advertising directed at them appears inherently manipulative and unfair. Even Americans on the secular Left agree with religious conservatives that desire, when awakened through marketing, may destroy the child's innate simplicity. It may weaken the youngster's later ability to be creative, make rational judgments, or defer gratification. These attempts to protect childhood from aggressive marketers have not been particularly successful. Still, the very difficulty in the United States of imposing any restrictions on markets has made these arguments central to constrain consumption.

Protecting children from the market was a serious public policy issue in the early twentieth century, culminating only in the late 1970s. Despite the potential advantage of selling directly to children, until the 1950s, merchandisers were very careful not to offend the sentiments of parents. The implicit rule was this: Because children lacked the rational capacity of the adult, they should not be "lured," through advertising, into wanting a toy or a sweet. Until the 1930s, toy makers appealed primarily to parents, not children, and even then, toy and candy companies did not advertise on children's radio programs. The merchandisers' moral and economic self-constraint meant that legislation was unnecessary.[33]

In the two decades after World War II, however, the situation changed dramatically. New sugared breakfast cereals and new toys based on licensed characters from film and TV hit the market. Aggressive and direct TV advertising to children seemed to break the old unwritten contract with parents.[34] Moreover, both the increasing powers of corporations and a commercial libertarian culture limited any constraint—even for the sake of the children. In this context, a new call for protecting children from commercialism emerged by the 1960s.

The division between the educational and the commercial was not always easy to discern. In the 1950s, even advocates of developmentally sound children's programs failed to separate them. Former first-grade teacher and a Ph.D. in education, "Miss Frances" Horwich, noted for her gentle and maternal style on her *Ding Dong School* program, called for educators, not scriptwriters, to decide the content of children's programs. Her morning show on NBC contrasted with the carnivalesque afternoon *Howdy Doody*, in which the clown Clarabell repeatedly squirted seltzer water in unsuspecting faces. Still, Horwich allowed a Tiny Tears doll to be perched on a book she read on live TV and then used this sweet but commercial image in an advertising campaign, during which Miss Frances made appearances at department stores. Her long-running successor, Bob Keeshan as Captain Kangaroo, took pride in his child-oriented program. Nevertheless, in 1957 he rode a toy tractor supplied by its manufacturer during his show to bring in advertising revenue. This in-show commercial (later condemned as "host" advertising) clearly broke the barrier between children's sheltered world of imagination and learning and the commercial world of manipulative advertising, but neither Horwich or Keeshan saw it that way.[35]

By the mid-1960s, however, the stakes had clearly risen. The small-time huckstering by Keeshan and Horwich had given way to the ad-intense programming of *The Mickey Mouse Club*. Despite complaints from reviewers when it first appeared in 1955, *The Mickey Mouse Club* proved the profitability of the hard sell to kids. Mattel, the first toy company to use this TV show for daily (rather than holiday) advertising, saw its sales rise from $6 million in 1955 to $25 million in 1960. Abandoning parent-oriented salespeople like Miss Frances, Mattel produced a new "host," Matty, a boy cartoon figure on the air at 5:00 P.M. weekdays. Matty appealed directly to children (by no means a moralizing adult) and, as important, indifferently presented "Casper the Friendly Ghost" cartoons and Mattel commercials. The distinction between programming and advertising vanished. In 1969, Mattel produced the Hot Wheels TV cartoon series to advertise a new line of toy cars. This was little more than a logical extension of a now-established tradition, but growing sensitivity to the conflict between commercialism and childhood led the Federal Trade Commission (FTC) to pressure Mattel not to advertise the toy on the program.[36]

An increasingly more interventionist Congress and Supreme Court also began to demand more action from moribund regulatory agencies, especially the FTC, which regulated advertising content, and the FCC, which issued TV licenses. In 1969, the Supreme Court directed the FCC to more vigorously enforce its licensing authority by demanding that stations offer "public interest" programming (especially for children).[37]

The impetus for sheltering the child from commercialism culminated in the 1970s. Newton, Massachusetts, homemaker Peggy Charren had formed Action for Children's Television (ACT) in 1968 to pressure the TV networks into providing educational children's TV. In 1971 it demanded the banning of ads on kids' TV, claiming that commercials interfered with parents' rights to educate their own children. This campaign applied the doctrine of protected innocence in the age of commercial television.[38]

Similarly, consumer advocate Robert Choate created the Council on Children, Media, and Merchandising to publicize concerns that ads for sugared cereal, candy, and soft drinks designed for children were undermining the nation's future health. When kids were exposed to twenty ads per hour of viewing, school and parental appeals to healthful eating were lost. The result, Choate proclaimed, was that 25 percent of Americans were overweight. Ads for Cookie Crisp cereal that told the child to "change your dish into a cookie jar" jarred the ears of Americans in the 1970s. Six consumer organizations appealed to the FTC to ban ads directed to children under the age of twelve, to eliminate all ads for artificially sugared foods, and even to reduce ads to six minutes per hour of children's television.[39]

In response to mounting criticism, the National Association of Broadcasters recommended new standards (that the FCC embraced) in 1974. TV networks and stations were to reduce advertising from 16 to 12 minutes per hour of children's programming on weekdays and allow only 9.5 minutes per hour on weekends. The guidelines condemned programs that featured and thus advertised toys in their story lines and denounced "host" advertising. Although these rules affected only 10 percent of programs, they protected children from unlimited advertising and commercialism.[40]

The pressure on advertising to children, however, did not let up. Widely read books, including Ron Goulart's *The Assault on Childhood* (1969) and Marie Winn's *The Plug-In Drug* (1977), suggested that too much TV was breaking up American family life, reducing children's contact with real people as opposed to emotionally appealing celebrities, and replacing education with entertainment. In this climate of growing concern about the loss of childhood innocence, it is no surprise that we see the most daring examples of defending childhood against the advertising and entertainment market.[41]

In 1977, the new FTC chair, Michael Pertschuk, began to target advertising directed explicitly toward children. The next year, he told *Newsweek* that he was committed to stopping the "commercialization of children" that "has crept on us without scrutiny or action." Such a ban on ads during children's programs would defend parents' right to raise their children without the interference of advertisers. By their very nature of appealing to the innocent young, these ads could be deemed "unfair" because children were not rational agents in a commercial exchange. Pertschuk saw this as an opportunity for drawing a boundary that limited market speech at a moment when consumers were concerned about both ads and their impact on children. Again, in response to this rising tide in favor of regulation, the networks made token efforts to appease critics. For example, in 1978, NBC aired informational spots such as "Junior Hall of Fame" and "Ask NBC News."[42]

But the pressure continued. In 1978, the FTC considered prohibiting ads directed at children under eight years of age, banning all commercials for sugared foods on kids' programs, and even outlawing all other kidvid ads. The FTC argued that commercials directed at children under eight were inherently deceptive and thus "unfair" because such young children did not understand their purpose. The FTC report even claimed that parents should not have to compete with commercials in raising their children.[43]

This effort, however, was short-lived. Ad makers attacked any interference with the "right" of children to have information about products.[44] In 1978, even the *Washington Post* mocked the FTC for its attack on kid ads, accusing the agency of undermining parental authority by replacing family responsibility to monitor children's TV watching with government regulation.[45] In November 1978, lobbyists for the junk-food industry convinced a U.S. district judge that Pertschuk had prejudged the ban on sugar before proper hearings, thus prohibiting him from personal involvement.[46] In hearings held in 1979, industry representatives stressed their right of commercial free speech. The Grocers' Manufacturing Association even claimed that sugar cereals were better for kids than peas and carrots. The tide had turned. In the spring of 1980, Congress suspended the FTC's proposal to ban "unfair" ads (rather than openly deceptive ones), in effect derailing the argument that ads directed toward children were inherently a threat to their innocence.[47]

Ronald Reagan's subsequent election as president in November 1980 and his appointment of Mark Fowler to the FCC in 1981 intensified this trend: Fowler suggested that public TV could take over the role of providing quality children's programming if the advertising market would not pay for it. In response to the government's signal, CBS gradually pushed Captain Kangaroo off the air on weekday mornings to make room for high-rated "news" programming. Finally, in January 1983, following a Justice Department antitrust suit against the NAB, this voluntary organization scrapped its code that had set standards for public service programming and ad limits since the early 1950s. Fowler followed suit by ending the obligation that TV stations offer children's programming and eliminated controls on the number of TV ads.[48]

The deregulation of children's TV allowed merchandisers to transform kids' programs into ads. Cartoon shows created by or for toy companies to promote action figures became common in the 1980s. These program-length commercials (PLCs) kept the toy line daily in front of the child. No longer did an entertaining cartoon figure become a licensed toy or doll only after achieving "fame." The point of the new-style program was to advertise a toy line and only secondarily to entertain.[49]

Despite widespread support for deregulation, these consequences of Fowler's FCC policies were not popular. In 1985, Congress passed a bill that would have restored children's TV programming and advertising regulations. Although Reagan pocket vetoed the bill, his action was soundly denounced in the press. Finally, in 1990 the Children's Television Act restored limits on kidvid ads (12 minutes per hour on weekdays and 10.5 minutes on weekends). It also required that the networks provide at least seven hours of children's programming per week. A highly significant loophole was the exclusion of cable channels from the law at a time when the old networks were losing audience share.[50] The FCC made no attempt to eliminate toy-based programming. *Power Rangers* and other program-length commercials continued to rule the airwaves.[51]

In 1999, Newton Minow, FCC chair in the Kennedy years, called for the restoration of the NAB code, especially in recognition of the "special needs of children." The abolition of the code only opened the airwaves to "shock jocks and video vultures." A code of good taste and responsibility, Minow argued, was not a threat to free speech. However, despite the wide-ranging support for protecting children, nothing came of this appeal.[52]

## Saving the Innocent from Sex and Smoke

Reformers failed to make childhood a wedge against commercialization, but that did not mean adults ceased trying to restrict markets in the name of innocence. The spread of legal gambling and home shopping networks, unrestricted advertising on TV, and the widening market for pornography and guns kept the politics of innocence alive.[53] While government interference in advertising to children had failed by 1980, similar intervention succeeded in restricting children's exposure to profanity and obscenity. A radio airing of George Carlin's twelve-minute monologue "Seven Dirty Words" in 1973 was heard in the early afternoon by a father and his young son. The FCC took the father's complaint to court, arguing that the hour of the day on which the monologue was broadcast exposed innocent children to Carlin's obscenity. The radio station insisted that it was the parents' responsibility to monitor their children's listening. The Supreme Court upheld the FCC, arguing that "broadcasting is uniquely accessible to children, even those too young to read. The government's interest in the well-being of its youth and in supporting parental claims to authority in their own household justified the regulation of otherwise protected expression."[54]

This position was virtually identical to the claims of the FTC in 1978 against advertising to children. Thus, it is not surprising that free-marketeer Mark Fowler at the FCC resisted applying this ruling in the 1980s. Yet, under pressure from the religious Right, Fowler enforced this "indecency" standard in 1986, declaring his intent "to drive lewd programming off the air." A decade later, the Communications Decency Act followed through on these concerns for the Internet age, prohibiting "indecency," the display of any sexually oriented material, on the Internet to a minor. The vagueness of this legislation resulted in a successful court challenge and a narrower law obliging pornographers to exclude access to minors. Clearly, Americans were eager to protect children from dirty words and pornography but not to shelter them from consumer desire.[55]

Still, because there were few legal and moral restraints on the pursuit of youth markets, the old call for protecting the most vulnerable consumer was not to be silenced. In the 1990s, the politics of innocence had the greatest potential impact in the area of restricting tobacco consumption. For thirty years, public disapproval of smoking had grown: in 1964, manufacturers were required to print a health warning on each cigarette pack; in 1971, all TV and radio advertising for tobacco products was banned; and by 1984, thirty-four states had outlawed smoking from many public places. The individual's right to be free of tobacco-polluted air trumped the free-market right to indulge.[56]

This left an opening for turning smoking into a child protection issue. In 1984, despite nominal evidence, the surgeon general warned that passive smoking endangered toddlers and the unborn. He urged parents to quit for the sake of their kids. A larger issue was the fact that restrictions on ads and health warnings had done relatively little to diminish youth tobacco use. While cigarette smoking had declined sharply among adults (dropping from 42.5 percent in 1965 to 25.5 percent in 1990), underage smoking had remained relatively steady since 1980. About 30 percent of high school seniors smoked in the early 1990s, even though state laws prohibited the selling of tobacco products to anyone under eighteen years of age. The simple fact was that cigarette makers kept introducing new generations to the habit. They did this by shifting ad dollars from TV and radio to magazines and billboards, and by sponsoring sports and cultural events where they prominently displayed their logos. Because an estimated 90 percent of adult smokers adopted the habit before they were twenty (60 percent began by thirteen years of age), the tobacco companies realized their future customers were mostly underage.[57] This was a perfect issue for child protection on legal, moral, and health grounds. In 1989, crusading congressmen Thomas Luken and Mike Synar introduced a bill based on a proposal of the American Medical Association to ban tobacco ads likely to be seen by children.[58]

By the end of the 1980s, merchandisers seemed to be growing more aggressive in pushing tobacco on the young. In 1988, a very visible and successful tobacco ad campaign brought the issue to a head. For many, R. J. Reynolds's ads featuring Joe Camel, a hip-looking, cartoon character with a cigarette dangling from his lips, were targeting children. Joe's image appeared on billboards and magazine ads but also on beach towels, baseball caps, windbreakers, and even candy cigarettes. He even had a cameo role in the children's movie *Who Framed Roger Rabbit?* As a cartoon figure, Joe may have appealed to young children, but, more important, his swagger and dress surely represented for older children the very essence of the cool. Sales of Camel cigarettes to underage smokers increased from under 1 percent in 1989 to 33 percent in 1991. The company claimed that peer pressure and imitation of parents, not its ads, governed teens' decision to smoke. But the AMA, the American Cancer Society, the surgeon general, and twenty-seven state attorney generals demanded that Reynolds drop the Joe Camel campaign. President Clinton joined in, linking advertising to the vulnerability of children and accusing Reynolds of "unscrupulous marketing campaigns that prey on the insecurities and dreams of our children."[59]

Protecting children's health attracted support across the political spectrum. Even more, in an age when government regulation of any kind was suspect, this was a practical avenue for limiting tobacco use in general. While Supreme Court decisions in the 1970s had extended the rights of commercial speech, the Court still recognized the principle of "deceptive" ads and the government's interest in protecting children from them. Youths under eighteen years of age were, by law, not free agents in any purchase of tobacco products. When children were lured into smoking through cigarette ads and became addicted to the habit, the tobacco industry could no longer argue that these smokers knowingly accepted health risks (like adults, who presumably had read the government-sanctioned health warnings and thus understood tobacco's dangers). This was because children presumably lacked the knowledge and intellectual maturity to make a free decision to smoke despite risks, and so when the tobacco industry advertised to children, antito-

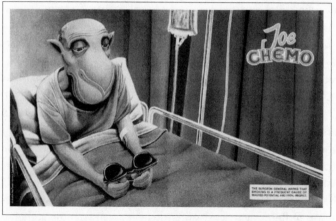

**6.2**
One of a series of satirical "ads" produced by Adbusters and used in campaigns to discourage children from smoking. Here Joe Camel has been transformed into Joe Chemo, obviously receiving chemotherapy to treat his lung cancer. The cool here has been turned on its head. Image courtesy of www.adbusters.org.

bacco reformers could raise the old issue of the "fairness" of these ads. The legal argument was that these messages evoked emotional responses to which children were vulnerable rather than communicating information (as in "protected" speech). Still, this was not an easy case to make. Despite public outcry, the FTC in 1994 narrowly opposed issuing a complaint against the makers of Camels. While advertising and tobacco executives were relieved, the Joe Camel incident created momentum for protecting the innocent with additional tobacco controls.[60]

Under the Clinton administration, the battle shifted to the Food and Drug Administration (FDA), an office with the authority to regulate the sale and production of legal drugs. The FDA took the bold step of trying to make nicotine in cigarettes a regulated drug. This was a legal stretch, for tobacco had never been regulated as a drug, and the FDA realized that banning tobacco outright was politically impossible. In 1994, the FDA decided on a parallel and ultimately safer course—to reduce tobacco access and advertising appeals to youth—and yet "not restrict the use of tobacco products by adults." The FDA proposed banning cigarette vending machines and restricting the emotional appeal of color and graphic advertising in magazines to which minors might have access, outlawing tobacco billboards within one thousand feet of a playground or school, and preventing cigarette logos from publicizing sponsorship of sporting or other cultural events. The report even argued for a two dollar tax per pack to create a substantial economic barrier to underage smoking. The idea was to wall off children from the pied pipers of nicotine.[61]

These were clever efforts to redefine this obvious attack on free markets to protect the vulnerable child. Indeed, the FDA argued that nicotine addiction was a "pediatric disease" that would prematurely shorten the lives of a third of young tobacco users. Underage smokers could not make a fully informed decision (as assumed in a genuine free-market situation), and because smoking is addictive, these smokers as adults and thus free agents would be physically unable to reverse an earlier "unfree" decision. As FDA chair David Kessler put it, kids could outgrow a decision to dye their hair orange, but when the million children who start smoking every year become addicted to tobacco, that habit carries into their adult years. The tobacco companies objected that the FDA's restrictions on marketing cigarettes to children would undermine free speech and impede adult access to information about tobacco products. In the name of sheltering the innocent, Kessler rejected the sacred "right" of tobacco companies to push their disease-causing product.[62]

President Clinton joined the fray with his "save the kids" rhetoric in defense of Kessler's proposals: "Children every day are bombarded by massive marketing campaigns that play on their vulnerabilities, their insecurities, their longings to be something in the world." Armed with a federal judge's approval, the FDA went on to issue new restrictions on the over-the-counter sales of tobacco, requiring clerks to "card" anyone appearing to be younger than twenty-seven and training undercover agents to enforce their compliance. Fearing FDA use of its trump card—regulating nicotine in cigarettes—and terrified by unrestricted class action suits undertaken by victims of tobacco use, the tobacco industry in 1996 and 1997 negotiated settlements with state attorneys general. In June 1997, a settlement between thirty-nine states and the tobacco companies would have required the payment of $368.5 billion to the states (over twenty-five years), along with severe controls over advertising to kids.[63]

Many antitobacco reformers thought this was not enough, and in March 1998, congressional supporters demanded a much larger settlement (up to $516 billion) and an additional $1.10 tax per pack. In response to this pressure, the cigarette companies walked out on negotiations, opting to launch a $40 million ad campaign against any new law. Allies in Congress defeated legislation by attacking new cigarette duties (ostensibly designed to price children out of the market) as a "new tax burden" and a new government intrusion into personal freedom. In August, another blow came: a federal appellate court ruled that the FDA could not regulate tobacco as a drug, giving the cigarette companies renewed leverage. Later that year, an out-of-court settlement between the tobacco companies and forty-six states reduced the earlier settlement to $206 billion in exchange for ending state suits against the companies. The cost to tobacco was far less than the $516 billion demanded in Congress and likely would be easily absorbed. Significantly, however, the ban on advertising to children remained in place.[64] The politics of innocence is bound to shape the future debate about gun control, pornography, alcohol, and, more broadly, commercialization.[65] Not only are there few legal means of challenging the market, but Americans still believe that the innocence of children is sacred.

On balance, however, what has been the impact of efforts to set the boundaries of innocence? Despite the breadth of support and centrality of protecting innocence in the United States, this enterprise has been surprisingly ineffective. Over the long run, movies, video games, and other media have become far more violent and sexually explicit. Today, the PG-13 film rating is less a warning to parents than an allurement to thirteen-year-olds, a symbol of their escape from the childish fare of G or PG movies. Moreover, PG-13-rated films are filled with violence, profanity, and sex talk, leaving out little but nudity and copulation. The genteel culture and values that so many hoped to preserve in the attack on comics in the 1940s and 1950s are lost to all but snobs, religious conservatives, and old-fashioned English or music teachers. Since the 1970s, superhero stories from the comic books have supplied the themes of big-budget, blockbuster films. Only those willing to isolate their families and ignore the charge of elitism can block their children's "right" to modern commercial culture.

Nevertheless, although the boundary has been repeatedly pulled back, almost all Americans insist that they still need a line to protect children (and perhaps themselves) from unrestrained desire. They have little difficulty devoting emotion and resources toward protecting children from sex and especially sexual predators. The desire for a line comes out also in their efforts to shelter the young from tobacco (and other drug) addiction. There may be no consensus on the parent's right to restrict children's exposure to advertising or society's obligation to delay the onslaught of commercial persuasion. This, however, is largely due to the massive financial and political power of the merchandisers, not a widespread belief that four-year-olds have a "right" to unlimited commercial messages.

So why have boundary makers been so unsuccessful? It large part, it is because Americans have been unable to reach a consensus about what they want to shelter the child from. This failure is one consequence of long-waged and continuing cultural wars. The rhetoric of child protection shared across the political and cultural spectrum often obscures the huge gulf separating the cultures of the religious Right from the secular Left, and this greatly impedes any real challenge to the commercialization of the cool. This division is typically expressed in the conflict between the traditional fear of concupiscence and the modern faith in diffused and benign desire. Each camp is further befuddled by its own contradictions. The laissez-faire faith of American conservatives compromises their traditionalist impulse to protect children, while the tolerant tilt of modernism is muddled by the pro-regulation belief of American liberals.

Underlying all this is a basic conundrum in modern child rearing: the need for boundaries and yet the inability to create them has much to do with adults' wanting the wondrous child and yet their disappointment when their Gismos become Gremlins. Parents cannot do without their "naughty" children who take them out of their rationalized lives at work and their disappointing lives at the mall. How can adults, who perhaps secretly enjoy the crude and immature boyishness of *The Man Show* or the outrageous self-indulgence of the *Anna Nicole Smith Show*, seriously draw a line against their thirteen-year-olds viewing *Austin Powers in Goldmember* despite its bathroom humor? And who can envision a return to the goody-two-shoes culture of *Tom Swift* or even *Nancy Drew*? The dialectics of the cute and the cool are so intertwined with the often positive values of children's autonomy and openness to change that it is no wonder so many are confused.

# Rethinking Innocence

I nnocence may define the modern child, but it has done so with great ambiguity. Adults' searches for wonder in the inexperienced response of the young have produced much disappointment and frustration, but so have attempts to shelter the innocent child from the world's temptations. One version of the innocent presumes virginal sanctity in the spontaneous child, the other, a vulnerable but malleable creature on a course to maturity. All this has left modern parents rehearsing again and again the same frustrations as they endlessly shift between permissiveness in search of the self-actualizing youngster and control in an effort to mold the superchild. There is no simple solution to the dilemma, and any answer will require us to go beyond conventional child-rearing strategies to thinking about how adults use children to cope with their own contradictions.

## A Half Century of Frustration

T he central debate over innocence has been whether the parent or the child knows best, whether childhood was a guided journey led by skilled parents or a time of life enjoyed by children and admired by adults. In 1946, the editors of *Parents* magazine, reflecting on their twentieth anniversary, noted a "swing away from the rigid emphasis on 'child training' to happier, more relaxed family living." The founders of the magazine in the mid-1920s had been an "almost prayerful group" of experts who surrounded the child and "decided what was to be done to him and then urged parents to go at it hammer and tongs." While the behaviorism that originally inspired this group had gone out of style, the real problem was "all this was hard on parents." Mothers especially said they "wanted to feel free to love their babies." And new authorities like Adolph Meyer and Arnold Gesell gave them permission by insisting that parents could not spoil the baby. Freudians assured them that "fixations" could result only from rigid toilet training and harsh repression of desires. This message was repeated over and over in the 1950s and 1960s, culminating with the arch-permissive expert Haim Ginott, who insisted on the most indirect persuasion: don't say "go to bed" but "I bet you wish you could play all night."[1]

Yet, despite the permissive messages embedded in ads and much child-rearing advice, Americans never felt comfortable with the celebration of children's desires. Concerns about the mother smothering the child with affection lasted long beyond John Watson's diatribes against it. Even before permissiveness had really even taken off in the postwar years, the intellectual historian George Boas could, in 1938, attack a "maleficent paidocracy" for displacing the old "benevolent paternalism." The modern rule of the child has made youth not only the "focus of all our thought but also the model for our behavior." He lamented that "our women dress and act like girls, our men like undergraduates. . . . Hence the passion for 'cuteness' in our houses [and] pets." While "no real child ever wanted to be cute," Boas insisted, "no adult that wanted to be a child ever failed to." Children who were taught that "their desires and personalities are sacred" inevitably suffer false expectations as adults. According to Boas, for children the real "god is appetite." They want only their "gang." Ignorant of reason, impatient with debate, they are "natural born fascists." While "our problem is to thicken the coat of civilization," our quest for the "childlike and innocent" is only leading to barbarism.[2]

Perhaps, on the eve of an irrational war, this attack on modern child rearing is understandable. Yet even during the height of the baby boom euphoria with the child-centered life, M. Harari, writing in the Catholic magazine Commonweal, rejected the modern obsession with pleasing the child. Harari denied that authoritarian parents victimized children. The problem was quite different: because we no longer recognize life as a "gift," we expect that personal "love be the source of life." Inevitably, when the parent's love is not perfect, children resent the relationship, and because no one is really ever guilty, the young cannot even forgive the less than perfect mother or father.[3]

The odd article in Better Homes and Gardens argues as early as 1952 that mothers should have outside jobs and advocates the "intelligent neglect" of kids. More important, in 1954, scarcely eight years after the appearance of his first edition of *Baby and Child Care*, Benjamin Spock was already suggesting a reversal of the "overpermissiveness trend." He warned against the "tyrannical character" of eight-month-old babies who never sleep and the right of parents to expect "politeness and cooperation" from their older children. In 1959, the often-cited anthropologist Margaret Mead observed that postwar parents may have rebelled against their own authoritarian upbringing and even "secretly encouraged naughtiness," but that was temporary, and now parents would find a happy medium.[4]

In many revisions of his child-rearing manual and in popular articles, Benjamin Spock tried to correct the common perception that he was the father of permissiveness. While condemned by popular preacher Norman Vincent Peale for producing a generation of self-indulgent youth, in 1968 Spock himself offered a surprisingly moderate perspective. Spock recognized that parental deference to children's wishes "makes for geniality between the generations," but he worried that the youth "develops merely an affectionate regard for his parents." Permissiveness was rooted in a popular reaction to Victorian propriety and formality. This response, Spock insisted, was misguided. It produced a corrosive cynicism toward marriage and the "dignity of man" because it failed to instill idealism in children. For the young to have positive models later in life, they had "to adore, be inspired by and pattern themselves after their parents," rather than the opposite. Of course, "these intense loves become suppressed in middle childhood and sublimated" into learning, hero worship, religion, and romantic love. But when parents lack standards, their children become disenchanted with life and lose the capacity for the mutual respect and civility upon which civilization depends. The liberal Spock, with his gentle methods and support for the youth-led peace movements of the 1960s and 1970s, also insisted that children should idealize their parents rather than parents glorify their children's wishes and longings. Yet his answer would not satisfy many because, as a mediator between authority and permissiveness, his position only reflected the ambiguity of the age rather than really resolved it.[5]

Not surprisingly, less nuanced critiques of permissiveness prevailed. Antidotes varied from Parent Effectiveness Training courses and professional reprogramming of indulged children to bringing God back into the homes and classrooms, "Dare to Discipline" manuals, and frequent "reassessment" of the no-spanking admonition of experts. Experts regularly advocated "authoritative" rather than authoritarian or permissive parenting. Nevertheless, it was hard to define a middle ground where both parents and children had rights, and civility and order were prerequisites for happy family life.[6]

Rethinking Innocence

193

The problem was not only concern about permissiveness but also about its opposite—overprotecting and overguiding the child. The obsessive drive of "yuppie" parents of the 1980s to raise "superbabies" was the most recent and most glaring example. Many young mothers, new to and excited about working in the corporate world, understood child rearing as a "business" and tried to apply the same principles of efficiency they used at work to help their toddlers "reach their goal." Prudently, they prepared their offspring to get into the right college by getting them into the right day care center. Developmental child-rearing principles were taken to extremes, even perverted. Some parents embraced the doctrines of Glenn Doman in his book *How to Teach Your Baby to Read* (1964) and his Better Baby Institute (founded in 1977). Doman claimed that seven-month-olds could master basic math and infants could read at one year of age (using flash cards). Parents played classical music to help their newborns develop the left side of their brains. It did not matter that academic experts warned that babies were incapable of such learning or that children who were allowed to play caught up with earlier achievers by the fourth grade. Like Ellen Key before them, these parents believed that their investment in the "right" educational toy, software, summer camp, or home teaching program would help their offspring avoid the temptations of an indulgent society and gain the competitive edge to win the brass ring of success.[7]

Experts warned against pushing children too soon into adult roles. The media regularly mocked overachieving parents for their vanity and obsessiveness, as well as their cruelty in denying their children playtime. In the 1960s, popular magazine articles warned against rushing preteens into dating and dances. "When children try to grow up too soon, they actually find the real step toward maturity so difficult to take, they may never really grow up at all," claimed Judson Landes of the University of California. He criticized parents who sent their children to dance schools and charm classes, denying them their right to play freely. Dress-up dances for sixth graders only created jaded children. Joshua Meyrowitz echoed these views in 1982 when he complained that "children do not seem childlike anymore." The look of Brooke Shields had replaced Shirley Temple. Kids had become "adults imprisoned in children's bodies." Others complained that children were forced to compete in adultlike clubs, sports, music, and parties at ten years of age when they needed to be lazy and play. In the 1960s and 1970s, University of Chicago psychologist Bruno Bettelheim regularly warned parents against pushing their children in school.[8]

Through all this confusion, there remained an abiding problem. Adults were caught between their desire to worship the child and their attempt to mold the child. The culture seemed to demand that children be divided into idealized states of immanence and potential, of present perfection and future possibility, and no one seemed to like the consequences of either approach.

Unsurprisingly, there has been an increasingly vocal rejection of child rearing altogether. Although rare for the time, a series of articles in the late 1930s in the *American Mercury* dared to say what some were beginning to feel—that the whole enterprise of both the wondrous and the guided child was a miserable disappointment. In 1937 a mother wrote an article titled "I Do Not Like My Children." She admitted that she was happy to be rid of her children after twenty years, having succeeded only in raising four demanding, vain, and self-centered people. Her life had been "torn off in little bits by these children." A letter to the editor responded by blaming the whining mother for her disappointment, insisting that "your sacrifices only weakened these children." But the traditional appeal to tough parenting was not enough for another anonymous writer in an essay entitled "No Children for Me!" He simply complained that children today (1938) are "ill-mannered and selfish" and that he, for one, would not sacrifice for twenty years just to add another body to the mess of humanity. Naturally, *Parents* magazine in an article called "Why Have Babies?" defended parenthood as "the height and depth of human experience," but it admitted that children "mean pain and suffering and give you anxiety or leave you to the entrails of despair." Even the conventional *American Home* could publish in 1944 a piece entitled "I've Raised Three Selfish Little Savages." The author blamed "progressive" child rearing for making her children believe "they have priority over everything and everybody" and sarcastically complained that expensive schools taught soap carving instead of math and history.[9]

As the baby boom generation was coming to maturity in the 1970s, there again emerged expressions of doubt about raising children. Research at the University of Michigan's Institute for Social Research found couples without children were more "satisfied" than those with offspring.[10] This finding corresponded to a sharp drop in childbearing (a 51 percent decrease in the total fertility rate from 1960–64 to 1975–79).[11] Nonfertility rites in Central Park and the creation of the National Organization for Non-Parents symbolize this trend. Such groups were hardly representative (the National Alliance for Optional Parenting claimed only two thousand members). Still, many women were anxious not to follow their mothers' path, sacrificing friends, marital bliss, and career for the sake of children.[12] For some, neither the emotional appeal of the wondrous child nor the intellectual and moral challenge of the sheltered and molded child seemed to justify the sacrifice.

## Challenging Rites of Wonder

E ven in the 1970s, the rejection of childbearing was still a relatively rare and extreme response. More common were challenges to the rituals of childhood wonder. While many condemned the commercialized sentimentalism of Christmas, if anything the rites of gift giving to children became ever more elaborate by the end of the twentieth century. Other sites of wondrous innocence, however, were far more vulnerable, especially Halloween and the Disney vacation.

Halloween was always the most suspect ritual of wondrous innocence because its archaic qualities had never been entirely suppressed. Unlike birthdays and even Christmas, it remained a community celebration. Halloween did not use children to let adults withdraw into domesticity. Instead, it invited children to go out and trick-or-treat. Halloween also retained associations with the violent and irrational traditions of mumming and the pagan occult that could not be as easily tamed and disguised as they had been for Christmas and other holidays. Parents have long been wary of sending their small children out into the night. An article in *Parents* in 1971 suggested limiting trick-or-treating to the hours of four to eight, confining children to their own neighborhood, and accepting only wrapped candy. In 1982, however, widespread publicity surrounding an incident of the lacing of Tylenol pain medicine with cyanide induced fears similar to the old anxieties that adults would put razor blades or pins into trick-or-treat apples. There were many false reports that adults were putting "angel dust" and poisons into Halloween candy. By 1983, various civic groups were organizing to ban trick-or-treating and to replace it with community parties. In 1984, hospitals even offered to X-ray children's candy bags for dangerous objects. In hopes of assuaging parents' fears that trick-or-treat candy was poisoned, the police chief of Omaha suggested that householders put pencils and hair clips instead of candy in the sacks of trick-or-treaters. The mayor of Los Angeles in 1985 organized a "kids' day" on Halloween to woo children from their traditional rounds with a community party featuring baseball stars. Many towns and cities shifted trick-or-treating to a Saturday afternoon. Experts insisted that practically all reports of adult malice were false, and newspaper editorials lamented this "moral panic." In fact, the scare abated by the end of the 1980s. Still, it is at least a little strange that parents would feel safer taking their children to the mall for trick-or-treating than letting them visit their neighbors. Little could be more telling about the decline of community trust than this.[13]

Despite efforts of reformers of the 1930s and 1940s to make Halloween a day of the cute, the underlying rules of the new Halloween that had made it charming were eroding. In the mid-1980s, adults complained of the rudeness of children who shouted "Me first!" or neglected to say thank you during the trick-or-treat ritual. One householder complained that she had to give "candy to other people's children" who walked on her lawn and trampled her shrubs in the mad rush for more goodies and moaned about greeting a greedy "six foot teenager" on her porch, crashing the party of wondrous innocence. A member of the Grey Panthers (a group of elderly activists) even complained that Halloween masks abused seniors by making old people look hideous.[14]

At the same time, newspapers reported with increasing alarm incidents of vandalism around Halloween. Despite the best efforts of earlier reformers to infantilize Halloween, the old traditions of "tricking" survived, and some grew more dangerous. For example, in 1974, the *New York Times* reported that the town of Union, New Jersey, had banned the selling of eggs to anyone less than eighteen years of age due to recent Halloween "eggings" of windows. Interestingly, a group of sixth-graders from the town protested this infringement of their rights. Twelve years later, New York suburbanites complained that local stores were actually promoting the sale of shaving cream to kids who had no legitimate need for this product. Much more serious were stories of arson in Detroit on "Devil's Night," the evening before Halloween, that forced police to institute a dusk-to-dawn curfew in 1986. As late as 1995, inner-city teens were still setting hundreds of fires, and Detroit was not alone. In 1998, a gathering of one hundred thousand in Los Angeles led to the arrest of about six thousand youths for vandalism. In urban America, riot and destruction seem to have replaced the pranks of the past.[15]

Another threat to the wonder of trick-or-treating came from the religious Right. Rejecting the long-established practice of passing on to children sanitized versions of old community and even pagan traditions, these new "Puritans" wanted to shelter children from anything that could potentially threaten their Christian values. For some, this led to the belief that, because of the pagan origins of Halloween, trick-or-treating was a form of devil worship. In the 1970s, some fundamentalist Protestant churches tried to turn Halloween into an opportunity to evangelize. They transformed the traditional haunted house into a scare house featuring sights of the gruesome deaths of Christian martyrs and the beheading of John the Baptist that ended in tables of religious literature promising salvation. In the 1980s, some churches gave children cartoon books that warned of the dangers of burning in hell and even stories that recalled the panics about poisoned candy, a fate that might await them if they did not embrace Christ. Some conservative Christians went a step further, claiming that Halloween was satanic. It not only taught children to threaten "tricks," they argued, but also celebrated Satan's holiday by featuring devils, witches, and ghouls, encouraging children to commit demonic acts and even murder. The decline of traditional Christianity, accelerated by the banning of prayer in the schools, declared fundamentalist firebrand Ralph Forbes, should not be compounded by the worship of Satan in the schools on Halloween. In 1986, he unsuccessfully filed a lawsuit in Arkansas (literally, in the name of Jesus Christ) against the celebration of the "Devil's Holiday" in the schools. Little changed in the 1990s. A southern California fundamentalist church of thirty thousand members produced a video *Halloween, Trick-or-Treat*, which claimed that the holiday, with its pagan roots, encouraged Satan worship and made children want to kill. In 1997, some 225 churches bought a "packaged" haunted house that displayed abortions, satanic murder, teen suicide, and the funeral of a homosexual victim of AIDS.[16]

Although all this was certainly a minority view, pressures from religious conservatives led school districts to replace Halloween crafts and costume parades with "neutral" activities: in Frederick County, near Washington, D.C., the public schools tried to make National Book Week an acceptable alternative. Elsewhere, elementary school principals asked parents to forgo costumes featuring supernatural or evil themes. In Ohio and New York, schools replaced Halloween celebrations with harvest festivals. In an effort to invent a new and more wholesome tradition, one Kansas City elementary school principal dressed as Johnny Appleseed and asked his pupils to do the same. Some schools even banned Halloween. All this, emerging only in the 1980s, was part of a broader conservative religious response to non-Christian customs and growing belief in the coming of the Antichrist. Yet it also was an assault on modern Halloween, the passing of pagan and saturnalian traditions on to children.[17]

Of course, in the 1980s and 1990s many adults protested this assault on Halloween. In newspapers from all regions, opinion pieces insisted that Halloween had nothing to do with Satanism. Instead, it was a kids' day for indulgence and exploration of the unknown. What is wrong, asked one editorial, with a "ghost in a flowered sheet" or a "pint-sized Superman, and a toddler with a cotton bunny tail sewed to the rear of her pink pajamas?" This was all perfectly innocent. Not only was Halloween one of the few surviving saturnalias in the modern world, but it was enhanced by its being passed on to children. Child-rearing experts endorsed Halloween for giving the young the illusion of power and thus emotional release when they dressed up as monsters or even cartoon characters. Even the conservative Protestant

7.1
Halloween in the modern age, with adults taking back
their holiday at a Toronto party in the late 1990s.
Courtesy Nicholas Rogers.

*Christianity Today* editorialized that we "mock" rather than worship the devil
on Halloween and that the holiday is as much a part of children's culture as
Christmas. Time and again, defenders of Halloween insisted that its sanctity lay in the fact that they had enjoyed it as children and thus so should
their children. They identified trick-or-treating with the wondrous innocence they had experienced and wanted to see again in their children.[18]

Nevertheless, Halloween was threatened from still another front. Adults'
pleasures were dominating the holiday again. By the 1980s, adult Halloween
costume parties had become common. In 1987, the *Washington Post* reported
that Halloween had become a "paean to the powers of the imagination," an
opportunity for adults to "upend etiquette." They could join one of the many

costumed balls throughout Washington or the crowd of one hundred thousand who rushed into Georgetown streets for Halloween fun. Even bigger was New York's Greenwich Village Halloween parade. Adults wanted their saturnalia back. "Spooktacular" orchestra concerts featuring the "Danse Macabre" and "Night on Bald Mountain," silent horror movie shows, spooky story readings on southern plantation grounds, and parades were some of the innovations attracting adult revelers in the 1990s. By 1999, an estimated 44 percent of twenty-five- to thirty-four-year-olds attended Halloween parties (with 62 percent of eighteen- to twenty-four-year-olds dressing up in Halloween costumes).[19] The classic moment of wondrous innocence when the neighbor happily greets the naughty-looking six-year-old dressed as the devil and stuffs candy into her outstretched bag remains, of course. Yet Halloween is no longer so innocent, nor is childish wonder so central to its celebration.

Even the Meccas of the cute, Disneyland and Disney World, had to compromise their child-centered image and ambience with new adult and age-segmented programs. In 1996, the Disney Institute at Walt Disney World offered unusual adult "crafts" (animation, orchestra conducting, and sixty other "if onlys" activities that adults always wished they had learned when younger). This was in keeping with Disney's celebration of adults' nostalgia for childhood, but innovations went further. The company added a "Boardwalk" and many adult nightlife attractions. A year earlier, Disney World even opened a Wedding Chapel. In 1999, the Florida operation went one step further with the Disney Magic Cruise Ship, which featured distinct age-graded activities on board and at its destination, a Disneyfied "deserted island," called Castaway Cay. The ship included, of course, a Mickey Mouse–shaped pool but also an adult-only pool where, it was boasted, Disney music would never be played. Clubs for children, teens, and adults featured age-appropriate activities. On the Cay, a $25 million artificial peninsula separated beaches designed for families with young children from special shoreline places for teens and adults! So much for family togetherness and the child's appeal to adults. On the West Coast, in 2001 Disney opened a new theme park, Disney's California Adventure catering to more mature crowds. The now familiar age-segmented scheme guided the decision to offer tapas at its restaurants and drinks at a nightlife zone called Downtown Disney. This change reflects the decline of the two-parent family with children (only 25 percent of American households in 2000). It also was an accommodation to the general aging of the population. Even if adults would have loved to bring children with them to Disney parks, many did not have them and were perfectly happy to visit without them. Disney had become an intense experience for money rich, but time poor, Americans eager for a "throbbing all-day, all-

*[handwritten margin note: more Disney created adult programs]*

night playground." The earlier Disney message of childhood nostalgia had not disappeared, but by the 1990s it was not the only message.[20]

Disney's efforts to accommodate the childless and nontraditional lifestyle inevitably raised controversy when religious conservatives heard about Disney's overtures to homosexuals. Company sponsorship of "gay and lesbian days," Disney company benefits to gay employees, and Disney advertisements in the gay-oriented *Out Magazine* led to church boycotts of Disney products in 1997. This tactic may not have been successful (even church members, unwilling to disappoint their children, ignored their religious leaders), but it is symptomatic of change. Moreover, the emotional reaction to Disney's affront to conservative family values suggests just how successful Disney had been in identifying itself with innocence. In a time when wonder had become one with Disney, the religious Right could see the gays' presence at Disney World as a defilement of this holy site. It had become sacred not in the Christian but in the Disney sense.[21]

Although Disney did not give in to these demands, the company certainly did not abandon the theme that had made it America's shrine to wondrous innocence. In recent years, American families have become even more obsessed with the identification of childhood with the vacation, especially to Disney. Families with less time for each other at home tried to make up for it on vacation (with 72 percent of vacations built around family in 1992). While Disney was hardly the only destination, businesses recognized this need when they booked conventions in Orlando and invited participants to bring the kids. Holiday Inns at Disney locations offered special single-parent programs for kids to share "quality time" with noncustodial parents. So important had this pilgrimage become that otherwise academically oriented parents pulled their children out of school to take them to Disney ahead of the spring break or Christmas crowds. Moreover, the Children's Wish Foundation regularly sponsored trips to Disney for terminally ill children—a generous gesture that affirmed the quasi-religious significance of Disney to both child and parent.[22]

Despite all the doubts and disappointment, Americans have hardly given up their love affair with wondrous innocence. Across the past century, over and over its hymn of praise was and is sung. Echoing the romantics of the early nineteenth century, a writer in *House Beautiful* intoned in 1902: "Man himself, the work of the creator, breathes more grace the fresher he is from His hand ere the innocence of childhood is sharpened to sophistication by the veneer of the world. The pity is that these dainty, artless, satisfying little creatures don't keep well." In 1943 *Parents* insisted: "The child brings you his curiosity, his wonder, his delight. . . . You will be taken back to the moral simplicities and truths which our harassed, mature life often allows us to forget." In 1955, baby boom mothers read in *McCall's* that at Christmas, children "naturally step into the spirit of giving and friendship." Despite all the frustrations of the 1960s and 1970s, in 1981, *Christianity Today* taught that children have a "grace that brings delight." Having children is "one of God's basic modes of supplying grace." And in 2001, the *National Catholic Reporter* repeated the old refrain: with the arrival of a child, "the initial promise of creation is renewed," even though the article admitted that promise eventually fades.[23] Despite all the disappointments and challenges, the look and appeal of wondrous innocence survive along with its paired opposite, sheltered innocence. And given the way that modern parents imagine the child and use these images for their own purposes, it may be inevitable that disappointment and frustration with the results will continue indefinitely.

## Wonder, Shelter, and Rethinking Innocence

The wondrous child and sheltered child have competed in the modern family for over a century; and, across that time, both ideals have led to many surprises and disappointments. The nineteenth century's baby fresh from God became the twentieth century's child spontaneously delighted with ever higher piles of consumer goods and experiences. Today, advertising and merchandising reduce wonder to spending, exaggerate the value of immediate and private worlds of fantasy and possession, and define the childlike even as they ultimately deprive the young of innocence through the promotion of a hedonistic culture.

*Consumerism takes over wonder*

The commercialization of wonder was a product of aggressive marketing, revolutionary media, and an increasingly child-centered, child-indulgent family. Manufacturers did not merely manipulate nostalgic and insecure parents, or exploit naive and impressionable children. Rather, children's consumer goods and media met the changing needs of a new family as it evolved after 1900. In the first generation of commercialized wonder, parents' gifts gave the young and old alike an entry into a timeless past and exciting future and provided relief from the prosaic, impersonal, and calculating worlds of modern adult life. Images of the cute were projected onto their children's culture and experience. At the same time, parents found in these goods expressions of their growing empathy for the emotional and social complexity of their offspring and respect for their autonomy. Innocence, however, based on fresh exposure to novelty and desire led almost inevitably to its opposite—

satiation and obsession. After a few years of exposure to the consumer gift culture, the cute child surrounded by generous parents was transformed into the cool youth seeking freedom from the adult world. Gizmos became Gremlins, at least, in the eyes of disappointed parents. The result for adults was a deep and multifaceted ambiguity about the commercial culture—embracing it to find an emotional connection with the child but attacking it when that bond broke down.

Is there any alternative to this path from the cute to the cool? This depends on whether wonder can be separated from commercialism. Some cynics doubt it. After all, did not commerce create the "look" of the cute child "naturally" responding to the "surprise" of the new, sensuous, and bountiful commodity? At least, one could argue that merchandisers have kidnapped the romantic idea of the godlike child. And, having been raised as a wondrous babe in the hothouse of consumerism, the worshiped child no longer recognizes its romantic ancestors. Still, many are unwilling to adopt this cynical conclusion. Cultural critics ranging from Gary Ruskin of the liberal Commercial Alert to Kay Hymowitz of the conservative Manhattan Institute have insisted that ads directed toward children are a growing threat to what is delightful about the child. The implication is clear: wondrous innocence could and should stand apart from the commercial expression of it.[24]

There is certainly evidence that this is possible. Anyone who has taken a young child to the vistas of the Grand Canyon may know that the sensual and emotional intensity of a video game may not be necessary to evoke wonder. Yet parents also experience disappointment when their child prefers a Gameboy to the splendors of forest and sea. Product makers have learned how to improve on nature, making their delights more delightful. The child-rearing experts of the early twentieth century recognized this dilemma. They suggested that parents needed to intervene and teach children to enjoy simple things and that "true" wonder went beyond immediate gratification and required experience. Indeed, they insisted that wonder is sustained, transformed, and even elevated by the attainment of skills, learning, and maturity. The seasoned naturalist may not see the Grand Canyon the way a child does for the first time, but the eyes of experience bring to the encounter a many-sided satisfaction and an understanding that the wondrous child cannot possibly know. The romantics may be right that the fresh and uninterpreted vision of the child may renew the jaded adult, but child development experts remind parents that knowledge and experience alone will sustain the child's wonder and overcome the otherwise inevitable onset of boredom (an emotion at the heart of the cool). Adult frustration with the commercial idea of the wondrous child led to attempts to isolate children and impose a strict religious or rationalist upbringing. Much of this reaction is confined to self-circumscribed communities and symbolic protests against modern Halloween or Christmas. Most parents today, however, try to follow a more difficult path—to balance the wondrous child with the sheltered child and thus to nurture the delights of both spontaneity and experience.

The idea of protecting the innocent from the adult world may have survived the twentieth century, but the child-rearing expert's attack on immediate gratification has failed on many fronts. One of the hallmarks of sheltered innocence, the educational toy, has hardly displaced the novelty plaything—rather, the opposite is true. Efforts to promote history, geography, and nature programs on television have long faced an uphill battle, and attempts to restrict children's TV advertising have met with little success. Yet parents, frustrated with the consequences of aggressive marketing to kids, continue to try to draw the line. Some admire the austere models of early twentieth-century child development experts and long for a wall between children and adults that they believe once protected the young from sin and concupiscence (if they are religious) or inhumane and irrational values (if secular). Most recognize, however, the impossibility of putting the genie back in the bottle and are unwilling to suppress the wondrous child, even in its commercial form.

The question of where or even if to draw a line has been debated continuously since the 1930s and, like the wondrous child, the very idea of sheltered innocence seemed to be in question by 2000. Shortly before his death, writer and comedian Steve Allen lamented in his *Vulgarians at the Gate* that media moguls have sacrificed the innocence of children for profit. Allen reaffirmed all the arguments used against movies in the 1930s, comics in the 1950s, and video games since the 1980s. Such critics continually demand curbs on the exposure of the young and vulnerable to violent and sexually explicit films, videos, and music.[25] In response, free-speech advocates like Marjorie Heins of the American Civil Liberties Union reject any censorship of children's media as a humorless and blunt attempt to eliminate "fun" and to deny the catharsis experienced in viewing violent and otherwise offensive media. Often the real intent of the censors, Heins argues, is to impose their morality on everyone in the name of protecting "innocence." She insists that freedom of speech in media and ads gives children the freedom to make choices and thereby has empowered them. Heins, like so many before her, sees only the adult censor and not the possible need to shelter the child.[26]

Crusaders, be they against tobacco, pornography, media violence, or even unchecked commercialism, use children's innocence to advance their agenda, often trying to make their own standards obligatory for adults and children alike. Heins is correct that advocates of the sheltered young may also needlessly delay or even deny children the right to grow up—to have the experiences that ultimately mean the loss of innocence but give the child the knowledge to participate freely in the adult world.

The problem with this approach, however, is that it tends to deny the reality of innocence, the difference between the adult and the child. Moreover, in America's free-market and free-speech society, the politics of sheltered childhood may be practically the only way to constrain the market in sex, tobacco, and media violence. Those sensitive to the special needs of children and to the moral power of those needs, embrace the ideal of sheltered innocence. Clearly wonder and shelter remain central to contemporary child rearing. The larger question remains whether they serve primarily the needs of adults or children.

The child increasingly has borne the obligation of imposing cultural standards on a society that is at war with itself over such standards. Should America prohibit the airing of "dirty words," restrict ads on children's TV, ban violent images from movies and video games seen or played by children, or all three? This question points to a cultural divide in modern America that, in the end, suggests that sheltering innocence may be more about the deep moral conflicts among adults than the needs of children.

The difficulty with using childhood innocence as a battering ram against the cultural or economic status quo is that doing so can obscure the needs of all children. A long-lasting critique of the modern idealization of the child has been that it is almost never applied universally but rather to the offspring of the dominant middle and upper classes in the richest parts of the world. The contrast between the youngster showered with gifts at Christmas and the child obliged to work in a sweatshop to make them is the classic example of this failing. Efforts to protect the suburban child from the threat of urban street culture reveal the same narrowness.

These ambiguities and confusions in the modern celebration of childhood suggest a still more subtle issue. Adults use both ideas—of the wondrous child and the sheltered child—to cope with the contradictions of modernity. Members of the older generation deal with these ambiguities by splitting the child's world. They insist that children be protected from premature contact with the worlds of work and business by confining them to schools designed to prepare them for the market. Emphasis on standardized testing, academic tracking, and summer educational enrichment, especially among middle-class parents, all point to this ever-present concern about enhancing offspring's life chances in a competitive world. At the same time, these adults impose on children a wondrous innocence that rejects work, competition, and social responsibility for a world of consumption. They project onto the young their own segmented lives— instrumentalist work and consumerist play. They extend to the sheltered child their hope for success and power while they seek in the wondrous child the delight they have lost in their own lives as affluent consumers. Naturally, this leads kids to be pressured too early to be successful in schools and sports. And it leads also to adults' disappointment when children no longer can or will play with them.

Modern childhood also serves the contradictions of modern life by both limiting and rationalizing the expansion of adult desire. The young necessarily place constraints on adult libido—obliging men and women to sacrifice and confine pleasure seeking to the home and to forgo satisfactions for the sake of future generations. More subtly, the innocent oblige adults to refrain from behaviors that threaten the unprotected. Sheltering innocence is one of the few arguments against unlimited private pursuit of gain and pleasure in a market economy. Opponents of tobacco addiction could win only when claiming to save the children. At the same time, the young let adults open that valve of desire, justifying not only adults' spending hundreds of dollars on children in the name of Santa but also their spending lavishly on themselves, serving their own "inner" childs. Freedom from and access to desire have become so confusingly interlaced that neither children nor adults can easily sort out when and what the young should be exposed to. Adding to the confusion, as children grow up in a culture that shelters them from desire and yet treats them as depositories of desire, they rebel against limits. They associate constraint negatively with the sheltered innocence of childhood and with parents' efforts to prolong the "cute." At the same time, children extend parents' gift of freedom into their own world of fantastic desire (sometimes expressed as sexuality in girls and action or violence in boys).

The adult's quest for wonder in the child also leads grown-ups to long for the cute and the cool in themselves. The man who acts the part of a teddy bear forever looking for someone to care for him shares a lot with the man who collects the superhero comic books of his youth. Ultimately, there is much in common between the woman who cultivates herself as a baby doll and the girl who dresses like a whore. Children flee innocence "prematurely," while adults long for a childlike look and experience.

Modern ideas about the innocent child have long been projections of adult needs and frustrations. In the final analysis, modern innocence has let adults evade the consequences of their own contradictory lives. Ultimately, the solution to the ambiguities of modern child rearing will require a more mature resolution to the contradictions of modern life.

The history of the wondrous and sheltered child points to no simple formula for overcoming modern frustrations and contradictions in child rearing. There is probably no reason to think that child rearing at the beginning of the twenty-first century is any more a failure than it was at the beginning of the twentieth—even if the deficiencies and disappointments are different. At best, this history suggests that balances between shelter and wonder can be struck if adults think seriously about children's needs for shelter and wonder, and less their own. Modern empathy for the young can and has transcended selfish adult uses of innocence. It is that possibility that makes this story useful today.

Balance between shelter & wonderous without parents needs involved

# Notes

## Chapter 1

1. Anne Higonnet, *Pictures of Innocence: The History and Crisis of Ideal Childhood* (London: Thames and Hudson, 1998), 87, 91.

2. Elaine May, *Barren in the Promised Land: Childless Americans and the Pursuit of Happiness* (New York: Basic Books, 1995), 10, 19, 232, 253, 255.

3. "Broadening the Mind into the Magic Kingdom," *Economist*, 23 Mar. 1991, 20.

4. J. Conrad, "Lost Innocent and Sacrificial Delegate—The JonBenet Ramsey Murder," *Childhood* 6 (1999): 313–51; James Kincaid, *Erotic Innocence: The Culture of Child Molesting* (Durham, N.C.: Duke University Press, 1998), 18.

5. Higonnet, *Pictures of Innocence*, 1–96.

6. Kincaid, *Erotic Innocence*, chap. 1; Kincaid, *Child-Loving: The Erotic Child and Victorian Culture* (New York: Routledge, 1992), 64, 79.

7. *Los Angeles Times*, 29 Mar. 1996, A1.

8. For example, William Bennett, *The Educated Child: A Parent's Guide from Preschool Through Eighth Grade* (New York: Free Press, 1999); Bennett, *The Book of Virtues: A Treasure of Great Moral Stories* (New York: Simon and Schuster, 1993).

9. Michael Medved, *Hollywood vs. America: Popular Culture and the War on Traditional Values* (New York: HarperCollins, 1992); Michael Medved and Diane Medved, *Saving Childhood: Protecting Our Children from the National Assault on Innocence* (New York: HarperCollins, 1998); Dana Mack, *The Assault on Parenthood: How Our Culture Undermines the Family* (New York: Simon and Schuster, 1997); Steve Allen, *Vulgarians at the Gate: Trash TV and Raunch Radio, Raising the Standards of Popular Culture* (New

York: Prometheus Books, 2001); Cornel West, *The War against Parents: What We Can Do for America's Beleaguered Moms and Dads* (New York: Houghton Mifflin, 1998); Hillary Clinton, *It Takes a Village: And Other Lessons Children Teach Us* (New York: Touchstone, 1996).

10. Kincaid, *Child-Loving*, 341–443. See Debbie Nathan and Michael Snedeker, *Satan's Silence: Ritual Abuse and the Making of a Modern American Witch Hunt* (New York: Basic, 1995); Philip Jenkins, *Moral Panics: The Changing Concept of the Child Molester* (New Haven, Conn.: Yale University Press, 1998), 166–74.

11. Sissela Bok, *Mayhem: Violence as Public Entertainment* (Reading, Mass.: Addison-Wesley, 1998); Deirdre Donahue, "Struggling to Raise Good Kids in Toxic Times," *USA Today*, 1 Oct. 1998, 1D.

12. "Malls Aren't Kidding Around with Security," *Chicago Sun-Times*, 13 Oct. 1996, 28; "Area Malls Watch Minnesota's Chaperon Policy," *Seattle Times*, 5 Sept. 1996, C1.

13. "School Codes without Mercy," *New York Times*, 12 Mar. 1997, A1; Ellen Goodman, "Zero Tolerance Should Not Be Tolerated," *Houston Chronicle*, 9 Jan. 2000, 6.

14. "Of Arms and the Boys," *Time*, 6 July 1998, 58; "End of Innocence," *Los Angeles Times*, 12 Aug. 1998, 6; Louisville (Ky.) *Courtier-Journal*, 6 Dec. 1998, 1; and, especially for the statistics, Janet Dolgin, "The Age of Autonomy: Legal Reconceptualization of Childhood," *Bridgeport Law Review* 18 (1999): 421 ff.

15. *In These Times*, 11 July 1999, 6.

16. "Truth about Tweens," *Newsweek*, 18 Oct. 1999, 62; and "Selling Innocence," *Ottawa Citizen*, 28 Sept. 1998, A13; "Innocence on the Line," *Guardian*, 14 Nov. 1999, 1.

17. "Growing Up Old," *U.S. News & World Report*, 7 Apr. 1997; Lauren Greenfield, *Fast Forward: Growing Up in the Shadow of Hollywood* (New York: Melcher Media, 1997); "No Room for Children in a World of Little Adults," *New York Times*, 10 May 1998, 4; James Côté and Anton Allahark, *Generation on Hold: Coming of Age in the Late Twentieth Century* (New York: New York University Press, 1996), 16–17.

18. "Innocence on the Line," 1.

19. Neil Postman, *The Disappearance of the Child* (New York: Dell, 1982), 28, 46, 89–90.

20. Marilyn Brandbard, "Sex Differences in Adult's Gifts and Children's Toy Requests at Christmas," *Psychological Reports* 56 (1985): 969–70.

21. John Locke, *Some Thoughts on Education* (Cambridge: Cambridge University Press, 1968), 211–12.

22. Steve Berg, "The End of Innocence," *Minneapolis (Minn.) Star Tribune*, 22 May 1997, 20A.

Chapter 2

1. John McEvoy and Peggy McEvoy, "Talk with a Toy King," *Reader's Digest*, Jan. 1955, 125.

2. Ellen Key, *The Century of the Child* (New York: Putnam, 1909), 183, 3. Two similar books were C. Gilman, *Concerning Children* (Boston: Small Maynard, 1901), 38–39, 76–77; Kate Douglas Wiggin, *Children's Rights: A Book of Nursery Logic* (Boston: Houghton Mifflin, 1892).

3. Key, *Century of the Child*, 242–43. See also Ann Hulbert, *Raising America: Experts, Parents and a Century of Advice about Children* (New York: Knopf, 2003); Barbara Ehrenreich and Deidre English, *For Her Own Good: 150 Years of Experts' Advice to Women* (Garden City, N.Y.: Anchor Books, 1979), chap. 6; Harvey Green, "Scientific Thought and the Nature of Children in America, 1820–1920," in *A Century of Childhood 1820–1920*, ed. Mary Heininger et al. (Rochester, N.Y.: Margaret Woodbury Strong Museum, 1984), 121–39.

4. Key, *Century of the Child*, 107, 181–82, 111.

5. John Locke, *Some Thoughts Concerning Education* (Cambridge: Cambridge University Press, 1968), 58–59, 76–79, 192, 211–12.

6. Jean-Jacques Rousseau, *Émile*, cited in Sol Cohen, ed., *Education in the United States* (New York: Random House, 1974), 1207.

7. Maria Edgeworth, *Works*, vol. 1 (Boston: Samuel Parker, 1825), 19–20, 28–29; John Sommerfield, *The Discovery of Childhood in Puritan England* (Athens: University of Georgia Press, 1992), 30; Gillian Avery, *Behold the Child: American Children and Their Books, 1621–1922* (Baltimore: Johns Hopkins University Press, 1994), chap. 3.

8. Christina Hardyment, *Dream Babies: Three Centuries of Good Advice on Child Care* (New York: Harper and Row, 1983), 130–31; Philip Greven, *Spare the Child: The Religious Roots of Punishment and the Psychological Impact of Physical Abuse* (New York: Knopf, 1991), 60–72, 82–97; Greven, *Childrearing Concepts, 1628–1861* (Itasca, Ill.: F. E. Peacock, 1973), chap. 1; Horace Bushnell, *Christian Nurture* (1847; reprint, New Haven, Conn.: Yale University Press, 1967), 292.

9. Jacob Abbott, *Gentle Measures in the Management and Training of the Young* (New York: Harper and Brothers, 1871), 13–31.

10. Paula Fass, *The Damned and the Beautiful: American Youth in the 1920s* (New York: Oxford University Press, 1977), chap. 2 and p. 134; U.S. Department of Education, National Center for Educational Statistics, *Projections of Educational Statistics* (Washington, DC: U.S. Government Printing Office, 2001), table 3.

11. Mary Odem, *Delinquent Daughters: Protecting and Policing Adolescent Female Sexuality in the United States* (Chapel Hill: University of North Carolina Press, 1995), 13–17, 22–24.

12. Linda Gordon, *Heroes of Their Own Lives* (New York: Penguin, 1988), 59–63; Susan Thiophene, *In Whose Best Interest? Child Welfare Reform in the Progressive Era* (Westport, Conn.: Greenwood, 1982), 216–20; Joseph Hawes, *Children between the Wars: American Childhood, 1920–1940* (New York, Twayne, 1997), 72–74, 79; Robert Bremner, ed., *Children and Youth in America: A Documentary History*, vol. 2 (Cambridge, Mass.: Harvard University Press, 1971), 757–58.

13. Jean-Jacques Rousseau, "On Reasoning with Children," in *The Portable Age of*

*Reason Reader*, ed. Crane Brinton (New York: Viking, 1956), 122; Rousseau, *Émile or On Education* (New York: Basic Books, 1979), 43; Hugh Cunningham, *Children and Childhood in Western Society since 1500* (London: Longman, 1995), 67–70.

14. William Wordsworth, "Ode on Intimations of Immortality from Recollections of Early Childhood," in *Complete Poetical Works of William Wordsworth*, ed. Biss Perry (Boston: Houghton Mifflin, 1904), 354.

15. Cunningham, *Children and Childhood*, 73; Barbara Garlitz, "The Immortality Ode: Its Cultural Progeny," *Studies in English Literature* 6 (1966): 639–49.

16. Humphrey Carpenter, *Secret Gardens: A Study of the Golden Age of Children's Literature* (Boston: Houghton Mifflin, 1985), 10–11; Henry David Thoreau, *Walden, or, Life in the Woods* in *The Works of Thoreau*, ed. Henry Canby (Boston: Houghton Mifflin, 1937), 262.

17. John Gillis, *World of Their Own Making: Myth, Ritual and the Quest for Family Values* (New York: Basic Books, 1996), 83–85.

18. J. H. Plumb, "The New World of Children in Eighteenth-Century England," *Past and Present* 67 (May 1975): 4; Philippe Ariès, *Centuries of Childhood: A Social History of Family Life* (New York: Vintage, 1962), 118–19; Karen Calvert, *Children in the House* (Boston: Northeastern University Press, 1992), 149–53; James Steward, *The New Child: British Art and the Origins of Modern Childhood, 1730–1830* (Seattle: University of Washington Press, 1995), 80–83, 89, 109.

19. Anne Higonnet, *Pictures of Innocence: The History and Crisis of Ideal Childhood* (London: Thames and Hudson, 1998), 31, 32, 51.

20. William Blake, *Four Zoas* (Oxford: Oxford University Press, 1913), 9–10.

21. Lorraine Daston and Katharine Park, *Wonder and the Order of Nature, 1150–1750* (New York: Zone Books, 1998), 16, 20, 25.

22. Higonnet, *Pictures of Innocence*, 92; Tony Tanner, *The Reign of Wonder: Naivety and Reality in American Literature* (Cambridge: Cambridge University Press, 1965), 13.

23. Max Luthi, *Once upon a Time: On the Nature of Fairy Tales* (Bloomington: Indiana University Press, 1976), 44, 46, 47, 51, 64, 65, 95.

24. R. Rosenblum, *The Romantic Child from Runge to Sendak* (London: Thames and Hudson, 1988); L. M. Alcott, *Little Women* (1868; Boston: Little, Brown, 1946), 21, 88; Cunningham, *Children and Childhood*, 76; Jackie Wullschlaeger, *Inventing Wonderland* (New York: Free Press, 1995), 14–17; Carpenter, *Secret Gardens*, 106–14.

25. Anne Scott MacLeod, *American Childhood: Essays on Children's Literature in the Nineteenth and Twentieth Centuries* (Athens: University of Georgia Press, 1994), 116–20; MacLeod, *A Moral Tale: Children's Fiction and American Culture, 1820–1860* (Hamden, Conn.: Archon, 1975), 20–24; Calvert, *Children in the House*, 150, 152; Ruth Freeman, *American Dolls* (Watkins Glen, N.Y.: Century House, 1952), 19; Roland Caillois, *Man, Play and Games*, trans. Meyer Barash (New York: Free Press, 1962), 57–58, 111–40; Max von Boehn, *Dolls and Puppets*, trans. Josephine Nicoll (Philadelphia: David McKay, 1932), esp. chaps. 6–8.

26. Gillis, *World of Their Own Making*, chap. 5.

27. Frances Hodgson Burnett, *Little Lord Fauntleroy* (New York: Scribner's, 1886);

Kate Douglas Smith Wiggin, *Rebecca of Sunnybrook Farm* (New York: Grosset and Dunlap, 1903); Avery, *Behold the Child*, 68–70; T. J. Jackson Lears, *No Place of Grace: Antimodernism and the Transformation of American Culture* (New York: Pantheon, 1981), 144–45; Wullschlaeger, *Inventing Wonderland*, 18–20 , 27, 109–11.

28. Ruth S. Cowan, *More Work for Mother* (New York: Basic Books, 1983); Phyllis Palmer, *Domesticity and Dirt: Housewives and Domestic Servants in the United States* (Philadelphia: Temple University Press, 1990); Stanley Lebergott, *Pursuing Happiness* (Princeton, N.J.: Princeton University Press, 1993), chap. 6; Daniel Scott Smith, "Family Limitation, Sexual Control and Domestic Feminism in Victorian America," *Feminist Studies* 1 (1973): 40–57; Daniel Rodgers, "Socializing Middle-Class Children: Institutions, Fables, and Work Values in Nineteenth-Century America," in *Growing Up in America: Children in Historical Perspective*, ed. N. Ray Hiner and Joseph Hawes (Urbana: University of Illinois Press, 1985), 121–32.

29. Brian Sutton-Smith, *Toys as Culture* (New York: Gardner Press, 1986), chaps. 2 and 3 and p. 245; Sutton-Smith, *History of Children's Play: The New Zealand Playground, 1840–1950* (Philadelphia: University of Pennsylvania Press, 1981); E. Anthony Rotundo, *American Manhood: Transformations in Masculinity from the Revolution to the Modern Era* (New York: Basic Books, 1993), 31–35; Mary Ryan, *Cradle of the Middle Class* (Cambridge: Cambridge University Press, 1981), chap. 4; Calvert, *Children in the House*, 97–106.

30. David Nasaw, *Children of the City* (New York: Oxford University Press, 1985).

31. Heininger, *Century of Childhood*, 3–6; I make this point in more detail in Gary Cross, *Kids' Stuff: Toys and the Changing World of American Childhood* (Cambridge, Mass.: Harvard University Press, 1997), chap. 2.

32. Viviana Zelizer, *Pricing the Priceless Child: The Changing Social Value of Children* (New York: Basic Books, 1985), 3–21.

33. Ibid., 103–12; E. Wayne Carp and Anna Leon-Guerrero, "When in Doubt, Count: World War II as a Watershed in the History of Adoption," in *Adoption in America: Historical Perspectives*, ed. E. Wayne Carp (Ann Arbor: University of Michigan Press, 2002).

34. Colin Campbell, *The Romantic Ethic and the Spirit of Modern Consumerism* (Oxford: Blackwell, 1987), chap. 1.

35. Gary Cross, "Toys and Time: Playthings and Parents' Attitudes toward Change in Early Twentieth-Century America," *Time and Society* 7, no. 1 (1998): 12–17.

36. Cross, *Kids' Stuff*, 87–88; "Chronological History of *Playthings*," *Playthings*, Sept. 1938, 98–114.

37. Roger W. Cummins, *Humorous but Wholesome: A History of Palmer Cox and the Brownies* (Watkins Glen, N.Y.: Century House, 1973), 34, 38, 60–67, 210–11.

38. Rosamond Olmsted Humm, *Children in America: A Study of Images and Attitudes* (Atlanta : High Museum of Art, 1978), 33; Alison Mager, ed., *Child of the Past in Photographic Portraits* (New York: Dover, 1978); Kathy Merlock Jackson, *Images of Children in American Film: A Sociocultural Analysis* (Metuchen, N.J.: Scarecrow Press, 1986), 31–36; Paula Fass, *Kidnapped: Child Abduction in America* (New York: Oxford University Press, 1997).

39. Daniel Rodgers, *The Work Ethic in Industrial America* (Chicago: University of

Chicago Press, 1974), 132–34, 139–42; Avery, *Behold the Child*, chap. 5; Thomas Aldrich, *The Story of a Bad Boy* (1869; Boston: Houghton Mifflin, 1923), 2, 55; Mac-Leod, *American Childhood*, 69–76; Wullschlaeger, *Inventing Wonderland*, 109–12; Jackson, *Images of Children in American Film*, 42, 21.

40. Jacqueline Rose, *The Impossibility of Children's Fiction* (London: Macmillan, 1984), 1–9. Others emphasize the construction of innocence around adult sexual and power desires. See Joseph Zornado, *Inventing the Child: Culture, Ideology, and the Story of Childhood* (New York: Garland, 2001), chap. 4; and, especially, James Kincaid, *Child-Loving: The Erotic Child and Victorian Culture* (New York: Routledge, 1992).

41. Promoting child study were G. Stanley Hall's journal, *Pedagogical Seminary* (1891), and *Child Study Monthly* (1895); H. Clay Trumbull, *Hints on Child-Training* (New York: Appleton, 1894); E. L. Thorndike, *Notes on Child Study* (New York: Macmillan, 1903); William Shearer, *Management and Training of Children* (New York: Richardson Smith, 1904); Ennis Richmond, *The Mind of a Child* (New York: Longmans, Green, 1902); George H. Payne, *The Child in Human Progress* (New York: Putnam's, 1916).

42. Margo Horn, *Before It's Too Late: The Child Guidance Movement in the United States* (Philadelphia: Temple University Press, 1989); Benjamin Gruenberg, ed., *Outlines of Child Study* (New York: Macmillan, 1924); Lois Meek, *Interests of Young Children* (Washington, D.C.: American Association of University Women, 1926); "Editorial," *Parents*, October 1926 1.

43. White House Conference on Child Health and Protection, *White House Conference* (New York: Century, 1930), 45–48; White House Conference on Child Health and Protection, *The Home and the Child* (New York: Century, 1931), 3, 5, 46–47; White House Conference on Child Health and Protection, *The Young Child in the Home* (New York: Appleton, 1936), 7, 50; Molly Ladd-Taylor, *Mother-Work: Women, Child Welfare, and the State, 1890–1930* (Urbana: University of Illinois Press, 1994), 47–49.

44. William Forbush, *The Coming Generation* (New York: Appleton, 1912), 46; Green, "Scientific Thought and the Nature of Children in America," 121–38.

45. G. Stanley Hall, *Youth: Its Education, Regimen, and Hygiene* (New York: Appleton, 1918), 73–74; Dorothy Ross, *G. Stanley Hall: The Psychologist as Prophet* (Chicago: University of Chicago Press, 1972), 279–308; Steven Schlossman, "G. Stanley Hall and the Boys' Club," *Journal of the History of the Behavior Sciences* 9 (1973): 140–47; G. Stanley Hall et al., *Aspects of Child Life and Education* (New York: Appleton, 1921), 337–38; Luther Gulick, *A Philosophy of Play* (New York: Scribner's, 1920), chaps. 2–3.

46. Sidonie Gruenberg, *Your Child Today and Tomorrow* (Philadelphia: Lippincott, 1912), 255; Children's Bureau, *Backyard Playgrounds* (Washington, D.C.: Children's Bureau Publications, 1923); Orinne Johnson, "Every Child His Own Room," *Farmer's Wife* 33 (April 1930): 8.

47. Beatrix Tudor-Hart, *Play and Toys in Nursery Years* (New York: Viking, 1940), 58–59; Patty Smith Hill, "Avoid the Gifts That Overstimulate," *Delineator*, Dec. 1914, 22–23.

48. Ethel Kawin, *The Wise Choice of Toys* (Chicago: University of Chicago Press, 1934), 56.

49. Perris Leger, "Christmas Shopping for the Child," *Hygeia* 5 (1927): 608.

50. Gruenberg, *Outlines of Child Study*, 85–90.

51. Helen Wooley, "Before Your Child Goes to School," *Parents* (Oct. 1926), 8; Ellen Seiter, *Sold Separately: Children and Parents in Consumer Culture* (New Brunswick, N.J.: Rutgers University Press, 1993), chap. 2; Jonas Frykman and Orvar Loefgren, *Culture Builders: An Historical Anthropology of Middle-Class Culture* (New Brunswick, N.J.: Rutgers University Press, 1990).

52. Quotation from a speech to a Brooklyn PTA by Patty Hill, in "Patty Smith Hill," *Playthings*, Jan. 1921, 347.

53. Rare exceptions include Rose Alschuler and Christine Heinig, *Play: The Child's Response to Life* (Boston: Houghton Mifflin, 1936), 70–80; Josephine Keyren, "Parents as Companions," *Good Housekeeping*, Mar. 1933, 108.

54. Lears, *No Place of Grace*, 35–40; Stanley Coben, *Rebellion against Victorianism: The Impetus for Cultural Change in 1920s America* (New York: Oxford University Press, 1991), chap. 3; Joan Rubin, *The Making of Middle/Brow Culture* (Chapel Hill: University of North Carolina Press, 1992), 31–32.

55. Luther Emmett Holt's *Care and Feeding of Children* (New York: Appleton, 1894) and later editions published through 1943 advocated twenty-minute feedings, thus transferring the hospital schedule to the home; see also Hardyment, *Dream Babies*, 124, 128, 138.

56. Mary Read, *Mothercraft Manual* (Boston: Little, Brown, 1916), 91; and Mrs. Max (Mary) West, *Infant Care*, Children's Bureau Publication no. 8 (1914), in *Child Rearing Literature of Twentieth-Century America* (New York: Arno Press, 1972), 10.

57. Holt, *Care and Feeding*, 192–95, 82; John Watson, *Psychological Care of Infant and Child* (New York: Norton, 1928), 82; West, *Infant Care*, 60; Hardyment, *Dream Babies*, 157, 170–74. See also H. Cravens, "Child-Saving in the Age of Professionalism, 1915–1930," in *American Childhood: A Research Guide and Historical Handbook*, ed. J. M. Hawes and N. R. Hiner (Westport, Conn.: Greenwood, 1985), 414–89.

58. Hardyment, *Dream Babies*, 59, 75; Arnold Gesell, *The Mental Growth of the Preschool Child* (New York: Macmillan, 1925); Arnold Gesell and Frances Ilg, *Infant and Child in the Culture of Today* (New York: Macmillan, 1943).

59. Nancy Wiess, "The Mother-Child Dyad Revisited: Perceptions of Mothers and Children in Twentieth-Century Child-Rearing Manuals," *Journal of Social Issues* 34 (1978): 35–36, 40–42; Benjamin Spock, *The Common Sense Book of Baby and Child Care* (New York: Duell, 1945); Hardyment, *Dream Babies*, 225.

60. Henry Jenkins, *The Children's Culture Reader* (New York: New York University Press, 1998), 215. For a popular behaviorist approach, note Ada Harrt Arlitt, *The Child from One to Six* (New York: McGraw-Hill, 1930); Dan Beekman, *The Mechanical Baby: A Popular History of the Theory and Practice of Childrearing* (Westport, Conn.: L. Hill, 1977).

61. Margaret Ribble, *The Rights of Infants*, 2d ed (New York: Columbia University Press, 1965), 87; Martha Wolfenstein, "Fun Morality: An Analysis of Recent American

Child-Training Literature," in *Childhood in Contemporary Cultures*, ed. Margaret Mead and Martha Wolfenstein (Chicago: University of Chicago Press, 1955), 169–70, 172–74.

62. Penelope Leach, *Your Baby and Child: From Birth to Age Five* (New York: Knopf, 1977), 18.

63. C. E. Strickland and A. M. Ambrose, "The Baby Boom, Prosperity, and the Changing Worlds of Children," in Hawes and Hiner, *American Childhood*, 533–86; Shari Thurer, *The Myths of Motherhood: How Culture Reinvents the Good Mother* (Boston: Houghton Mifflin, 1994), 220–22, 246–49, 254, 258.

64. Seiter, *Sold Separately*, 7–26, 31–37.


Chapter 3

1. Definitions in *Merriam-Webster's Dictionary* (on-line edition).

2. For parental efforts to control negative emotions, see Peter Stearns, *Battleground of Desire: The Struggle for Self-Control in Modern America* (New York: New York University Press, 1999), esp. 3–29; and Stearns *American Cool: Constructing a Twentieth-Century Emotional Style* (New York: New York University Press, 1994), 95–137.

3. *Frank Leslie's Illustrated Weekly*, 31 Jan. 31 1885, 396; 12 March 1896, cover illustration.

4. Pear's soap ad and Quaker Oats ad, *Frank Leslie's Illustrated Weekly*, 14 Feb. 1885, 432; 17 Dec. 1896, back cover.

5. Images from *Harper's Weekly*, 15 Jan. 1870; 3 Sept. 1881, 596; 26 Feb. 1881, 149; *Frank Leslie's Illustrated Weekly*, 29 Aug. 1885, 29; 7 Nov. 1885, 88.

6. Images from *Harper's Weekly*, 9 Jan. 1870, cover; 21 May 1879, 328; *Frank Leslie's Illustrated Weekly*, 12 Dec. 1885, 261; and *Harper's Weekly*, 1 Jan. 1870, cover; 1 Jan. 1881, 4.

7. Anita Schorsche, *Images of Childhood: An Illustrated Social History* (New York: Mayflower Books, 1979), 30–31, 80, 148.

8. Robert Jay, *The Trade Card in Nineteenth-Century America* (Columbia: University of Missouri Press, 1987), 1–33, 99–103. I examined three sets of cards, comprising about eight hundred cards published in the 1880s and 1890s: "Scrapbooks of American Trade Cards, Tickets, etc. ca. 1880–ca. 1929," vols. 2–4; Charles Lathrop, "Scrapbook of American Trade Cards, 1881–ca. 1900?"; and "Trade Cards of San Francisco Businesses, 1881–1883," all in Bancroft Library Special Collection, University of California at Berkeley.

9. Lathrop, "Scrapbook"; "Trade Cards of San Francisco"; "Scrapbooks of American Trade Cards," vols. 1–2.

10. Lathrop, "Scrapbook"; "Trade Cards of San Francisco"; "Scrapbooks of American Trade Cards," vols. 1–2; Jay, *Trade Card*, 97.

11. "Trade Cards of San Francisco"; Lathrop, "Scrapbook"; "Scrapbooks of American Trade Cards," vols. 3–4; Alice Muncaster, *The Baby Made Me Buy It* (New York: Crown, 1991), 12, 24.

12. Kodak ad, *Harper's Weekly*, 26 Jan. 1901, 99; Nancy West, *Kodak and the Lens of Nostalgia* (Charlottesville: University Press of Virginia, 2000); quotation from Jean-Claude Gautrand, *Publicités Kodak, 1910–1939* (Paris: Contrejour, 1983), n.p.; Philip Hale, *Great Portraits of Children* (Boston: Bat and Guild, 1909), 1.

13. Word search in the on-line collection of *Harper's Weekly* (1857–1912) at http://app.harpweek.com; quotation from *Harper's Weekly*, 13 Jan. 1909, 13.

14. Leigh Schmidt, *Consumer Rites: The Buying and Selling of American Holidays* (Princeton, N.J.: Princeton University Press, 1995), 74; Bye Bye Kids ad, *Playthings*, June 1908, 102. See also Linda Richter, *Treasury of Kaethe Kruse Dolls* (New York: HP Books, 1984), 18–19, 103.

15. Miriam Formanek-Brunell, *Made to Play House: Dolls and the Commercialization of American Girlhood, 1830–1930* (New Haven, Conn.: Yale University Press, 1993), 104–5, 180, 182; Flossie Flirt ad, Sears and Roebuck catalog, 1931, 669, and Sears Roebuck and Co. catalog, 1927, 624, reprinted in Margaret Adams, *Collectible Dolls and Accessories of the Twenties and Thirties from Sears, Roebuck and Co. Catalogs* (New York: Dover, 1986), 60.

16. Patricia Schoonmaker, *The Effanbee Patsy Family and Related Types* (North Hollywood, Calif.: Doll Research Project, 1971), 1–15, 20–35, 50, 66; Effanbee ad, *Playthings*, July 1928, 7; Effanbee ad, *Playthings*, Jan. 1929, 29.

17. Formanek-Brunell, *Made to Play House*, 90–92, 109–16; Joleen Robinson, *Advertising Dolls* (Paducah, Ky.: Collector Books, 1980), chaps. 1–2.

18. Formanek-Brunell, *Made to Play House*, 4–5.

19. Matt Cartmill, *A View to a Death in the Morning: Hunting and Nature through History* (Cambridge, Mass.: Harvard University Press, 1993), 168–81.

20. Pat Schoonmaker, *A Collector's History of the Teddy Bear* (Cumberland, Md.: Hobby House Press, 1981), 227–41, 250–52, 280–82; Linda Mullins, *A Tribute to Teddy Bear Artists* (Grantsville, Md.: Hobby House Press, 1994), 74–80.

21. Butler Brothers, *toy catalog* (New York, 1910), 1910; Horsman ad for Billikens, *Playthings*, Sept. 1910, 35; Daniel Harris, *Cute, Quaint, Hungry, and Romantic: The Aesthetics of Consumerism* (New York: Basic Books, 2000), 4.

22. Norman Kline, *Seven Minutes: The Life and Death of the American Animated Cartoon* (London: Verso, 1993), 30–31, 35–40, 85, 129–130; Richard De Cordova, "The Mickey in Macy's Window: Childhood, Consumerism, and Disney Animation," in *Disney Discourse: Producing the Magic Kingdom*, ed. Eric Smoodin (New York: Routlege, 1994), 203–13.

23. Disney Studio handbook, quoted in Kline, *Seven Minutes*, 45.

24. Kathy Merlock Jackson, *Images of Children in American Film: A Sociocultural Analysis* (Metuchen, N.J.: Scarecrow Press, 1986), 24–25, 31–36, 45–46.

25. Eileen Whitfield, *Pickford: The Woman Who Made Hollywood* (Lexington: University Press of Kentucky, 1997), 128, 130–31, 154; Jackson, *Images Children in American Film*, 42.

26. Formanek-Brunell, *Made to Play House*, chap. 5; Joseph Schroeder, *The Wonderful World of Toys, Games, and Dolls, 1860–1930* (Chicago: Follett, 1971), 195; Shelley

Armitage, *Kewpies and Beyond: The World of Rose O'Neill* (Jackson: University Press of Mississippi, 1994), 102, quotation on 112.

27. David Longest, *Character Toys and Collectibles*, vol. 2 (Paducah, Ky.: Collector Books, 1992), 223–26; Ralph McCanse, *Titans and Kewpies: The Life and Art of Rose O'Neill* (New York: Vantage Press, 1968); Muncaster, *Baby Made Me*, 57–59.

28. Kline, *Seven Minutes*, 47; Jackson, *Children in American Film*, 60–63, 66–67, 71–72.

29. Daniel Rodgers, *The Work Ethic in Industrial America* (Chicago: University of Chicago Press, 1974), 132–34, 139–42; and Gillian Avery, *Behold the Child: American Children and Their Books, 1621–1922* (Baltimore: Johns Hopkins University Press, 1994), chap. 5.

30. Ian Gordon, *Comic Strips and Consumer Culture, 1890–1945* (Washington, D.C.: Smithsonian Institution Press, 1998), 13–14, 25; Marcus Klein, *Easterns, Westerns, and Private Eyes* (Madison: University of Wisconsin Press, 1994), chap. 2; Robert Harvey, *Children of the Yellow Kid* (Seattle: Frye Art Museum, 1998), 17–25; R. F. Outcault, *R. F. Outcault's the Yellow Kid : A Centennial Celebration of the Kid Who Started the Comics* (North Hampton, Mass.: Kitchen Sink Press, 1995).

31. "Comic Weekly," *New York World*, 18 Dec. 1898; 2 Feb. 1902; "Funny Side," *New York World*, 3 Feb. 1907; 10 Feb. 1907; 4 Dec. 1910; Clare Dwiggins, *School Days* (New York: Harper and Brothers, 1919); George Herriman, *Krazy Kat* (New York: Holt, 1946); M. Thomas Inge, *Comics as Culture* (Jackson: University of Mississippi Press, 1990), 22–23; Robert Harvey, *Art of the Funnies: An Aesthetic History* (Jackson: University of Mississippi Press, 1994), chap. 2; Winsor McCay, *Little Nemo: 1905–1914* (London: Evergreen, 2000); Richard Marschall, ed., *Complete Little Nemo in Slumberland* (Seattle: Fantagraphics, 1990).

32. "Buster Brown," *New York Herald*, 13 July 1902.

33. Gordon, *Comic Strips*, 43–47, 55, 80; Richard Outcault, *Outcault's Buster Brown and Company, Including Mary Jane* (New York: F. A. Stokes, 1907); Kenny Harman, *Comic Strip Toys* (Des Moines, Iowa: Wallace-Homestead Books, 1975), 5–7, 22–23; Longest, *Character Toys* 2:14; Reinhold Reitberger and Wolfgang Fuchs, *The Comics: An Anatomy of a Mass Medium* (Boston: Little, Brown, 1973), 12–13, 15; Judith O'Sullivan, *The Great American Comic Strip: One Hundred Years of Cartoon Art* (Boston: Little, Brown, 1990), 10–11.

34. Arthur Berger, *Comic Stripped American* (Baltimore, Md.: Penguin, 1974), 38–39, 44–45, Harman, *Comic Strip Toys*, 13–15; Reitberger and Fuchs, *Comics*, 34; Ron Goulart, ed., *The Encyclopedia of American Comics* (New York: Facts on File, 1990), 80; Rudolph Dirks, *Katzenjammer Kids* (Embee, N.Y.: Rudolph Dirks, 1921); Joe Musial, *The Katzenjammer Kids* (New York: Pocket Books, 1970).

35. Goulart, *Encyclopedia of American Comics*, 231, 232, 256.

36. See www.Skippy.com (Web site for Percy Crosby's estate); Goulart, *Encyclopedia of American Comics*, 86–87, 336–37; Percy Crosby, *Skippy* (New York: Putnam, 1929), 8, 43.

37. Barbara Bader, *American Picture Books* (New York: Macmillan, 1976), 266;

"Ketcham's Menace," *Newsweek,* 4 May 1953, 57; Hank Ketcham, *Dennis the Menace* (New York: Holt, 1952).

38. "Newly Weds," *New York World,* 6 Nov. 1904; 5 Dec. 1909; 12 Dec. 1909; 4 Dec. 1910; George McManus, *The Newly Weds and Their Baby* (Abion, Ohio: Saalfield, 1926); Goulart, *Encyclopedia of American Comics,* 245–46; O'Sullivan, *Great American Comic Strip,* 53–54; Reitberger and Fuchs, *Comics,* 30–31; Samstag and Hilder Bros. ad for Snookums toys, *Playthings,* Jan. 1910, 18.

39. Diana Cary, *Hollywood's Children: An Inside Account of the Child Star Era* (Boston: Houghton Mifflin, 1978), 48–53; Reitberger and Fuchs, *Comics,* 34; quotation from Leonard Maltin and Richard Bann, *Our Gang: The Lives and Times of the Little Rascals* (New York: Crown, 1977), 55; Jean Geddes, *Childhood and Children* (Phoenix: Oryx, 1997), 406.

40. Geddes, *Childhood and Children,* 406, 412; Wiley Umphlett, *Mythmakers of the American Dream: The Nostalgic Vision in Popular Culture* (Lewisburg, Pa.: Bucknell University Press, 1983), 156–57; "Movie of the Week," *Life,* 6 Nov. 1939, 37–40; "Judge Hardy and Son," ad, *Life,* 25 Dec. 1939, 1.

41. Marianne Sinclair, *Hollywood Lolitas: The Nymphet Syndrome in the Movies* (New York: Holt, 1988), 43–80; Anne Edwards, *Shirley Temple: American Princess* (New York: William Morrow, 1988), 28–31, 38, 75, 93–94, 97; Lori Merish, "Cuteness and Commodity Aesthetics: Tom Thumb and Shirley Temple" in *Freakery,* ed. Rosemarie Thomson (New York: New York University Press, 1996), 185–206.

42. Note Durbin's film *100 Men and a Girl;* Sinclair, *Hollywood Lolitas,* 60–80.

43. Jan Cohn, *Covers of the* Saturday Evening Post (New York: Viking, 1995), x–xii, covers by year, n.p.; cover, *Ladies' Home Journal,* (hereafter cited as *LHJ*), March 1913. In 1907, 1911, and 1916, for example, all the *Collier's* covers refer to stories, often with illustrations of famous people.

44. Cohn, *Covers of the* Saturday Evening Post, esp. 24 Dec. 1904; 6 May 1905; 23 Mar. 1907; 5 Feb. 1908; 5 Sept. 1908.

45. Ibid., esp. 1 Apr. 1911; 19 Oct. 1911; 28 Feb. 1914; 17 Oct. 1914; 29 Apr. 1922; 23 May 1925.

46. Among the many examples of the child's delight on Christmas morning are covers of the *LHJ,* Dec. 1935; *Parents,* Dec. 1946; Avondale Mills ad, *Saturday Evening Post* (hereafter cited as *SEP*), 21 Dec. 1948, 11. Summer scenes of child delight include the cover of *SEP,* 6 Aug. 1927.

47. Covers of *SEP,* 18 Oct. 1919; 16 Dec. 1933; covers of *Collier's,* 24 Feb. 1923; 4 Jan. 1930.

48. Covers of *SEP,* 9 Nov. 1929; 21 Oct. 1933.

49. Covers of *SEP,* 25 Nov. 1933; 22 Nov. 1952; Cohn, *Covers of the* Saturday Evening Post (covers of the 1930s through 1950s, especially 28 Sept. 1935; 12 Sept. 1936; 2 Sept. 1939; 23 May 1953). Note also Christopher Finch, *Norman Rockwell: 332 Magazine Covers* (New York: Artabus, 1994); Dave Hickey, "The Kids Are All Right: 'After the Prom,'" in *Norman Rockwell: Pictures for the American People,* ed. Maureen Hennessey and Anne Knutson (Atlanta: High Museum of Art, 1999).

50. Quaker ad, *LHJ*, Feb. 1913, 67; Fleischmann ad, *LHJ*, Dec. 1919, 64; Elisa Schement, "Showing Us the Way: Children in Early 20th Century Advertising" (B.A. honor's thesis, Pennsylvania State University, 2000).

51. Lifebuoy ad, *LHJ*, July 1925, 89; Ralston ad, *LHJ*, Feb. 1913, 39; Metropolitan Insurance ad, *LHJ*, Mar. 1935, 123; Investor's Syndicate ad, *Parents*, Apr. 1938, 61.

52. American radiator ad, *Collier's*, 9 Oct. 1926, 28; Perfection heaters ad, *SEP*, 12 Dec. 1914; GE ad, *American Home*, Nov. 1936, 3; Westinghouse ad, *SEP*, 19 Oct. 1925, 209; Denton ad, *LHJ*, Aug. 1919, 111; Lysol ad, *LHJ*, Nov. 1925, 207.

53. Viviana Zelizer, *Pricing the Priceless Child: The Changing Social Value of Children* (New York: Basic Books, 1985), 3–21.

54. Sun Maid ads, *SEP*, 17 Oct. 1914, 32; Spencer ad, *SEP*, 7 Dec. 1929, 131.

55. Kodak ad, *Collier's*, 28 Nov. 1908, back cover; Kodak ad, *SEP*, 30 July 1921, 71; Bell and Howell ad, *SEP*, 23 July 1927, 61; Cine-Kodak ad, *Time*, 20 Feb. 1928, 41; Kodak movie camera ad, *Parents*, May 1935, 41; "Priceless Pictures," *Parents*, Feb. 1937, 94; "Train Your Own Cinema Star," *Parents*, June 1938, 89; "Photographing Children," *American Photography*, May 1933, 294–99. See especially Nancy Martha West, *Kodak and the Lens of Nostalgia* (Charlottesville: University Press of Virginia, 2000), for a full treatment of this theme.

56. Bell and Howell ad, *Life*, 19 Apr. 1937, 13; Coca-Cola ad, *SEP*, 26 Dec. 1959, back cover; AT&T ad, *McCall's*, May 1958, 172.

57. National Lead Paint ad, *LHJ*, Sept. 1912, inside front cover; Uneeda ad, *LHJ*, July 1916, back cover; Campbell's ad, *LHJ*, Dec. 1933, 79.

58. Bissel ad, *LHJ*, Dec. 1929, 188.

59. Chevrolet ad, *Life*, 5 Apr. 1937, 50.

60. Pearl ad, *Collier's*, 15 Apr. 1916, 31; Mennen's ad, *Theatre Magazine*, 1909, cited in Muncaster, *Baby Made Me*, 5, 80–81; Cream of Wheat ad, *SEP*, 16 Dec. 1922, inside front cover; Jell-O ad, *LHJ*, Mar. 1919, 63; Johnson and Johnson ads, *LHJ*, Dec. 1935, 62; Aug. 1948, 149; Quaker cereal ad, *LHJ*, Nov. 1922, 48.

61. Kellogg ads, *LHJ*, Aug. 1911, back cover; Aug 1913, back cover.

62. Schrader Gauge ad, *SEP*, 21 Dec. 1930, 22; Listerine ad, *LHJ*, Nov. 1925, 85.

63. Beach Nut ads, *LHJ*, July 1913, 37; Mar. 1919, 65; and, for quote, May 1919, 43; Swift ad, *LHJ*, Mar. 1919, 66; Welch ads, *LHJ*, Oct. 1948, 247; Nov. 1948, 117.

64. Post ad, *LHJ*, Aug. 20, 1927, 36; Kix ad, *LHJ*, July 1948, 129; Lionel ad, *SEP*, 2 Dec. 1933, 77; Daisy ads, *SEP*, 12 Nov. 1926, 202; 11 Dec. 1926, 21; Laurence Greenfield, "Toys, Children, and the Toy Industry in a Culture of Consumption, 1890–1991" (Ph.D. diss., Ohio State University, 1991), 312–13; Meccano ad, *SEP*, 5 Dec. 1914, 56; Kodak ad, 16 Oct. 1948, *SEP*, 72.

65. Pearl ad, *LHJ*, Aug. 1919, 137; Fair soap ad, *LHJ*, Aug. 1919, 108; Ivory soap ad, *LHJ*, Aug. 1935, 2.

66. Cheramy perfume ad, *LHJ*, Feb. 1926, 75.

67. Johnson and Johnson ad, *SEP*, 20 Nov. 1948, 151; White sewing machine ad, *LHJ*, Sept. 1948, 202; Coca-Cola ad, *LHJ*, Apr. 1935; Seven-Up ad, *LHJ*, July 1952, 67.

68. Mallory ad, *Collier's*, 15 May 1911, 33; Kaynee ad, *LHJ*, June 1919, 166; Doubleknit ad, *LHJ*, Oct. 1919, 147.

69. Quaker ads, *LHJ*, Aug. 1925, 72; Oct. 1925, 106; Vitavose ad, *LHJ*, Jan. 1934, 60; Lifebuoy ad, *LHJ*, Sept. 1925, 105.

70. H. Jenkins, *The Children's Culture Reader* (New York: New York University Press, 1998), 227.

71. Stearns, *Battleground of Desire*, esp. 3–29; Stearns, *American Cool*, 95–137.

72. Woody Register, *The Kid of Coney Island* (New York: Oxford University Press, 2001), 288.

73. Joan Jacobs Brumberg, *The Body Project: An Intimate History of American Girls* (New York: Vintage Books, 1998); Kathy Lee Peiss, *Hope in a Jar: The Making of America's Beauty Culture* (New York: Metropolitan Books, 1998).


Chapter 4

1. Fascinating details are in A. R. Wright, *British Calendar Customs*, 3 vols. (London: Glaisher, 1936–40); Robert Muchembled, *Popular Culture and Elite Culture in France, 1400–1750* (Baton Rouge: Louisiana State University Press, 1985), 49–61.

2. Robert Malcolmson, *Popular Recreations in English Society* (Cambridge: Cambridge University Press, 1973), 21; William Addison, *English Fairs and Markets* (London: Batsford, 1953, 1979), 95–225.

3. Peter Burke, *Popular Culture in Early Modern Europe* (New York: Harper and Rowe, 1978), 178–204; Emmanuel Le Roy Ladurie, *Carnival in Romans* (New York: Braziller, 1979), 305–24; Mikhail Bakhtin, *Rabelais and His World* (Bloomington: Indiana University Press, 1984), chap. 1.

4. Christopher Gregory, *Gifts and Commodities* (London: Academic Press, 1982), 41; James Carrier, "The Rituals of Christmas Giving," *Unwrapping Christmas*, ed. Daniel Miller (Oxford: Clarendon, 1993), 64–65.

5. Penne Restad, *Christmas in America: A History* (New York: Oxford University Press, 1995), 4–5, 84; Frederick Douglass, *The Life of Frederick Douglass* (New York: New American Library, 1968), 84–85; Stephen Nissenbaum, *The Battle for Christmas* (New York: Knopf, 1996), 5–11; Leigh Schmidt, *Consumer Rites: The Buying and Selling of American Holidays* (Princeton, N.J.: Princeton University Press, 1995), 109–10; Elizabeth Pleck, *Celebrating the Family: Ethnicity, Consumer Culture, and Family Rituals* (Cambridge, Mass.: Harvard University Press, 1999), 45.

6. William Waits, *The Modern Christmas in America: A Cultural History of Gift Giving* (New York: New York University Press, 1993), chap. 2.

7. Restad, *Christmas in America*, 17–41, 91–104; Nissenbaum, *Battle for Christmas*, 14–45; John Pimlott, *The Englishman's Christmas: A Social History* (Atlantic Heights, N.J.: Humanities Press, 1978), 23–29, 120–24; James Barnett, *The American Christmas: A Study in National Culture* (New York: Macmillan, 1954), chap. 1; Katherine Richards, *How Christmas Came to Sunday Schools* (New York: Dodd, Mead, 1934); John Gillis,

A World of Their Own Making: Myth, Ritual, and the Quest for Family Values (New York: Basic Books, 1996), 71.

8. Schmidt, Consumer Rites, 113–20.

9. Nissenbaum, Battle for Christmas, 49–65; Karal Ann Marling, Merry Christmas: Celebrating America's Greatest Holiday (Cambridge, Mass.: Harvard University Press, 2000), 122–30.

10. Restad, Christmas in America, 30–35, 137; Nissenbaum, Battle for Christmas, chap. 5; Carrier, " Rituals of Christmas Giving," 160, 65–68; Russell Belk, "Materialism and the Making of Modern American Christmas," in Miller, Unwrapping Christmas, 75–104; R. Belk, "Materialism and the Modern U.S. Christmas," in Interpretative Consumer Research, ed. Elizabeth Hirschman (Provo, Utah: Association for Consumer Research, 1989), 115–35.

11. Restad, Christmas in America, 58–68, 96; Pimlott, Englishman's Christmas, 94, 110.

12. Restad, Christmas in America, 43, 44; Gillis, World of Their Own Making, 163–65; 185–86; Pleck, Celebrating the Family, 47.

13. Nissenbaum, Battle for Christmas, chap. 3, is especially insightful on these themes.

14. Miller, "A Theory of Christmas," in Miller, Unwrapping Christmas, 18–22.

15. Jenna Weissman Joselit, "'Merry Chanuka': The Changing Holiday Practices of American Jews, 1880–1950," in The Uses of Tradition: Jewish Continuity in the Modern Era, ed. Jack Wertheimer (New York: Jewish Theological Seminary, 1992), 303–25; Pleck, Celebrating the Family, 68–69.

16. Nissenbaum finds an ad for children's Christmas books in a Salem, Massachusetts, newspaper from 1806, though by the 1840s candies became common, even caramelized sugar and chocolate molds in the shape of beetles, spiders, and cockroaches (early appealing to boys); Battle for Christmas, 136, 138.

17. Restad, Christmas in America, 70; James Carrier, "Gifts in a World of Commodities: The Ideology of the Perfect Gift in American Society," Social Analysis 29 (1990): 19–37; David Cheal, "'Showing Them You Love Them': Gift Giving and the Dialectic of Intimacy," Sociological Review 35 (1987): 150–69; Belk, "Materialism and the Making," 86–87, 94–95; Schmidt, Consumer Rites, 127; Waits, Modern Christmas, chap. 2; Brian Sutton Smith, Toys as Culture (New York: Gardner, 1986), 18, 23.

18. Restad, Christmas in America, 143, 151; Belk, "Materialism and the Making," 92–93; Michael Barton, "The Victorian Jeremiad: Critics of Accumulation and Display," in Consuming Visions: Accumulation and Display of Goods in America, 1880–1920, ed. Simon Bronner (New York: Norton, 1989), 55.

19. Belk, "Materialism and the Making," 89.

20. Waits, Modern Christmas, 238–40, offers excellent bibliographical notes. See also Barnett, American Christmas, chap. 2; Pimlott, Englishman's Christmas, chap. 10; Schmidt, Consumer Rites, 131–38; William Walsh, The Story of Santa Claus (Detroit: Gale, 1970); Francis Weiser, The Christmas Book (New York: Harcourt Brace, 1952); T. G. Crippen, Christmas and Christmas Lore (Detroit: Gale, 1971), 143–49; Gillis, World of Their Own Making, 103–4.

21. *The Children's Friend* (New York, 1821), quoted in Nissenbaum, *Battle for Christmas*, 73.

22. Schmidt, *Consumer Rites*, 138–40; Nissenbaum, *Battle for Christmas*, 169; and Thomas Nast, *Christmas Drawings for the Human Race* (1890; reprint, New York: Harper and Row, 1971).

23. Belk, "Materialism and the Making," 75–104; R. Belk, "Materialism and the Modern U.S. Christmas," 115–35. See also Barton, " Victorian Jeremiad," 55–71; and Schmidt, *Consumer Rites*, 151–59.

24. Cited in Restad, *Christmas in America*, 54.

25. Belk, "Materialism and the Making," 95.

26. Schmidt, *Consumer Rites*, 173.

27. William Leach, *Land of Desire: Merchants, Power, and the Rise of a New American Culture* (New York: Pantheon, 1993), 89–90; 337; Waits, *Modern Christmas*, 130–33; Schmidt, *Consumer Rites*, 114–45; "A Chronological History of the American Toy Industry," *Playthings*, Sept. 1938, 99.

28. Nissenbaum, *Battle for Christmas*, 246.

29. Sophie Swett, "The Crust of the Christmas Pie," *Harper's Young People*, 8 Jan. 1884, 149; Marling, *Merry Christmas*, 140–50.

30. "The Mother and Her Children at Christmas," *LHJ*, Oct. 1904, 28.

31. *The Snowman, Designer*, Dec. 1904, 176–80; "Christmas with the Children," *LHJ*, Dec. 1905, 19. For insight on the role of parlor plays in Victorian homes, see Karen Halttunen, *Confidence Men and Painted Women: A Study of Middle-Class Culture in America, 1830–1870* (New Haven, Conn.: Yale University Press, 1982), 153–90.

32. *LHJ*, Dec. 1905, 18; *New York Sun*, 21 Sept. 21, 1897. Good commentary is found in Marling, *Merry Christmas*, 241–42.

33. "A Holiday Spectacle," *Frank Leslie's Illustrated Newspaper*, 20 Dec. 1884, 284; Marshall Field, *toy catalog* (1892–93), 12–14; *Playthings*, Dec. 1912, 45; Jan. 1913, 117.

34. Woody Register, *The Kid of Coney Island: Fred Thompson and the Rise of American Amusements* (New York: Oxford University Press, 2001), 281–82; "Everybody Helps in Los Angeles," *Playthings*, Dec. 1930, 74; Marling, *Merry Christmas*, chap. 3.

35. Meridel Le Sueur, "Christmas and the Child," *Parents*, Dec. 1934, 16–17, 70–71.

36. Chinchy Russell, "Christmas Is the Face of the Child," *Parents*, Dec. 1941, 15. Similar descriptions are found in "Christmas Is for the Children," *Harper's Bazaar*, Dec. 1939, 32; "It's Just Not Christmas without Children," *American Home*, Dec. 1939, 13; "Is Christmas Just for Children?" *American Home*, Dec. 1964, 18; "Christmas is NOT for Children," *LHJ*, Dec. 1967, 58. Note also "Faces of Christmas," *Collier's*, 23 Dec. 1955, 41; "Christmas Letter," *Redbook*, Dec. 1979, 47, 90, 91.

37. "Christmas Is for Children," *Look*, 19 Dec. 1964, 48; "Can Christmas Bring the Generations Together?" *Redbook*, Dec. 1973, 27–28.

38. Examples of this ironic faith in children's simplicity include Edwin Aubrey, "Religion and Our Children," *Parents*, Dec. 1930, 11; Le Sueur, "Christmas and the Child," 70; "How Children Spread Simply Ideas," *Life*, 14 Dec. 1942, 141–42; "After Santa Claus, What?" *House Beautiful*, Dec. 1958, 127.

39. For example, see *St. Nicholas*, Oct. 1905, 24–25; "A Child's Christmas Party," *LHJ*, Dec. 1904, 26.

40. For example, "The Girl and the Poet" and "Jimmy's Christmas Gift," *LHJ*, Dec. 1905, 25, 10.

41. Magner White, "Experiences of a Department Store Santa," *American Magazine*, Dec. 1925, 45, quoted in Marling, *Merry Christmas*, 202.

42. *Parents*, Dec. 1943, 32; Dec. 1952, 44; "Are You Doing Too Much for Your Children?" *Home and Garden*, Dec. 1958, 92–93; and, especially, "Child's Own Wonder," *American Home*, Dec. 1964, 18, 89.

43. Haim Ginott, "Holidays and Children," *McCall's*, Dec. 1969, 14; "What Your Children Really Want for Christmas," *Redbook*, Dec. 1980, 81–83; "How We Beat the Christmas Greedies," *Redbook*, Dec. 1981, 32. Roper Center for Public Opinion, 4 Dec. 1989, cited in Pleck, *Celebrating the Family*, 225.

44. Judy Benjamin, "Santa Then and Now," *Psychology Today*, Dec. 1979, 36–38.

45. Nissenbaum, *Battle for Christmas*, 209–11.

46. Marling, *Merry Christmas*, 339–40; and Thomas Burns, "Dr. Seuss' *How the Grinch Stole Christmas*: Its Recent Acceptance into the American Popular Tradition," *New York Folklore* 2 (winter 1976): 191–204.

47. Pleck, *Celebrating the Family*, 73–82; Schmidt, *Consumer Rites*, chap. 4, esp. 226–33.

48. Mary Hazeltine, *Anniversaries and Holidays*, 2d ed. (New York: American Library Association, 1944), 207, 216–18, 123; N. M. Banta, ed., *Autumn and Winter Festivals* (Chicago: Flanagan, 1924); R. H. Schauffler, *Plays for Our American Holidays*, 4 vols. (New York: Dodd, 1928); Adelaide Linnell, *The School Festival* (New York: Scribner's, 1931).

49. Nicholas Rogers, *Halloween: From Pagan Ritual to Party Night* (New York: Oxford University Press, 2002), 11–21, 28–29, 40; David Skal, *Death Makes a Holiday: A Cultural History of Halloween* (New York: Bloomsburg, 2002), chaps. 1–2; Ralph Linton and Adelin Linton, *Halloween through Twenty Centuries* (New York: Schuman, 1950), chaps. 1–2; Christina Hole, *British Folk Customs* (London: Hutchinson, 1976), 91; Peter Opie and Iona Opie, *Language and Lore of Schoolchildren* (Oxford: Clarendon, 1959), 269–83; Tom Fawkner, "How the Pumpkin Lost Its Teeth," *Christian Century*, 29 Oct. 1980, 1033. Good sources are found in Tad Tuleja, "Trick or Treat: Pre-Texts and Contexts," in *Halloween and Other Festivals of Death and Life*, ed. Jack Santino (Knoxville: University of Tennessee Press, 1994), 95–102.

50. Jack Santino, "Halloween in America: Contemporary Customs and Performances," *Western Folklore* 42 (1983): 1–20; Roger Abrahams and Richard Bauman, "Ranges of Festival Behavior," in *The Reversible World*, ed. Barbara Babcock (Ithaca, N. Y.: Cornell University Press, 1978), 206; George Douglas, *American Book of Days* (New York: H. Wilson, 1938), 537–38.

51. Rogers, *Halloween*, 59–73. For contemporary accounts, note, for example, Ruth Kelley, *The Book of Halloween* (Boston: Lathrop, 1919); Bellamy Partridge and Otto Bettman, *As We Were: Family Life in America 1850–1900* (New York: McGraw-Hill,

1946), 24; Douglas, *American Book of Days*, 53; "Halloween Pranks and Pumpkins Are Traditional," *Life*, 3 Nov. 1941, 68–70, 68 for quotation; Alvin Schwartz, ed., *When I Grew Up Long Ago* (Philadelphia: Lippincott, 1978), 127–30.

52. See Pleck, *Celebrating the Family*, 30–31. Reports on parties in *LHJ*, Oct. 1902, 41; *Harper's Bazaar*, Nov. 1912, 578; *Playground*, Sept. 1927, 334–37 (for teens and adults); *St. Nicholas*, Oct. 1905, 1124; *Hygiea*, Oct. 1936, 890; *American Home*, Oct. 1936, 49–51 (for children); "Halloween Entertainment in Rural Schools," *LHJ*, Oct. 1913, 106.

53. Note, for example, the accounts in Henning Cohen and Tristan Potter, *Folklore of American Holidays* (Detroit: Gale, 1991), 381; Margaret Mead, "Halloween, Where Has All the Mischief Gone?" *Redbook*, Dec. 1975, 31–32.

54. "A Victim of the Window Soaping Brigade," *American Home*, Nov. 1939, 48; "New Tricks and Treats for Halloween," *American Home*, Nov. 1940, 95–96. Other articles illustrating Halloween reform include *Recreation*, Oct. 1941, 420; *American City*, Oct. 1941, 99; *Recreation*, Sept. 1946, 297; *Parents*, Oct. 1946, 60; *Rotarian*, Oct. 1949, 34; Rogers, *Halloween*, 81–82, 86–90; Tuleja, "Trick or Treat," 89.

55. "A Victim of the Window Soaping Brigade," 48; "New Tricks and Treats for Halloween," 95–96; "Trick or Treat," *SEP*, 1 Nov. 1941, 75; "Halloween: Pranks and Pumpkins Are Traditional," *Life*, 3 Nov. 1941, 69–70; "Trick or Treat," *American Home*, Oct. 1947, 150; Tuleja, "Trick or Treat," 88–90.

56. Tuleja, "Trick or Treat," 91–95. See also Brian Sutton-Smith, "What Happened to Halloween?" *Parents*, Oct. 1983, 64; Gregory Stone, "Halloween and the Mass Child," *American Quarterly* 11 (1959): 372–79; Erin Beck, "Tricker on the Threshold: An Interpretation of Children's Autumn Traditions," *Folk-Lore* 96 (1985): 24–28.

57. "Halloween Pranks," *Life*, 3 Nov. 1941, 8–70; "Hallowing Halloween," *Christianity Today*, 2 Oct. 2000, 5.

58. Ralph Linton and Adelin Linton, *The Lore of Birthdays* (New York: H. Schuman, 1954), 81–82; Linda Lewis, *Birthdays* (Boston: Little, Brown, 1976), 24, 49.

59. Pleck, *Celebrating the Family*, chap. 7; Marion Emrich and George Korson, *The Child's Book of Folklore* (New York: Dial: 1947), 98–99; Justin McCarthy, "Love and Patience," *Harper's Weekly*, 19 Feb. 1870, 122; Howard Chudacoff, *How Old Are You? Age Consciousness in American Culture* (Princeton, N.J.: Princeton University Press, 1989), chap. 6; Gillis, *World of Their Own Making*, 83–85; Schmidt, *Consumer Rites*, 94–96.

60. "Children's Birthday Parties," *Harper's Bazaar*, Jan. 1906, 80–82; Madeline Snyder, *My Book of Parties* (Garden City, N.Y.: Doubleday, 1929); Theodore Humphrey, *Food and Festival in American Life* (Ann Arbor, Mich.: UMI Research Press), 19–26; Wicke Chambers *Celebration Book of Great American Traditions* (New York: Harper and Row, 1983), 16.

61. Bess Hawes, "The Birthday: An American Ritual" (master's thesis, University of California at Berkeley, 1970), 19–26, 44, 50–57, 72–75; Mary Ellsworth, *Birthday Parties for Boys and Girls from One to Fourteen* (New York: Women's Press, 1951), 15.

62. Emily Post, *Children Are People* (New York: Funk and Wagnalls, 1940), 267;

"Something's Wrong with Children's Parties," *Parents*, Apr. 1935, 78; "His Party or Yours," *Parents*, Sept. 1948, 72; "Whose Party Is It Anyway?" *Better Homes and Gardens*, June 1948, 219–20; "Life Goes to an Ideal Child's Party," *Life*, 20 May 1946, 80–82; Ellsworth, *Birthday Parties for Boys and Girls*; Chambers, *Celebration*, 26, 28, 38; Frances Ilg, Louise Ames, Evelyn Goodenough, and Irene Andresen, *Gesell Institute Party Book* (New York: Harper, 1956).

63. Cindy Aron, *Working at Play: The History of Vacations in the United States* (New York: Oxford University Press, 1999); Jon Sterngass, *First Resorts: Pursuing Pleasure at Saratoga Springs, Newport and Coney Island* (Baltimore: Johns Hopkins University Press, 2001), 7–74, 117–45, 204–20, 227.

64. "The Best 2 Weeks Vacation for a Family," *LHJ*, June 1904, 24; "Time Off," *American Mercury*, Aug. 1929, 463–69; "Getting Acquainted with Your Family," *Craftsman*, Aug. 1916, 525–28.

65. Charles Mills, *Vacations for Industrial Workers* (New York: Ronald Press, 1927), 24–25, 149–51; "The American Vacation," *Fortune*, 14 (1936): 161; Gary Cross, *Time and Money: The Making of Consumer Culture* (London: Routledge, 1993), 79–82, 95–97.

66. "Try a Different Vacation," *Parents*, Aug. 1935, 16–17; "Vacation for the Family," *Parents*, June 1949, 35, 110; "Emily in Wonderland," *Look*, 15 May 1956, 94–99; "Life Goes on a Family Vacation," *Life*, 21 Aug. 1950, 100–102; "There's No Vacation Like a Family Vacation," *Parents*, May 1955, 48–49.

67. "Family Camping Trip," *Look*, 21 Sept. 1954, 730–74; "Try Station Wagon Camping," *National Wildlife*, Aug. 1971, 20; James Weeks, *Gettysburg: Memory, Market, and an American Shrine* (Princeton, N.J.: Princeton University Press, 2003), chap. 5.

68. Benjamin Spock, "Can Parents and Children Share Vacation Fun?" *Redbook*, June 1961, 20; see also *Life*, 3 Sept. 1971, 20; Orvar Löfgren, *On Holiday: A History of Vacationing* (Berkeley: University of California Press, 1999), 63–64, 273.

69. "Just the Two of Us," *Redbook*, May 1978, 72.

70. "Taking a Family Vacation," *SEP*, 13 June 1959; "Missing Them Is Half the Fun," *Today's Health*, Apr. 1972, 32–33.

71. William Addison, *English Fairs and Markets* (London, 1953), 95–225.

72. Judith Adams, *The American Amusement Park Industry: A History of Technology and Thrills* (Boston: Twayne, 1991), 3–6; Warwick Wroth, *London Pleasure Gardens of the Eighteenth Century* (London, 1896); Neil Harris, "Expository Expositions: Preparing for the Theme Parks," in *Designing Disney's Theme Parks*, ed. Karal Ann Marling (New York: Flammarion), 19–24; John Kasson, *Amusing the Million: Coney Island at the Turn of the Century* (New York: Hill and Wang, 1978), chaps. 1–2.

73. Kasson, *Amusing the Million*, 63–86; Kathy Peiss, *Cheap Amusements: Working Women and Leisure in Turn-of-the Century New York* (Philadelphia: Temple University Press, 1986), 128–36; Charles Davis, "The Renaissance of Coney," *Outing Magazine* 48 (1906): 516; Raymond Weinstein, "Disneyland and Coney Island: Reflections on the Evolution of the Modern Amusement Park," *Journal of Popular Culture* 26 (1992): 131–42.

74. Adams, *American Amusement Park Industry*, 12–15.

75. Register, *The Kid of Coney Island*, 300–303; *New York Times*, 18 Mar. 1928, 71.

76. For background, see, for example, Douglas Gomery, "Disney's Business History," in *Disney Discourse: Producing the Magic Kingdom*, ed. Eric Smoodin (New York: Routledge, 1994), 71–77; Richard Schickel, *The Disney Version: The Life, Times, Art, and Commerce of Walt Disney* (New York: Simon and Schuster, 1968), 263–66; and, especially, Karal Ann Marling, "Imagineering the Disney Theme Parks," in *Designing Disney's Theme Parks*, 55–79.

77. Disneyland shared much with the fantasy settings created at Luna Park and Dreamland on Coney Island a half century earlier. Marling, "Imagineering the Disney Theme Parks," 31–54; Randy Bright, *Disneyland: Inside Story* (New York: Abrams, 1987), 38–41; Weinstein, "Disneyland," 146–53.

78. See *A Disneyland Anthology* (Burbank, Calif.: Walt Disney Home Video, [1999?]) for laser disc copies of examples of Disneyland programs from the 1950s and early 1960s illustrating features on the four "lands" of Disneyland (the place). A fine history of Disneyland's origins is found in John Findlay, *Magic Lands: Western Cityscapes and American Culture after 1940* (Berkeley: University of California Press, 1992), chap. 2.

79. "What Hath Disney Wrought," *Newsweek*, 18 Oct. 1971, 38–43. Other commentaries include *Look*, 6 Apr. 1971, 17–20; *Time*, 18 Oct. 1971, 52. See also Walt Disney Productions, *Project Florida: A Whole New Disney World* (Burbank, Calif.: 1967); Eve Zibart, *Inside Disney: The Incredible Story of Walt Disney World and the Man behind the Mouse* (Foster City, Calif.: IDG Books, 2000), 72–112; Richard Foglesong, *Married to the Mouse: Walt Disney World and Orlando* (New Haven, Conn.: Yale University Press, 2001).

80. Paul Fussel quoted in "Disney's America," *Denver Post*, 6 Aug. 1995, 1; C. E. A. Lawrence, "In the Mick of Time: Reflections on Disney's Ageless Mouse," *Journal of Popular Culture* 20 (1986): 65–72; H. Elliott, "Disney Goes for Old Generations," *New York Times*, 5 May 1994, 5; Alan Bryman, *Disney and His Worlds* (New York: Routledge, 1995), 88–89.

81. Note, for example, Elizabeth and Jay Mechling, "The Sale of Two Cities: A Semiotic Comparison of Disneyland with Marriott's Great America," *Journal of Popular Culture* 15 (1981): 116–79; *Disneyland, the First Quarter Century* (Anaheim: Walt Disney Productions, 1979), 3; and *Walt Disney's Guide to Disneyland* (Anaheim: Walt Disney Productions, 1964), 4.

82. Smoodin, *Disney Discourse*, 10.

83. Beth Dunlop, *Art of Disney Architecture* (New York: Abrams, 1996), 25; and Marling, "Imagineering the Disney Theme Parks."

84. Margaret King, "Disneyland and Walt Disney World: Traditional Values in Futuristic Form," *Journal of Popular Culture* 15 (1981): 116–40; Jean Starobinski, "The Idea of Nostalgia," *Diogenes* 54 (summer 1966): 81–103, quotation on 103; Peter Fritzsche, "Specters of History: On Nostalgia, Exile, and Modernity," *American Historical Review* 106 (2001), 1587–1618.

85. Janet Wasko, *Understanding Disney: The Manufacture of Fantasy* (Cambridge:

Polity Press, 2001), 118; Disney quoted in Marc Eliot, *Walt Disney, Hollywood's Dark Prince* (New York: Birch Lane, 1993), 72.

86. The Project on Disney, *Inside the Mouse: Work and Play at Disney World* (Durham, N.C.: Duke University Press, 1995), 46; "Tenth Anniversary of Disneyland," 3 Jan. 1965 episode of *Disneyland*, in *Disneyland USA* (DVD recordings, 2001).

87. *Walt Disney's Guide*, 16, 22; "Dateline Disneyland," 15 July 1955 live broadcast, and "The Disneyland Story," 27 Oct. 1954 episode of *Disneyland*, in *Disneyland USA* (DVD recordings, 2001); *Disneyland, the First Quarter Century*, 17; A. Wasserman, "Loathing at EPCOT," *Industrial Design Magazine*, Mar./Apr. 1983, 39, quoted in Bryman, *Disney and His Worlds*, 156–57.

88. Bryman, *Disney and His Worlds*, 95; and Margaret King, "McDonald's and Disney," in *Ronald Revisited and the World of Ronald McDonald*, ed. M. Fishwich (Bowling Green, Ohio: Bowling Green State University Popular Press, 1983), 117. For a full treatment, see Henry Giroux, *The Mouse That Roared: Disney and the End of Innocence* (Lanham, Md.: Rowman and Littlefield, 1999).

Chapter 5

1. *Gremlins* (1984), Steven Spielberg, producer; and Daniel Harris, *Cute, Quaint, Hungry, and Romantic: Aesthetics of Consumerism* (New York: Basic Books, 2000), 19–22.

2. Emily Post, *Children Are People and Ideal Parents Are Comrades* (New York: Funk and Wagnalls, 1940), ix–x, 368.

3. Donna Lanclos, "Bare Bums and Wee Chimneys: Rudeness and Defining the Line between Child and Adult," *Children's Folklore Review* 12, no. 2 (2000): 7–48; and Iona Opie and Peter Opie, *Children's Games in Street and Playground* (Oxford: Clarendon, 1970).

4. *St. Nicholas*, Nov. 1923, 14–15; Nov. 1932, 44–45; Nov. 1933, 128; R. Gordon Kelly, *Children's Periodicals of the United States* (Westport, Conn.: Greenwood, 1984), 507–14.

5. Pat Schoonmaker, *A Collector's History of the Teddy Bear* (Cumberland, Md.: Hobby House Press, 1981), 41–42, 50–51, 227–41, 250–52, 280–82; Columbia Manufacturing ad (teddy bear), *Playthings*, Oct. 1907; "The Teddy Bear and the Doll at Christmas," *LHJ*, Dec. 1907, 80; "Stand Aside," *Harper's Weekly*, 4 Apr. 1907, 625; F. R. Bird ad, *Delineator*, Dec. 1907, 1151.

6. For example, Mace Company, *toy catalog* (1907), 115; On On Daga Indian Wigwam Co. ad, *Playthings*, Mar. 1910, 91.

7. Miriam Formanek-Brunell, *Made to Play House: Dolls and the Commercialization of American Girlhood, 1830–1930* (New Haven, Conn.: Yale University Press, 1993), 92, 106–7; and Gary Cross, *Kids' Stuff: Toys and the Changing World of American Childhood* (Cambridge, Mass.: Harvard University Press, 1997), 73–74.

8. Horsman doll ad, *Playthings*, May 1911, 3; Joseph Schroeder, *The Wonderful World of Toys, Games, and Dolls, 1860–1930* (Chicago: Follett, 1971), 158, 209.

9. Kenny Harman, *Comic Strip Toys* (Des Moines, Iowa: Wallace-Homestead Books, 1975), 5–7, 13–35, 51–56, 70–72; David Longest, *Character Toys and Collectibles* (Paducah, Ky.: Collector Books, 1992), 1:14–28.

10. "Editorial," *Toys and Novelties*, June 1913, 70.

11. For example, Lionel Trains ad, *American Boy*, Oct. 1918, 45.

12. Ruth Freeman, *American Dolls* (Watkins Glen, N.Y.: Century House, 1952), 36; Longest, *Character Toys*, 2:129–30.

13. Sears and Roebuck catalog, no. 171 (Chicago, 1935), 732; no. 173 (1936), 793; and no. 179 (1939), 896.

14. Ideal Toys ad, *Playthings*, Mar. 1936, 3; "Cash in on April's Double Header," *Playthings*, Mar. 1936, 64; Anne Edwards, *Shirley Temple: American Princess* (New York: Morrow, 1988), 28–31.

15. Disneyland episodes, "Story of Disneyland" (1954) and "Day in the Life of Donald Duck" (1 Feb. 1956), in *A Disneyland Anthology* (Burbank, Calif.: Walt Disney Home Video, [1999?]); Norman Kline, *Seven Minutes: The Life and Death of the American Animated Cartoon* (London: Verso, 1993), 17, 45, 53, 91–95.

16. Alva Johnston, "Mickey Mouse," *Woman's Home Companion*, July 1934, 12–13; "Mickey Mouse Is 8 Years Old," *Literary Digest*, 122 (2 Oct. 1936): 18–19; Bevis Hillier, *Walt Disney's Mickey Mouse Memorabilia* (New York: Hawthorn Books, 1986), 14; Robert Heide and John Gilman, *Cartoon Collectibles: 50 Years of Dime Store Memorabilia* (Garden City, N.Y.: Doubleday), 122–29, 134, 173–80; Kline, *Seven Minutes*, 106–9, 167–68; and Richard De Cordova, "The Mickey in Macy's Window: Childhood, Consumerism, and Disney Animation," in *Disney Discourse: Producing the Magic Kingdom*, ed. Eric Smoodin (New York: Routlege, 1994), 207–8.

17. Harris, *Cute, Quaint*, 52–74.

18. Caroline Burk, "The Collecting Instinct," in *Aspects of Child Life and Education*, ed. G. Stanley Hall (New York: Ginn and Co., 1907), 205–39.

19. E. Evalyn Grumbine, *Reaching Juvenile Markets* (New York: McGraw-Hill, 1938); E. Evalyn Grumbine, "Juvenile Clubs and Contests," *Printers' Ink Monthly*, May 1936, 22, 23, 56, 57; Roland Marchand, "Precocious Consumers and Junior Salesmen: Advertising to Children in the United States to 1940" (unpublished ms.).

20. David Zinman, *Saturday Afternoon at the Bijou* (New Rochelle, N.Y.: Arlington House, 1973), 288–300; Alan Barbour, *Saturday Afternoon at the Movies* (New York: Bonanza Books, 1–29; Jim Harmon, *Great Movie Serials: Their Sound and Fury* (Garden City, N.Y.: Doubleday, 1972), 2–5; Kalton Lahue, *Continued Next Week: A History of the Moving Picture Serial* (Norman: University of Oklahoma Press, 1964), 5–6, chaps. 4–10; William Cline, *In the Nick of Time: Motion Picture Sound Serials* (Jefferson, N.C.: McFarland, 1984), 7, 21–23; Buck Rainey, *Serials and Series: A World Filmography, 1912–1956* (Jefferson, N.C.: McFarland, 1999), 3–4, 92–93.

21. Orrin Dunlap, *Radio in Advertising* (New York: Harper and Row, 1931), 83; Jim Harmon, *Radio Mystery and Adventure* (Jefferson, N.C.: McFarland, 1992), 18–19, 24, 30–32, 102–3; Marilyn Boemer, *The Children's Hour: Radio Programs for Children, 1929–1956* (Metuchen, N.J.: Scarecrow Press, 1989), 7–16; Ray Barfield, *Listening to Radio, 1920–1950* (Westport, Conn.: Praeger, 1996), 109, 115, 121.

22. Matthew Pustz, *Comic Book Culture: Fanboys and True Believers* (Jackson: University of Mississippi Press, 1999), 27; Bradford Wright: *Comic Book Nation: The Transformation of Youth Culture in America* (Baltimore: Johns Hopkins University Press, 2001), 2–7.

23. Roger Sabin, *Comics, Comix, and Graphic Novels* (London: Phaidon Press, 1996), 27; Ron Goulart, *Comic Book Culture* (Portland, Oreg.: Collectors' Press, 2000), 8–13, 140–49; Michael Barrier and Martin Williams, eds., *A Smithsonian Book of Comic-Book Comics* (Washington, D.C.: Smithsonian Institution Press, 1981), 10–12, 149–51; Patrick Parsons, "Batman and His Audience," in *The Many Lives of the Batman*, ed. Roberta E. Pearson and William Uricchio (London: Routledge, 1991), 71; Donna Richardson, "Classics Illustrated," *American Heritage* 44, no. 3 (May–June 1993): 78–86.

24. Goulart, *Comic Book Culture*, 25–43.

25. Ruth Bahivin, "Psychological Aspects of Pediatrics: The Comics," *Journal of Pediatrics* 22 (1953): 633, cited in Parsons, "Batman," 70; Pustz, *Comic Book Culture*, 234.

26. Victory Appleton, *Tom Swift and His War Tank: or, Doing His Bit for Uncle Sam* (New York: Grosset and Dunlap, 1918); Victor Appleton, *Tom Swift and His Television Detector* (Racine, Wis.: Whitman, 1933); Edward Stratemeyer, *The Rover Boys in the Air, or, From College Campus to the Clouds* (New York: Grosset and Dunlap, 1912); Deirdre Johnson, *Edward Stratemeyer and the Stratemeyer Syndicate* (New York: Twayne, 1993), chaps. 3–4; John Dizer, *Tom Swift, the Bobbsey Twins, and Other Heroes of American Juvenile Literature* (Lewiston, N.Y.: Edwin Mellon, 1997), 1–10, 52, 324–31; Dizer, *Tom Swift and Company* (Jefferson, N.C.: McFarland, 1982); Carol Billman, *The Secret of the Stratemeyer Syndicate* (New York: Ungar, 1986), chap. 2.

27. Franklin Dixon, *The Shore Road Mystery* (New York: Grosset and Dunlap, 1928); Gary Westfahl, *Science Fiction, Children's Literature, and Popular Culture* (Westport, Conn.: Greenwood, 2000), 21, 25, 28, 33.

28. J. Harmon, *The Great Radio Heroes* (Garden City, N.Y.: Doubleday, 1967), 229–58.

29. Harmon, *Great Movie Serials*, 80–82, 145–53; Harmon, *Radio Mystery and Adventure*, 1, 6–10; Harmon, *Great Radio Heroes*, 229–58; Zinman, *Saturday Afternoon*, 369–74, 384, 415–17.

30. Carolyn Keene, *Nancy Drew Mystery Stories* (New York: Grosset and Dunlap, 1930), begins the series; Sherrie Inness, "The Ideology of Girls' Scouting Novels, 1910–1935," in *Nancy Drew and Company*, ed. S. Inness (Bowling Green, Ohio: Bowling Green State University Popular Press, 1997), 89–100; L. M. Montgomery, *Anne of Green Gables* (Boston: L. C. Page and Company, 1908).

31. Michael Denning, *Mechanical Accents: Dime Novels and Working-Class Culture in America* (New York: Verso, 1989), 18, 30, 45; Christine Bold, *Selling the Wild West: Popular Western Fiction* (Bloomington: Indiana University Press, 1987), 3–5, 10–15, 33, and chap. 3; Larry Sullivan and Lydia Schuman, *Pioneers, Passionate Ladies and Private Eyes: Dime Novels, Series Books, and Paperbacks* (New York: Haworth, 1996); Jeffrey Wallmann, *The Western: Parables of the American Dream* (Lubbock: Texas Tech University Press, 1999), 69–71, 95, 125, 128, 137.

32. Wallmann, *Western*, 16, 21, 39, 135; Harmon, *Radio Mystery and Adventure*, 219–25; Zinman, *Saturday Afternoon*, 153–55.

33. A few authors like mystery writers Dashiell Hammett and Raymond Chandler crossed between the pulps and slicks, but most did not. Authors were forced to use gimmicks and sensationalism (coincidences, conspiracies, ghosts, and "evil twins") to produce the 3,000 to 5,000 words a day required to make a living as a pulp writer. The division between the two genres probably grew in the 1920s, when the pulps became identified in the eyes of "slick" readers as "daydreams for the masses" and, because of their formulaic character, as "the incursion of the machine age into the art of taletelling"; Marcus Duffield, "The Pulps," *Vanity Fair*, June 1933, 26–27. See Ron Goulart, *Cheap Thrills: An Informal History of Pulp Magazines* (New Rochelle, N.Y.: Arlington House, 1972); Tony Goodstone, ed., *The Pulps: Fifty Years of American Popular Culture* (New York: Chelsea House, 1970); and especially Denning, *Mechanical Accents*, chap. 2; Erin Smith, *Hard-Boiled: Working-Class Readers and Pulp Magazines* (Philadelphia: Temple University Press, 2000), 18–34.

34. Raymond Chandler, *The Big Sleep* (New York: Knopf, 1939); Smith, *Hard-Boiled*, 56, 77–79.

35. Garyn Roberts, *Dick Tracy and American Culture: Morality and Mythology* (Jefferson, N.C.: McFarland, 1993), 3–6, 11, 31–53, 213; Harmon, *Radio Mystery and Adventure*, 27–40; R. M. Hayes, *Republic Chapterplays: A Complete Filmography of the Serials* (Jefferson, N.C.: McFarland, 1991), 20; Longest, *Character Toys*, 2:66.

36. The original story by Philip F. Nowland, "Armageddon-2419," appears in Lorraine Dille Williams ed., *Buck Rogers, The First 60 Years in the 25th Century* (New York: TSR, 1988), 19–46, along with an interesting selection of "Buck Rogers" strips.

37. Amy Sue Bix, *Inventing Ourselves Out of Jobs: American Debate over Technological Unemployment, 1929–1981* (Baltimore: Johns Hopkins University Press, 2000).

38. Roy Kinnard, *Science Fiction Serials* (Jefferson, N.C.: McFarland, 1998), 67–76; Harmon, *Great Movie Serials*, 27–33, 40–41; Pustz, *Comic Book Culture*, 30–32, 40; Rainey, *Serials and Series*, 215–18.

39. Goulart, *Comic Book Culture*, 27, 43–47; Kinnard, *Science Fiction Serials*, 63–67, 77, 102–3, 78, 156–57; Harmon, *Radio Mystery and Adventure*, 43–45, 197; Pustz, *Comic Book Culture*, 27–28; Rainey, *Serials and Series*, 102–4; Hayes, *Republic Chapterplays*, 56; Wright, *Comic Book Nation*, 8–21.

40. "Captain Marvel Battles the Plot against the Universe," *Captain Marvel* (Sept. 1949), in Barrier and Williams, *Smithsonian Book*, 79–80.

41. Richard O'Brien, *Collecting Toys* (Florence, Ala.: Americana Books, 1990), 175–76, 188, 197–210, 229–31; Peter Johnson, *Toy Armies* (Garden City, N.Y.: Doubleday, 1981), 105; Ruth Freeman and Larry Freeman, *Cavalcade of Toys* (Watkins Glen, N.Y.: Century House, 1942), 109.

42. Daisy ad, *American Boy*, Dec. 1934, back cover.

43. J. Fred MacDonald, *Don't Touch That Dial: Radio Programming in American Life, 1920–1960* (Chicago: Nelson-Hall, 1979), 42–44; Harmon, *Great Radio Heroes*, 109–14; Boemer, *Children's Hour*, 128–32; Arthur Berger, *The Comic-Stripped American* (Baltimore: Penguin, 1973), 79–101.

44. William Savage, *Comic Books and America, 1945–1954* (Norman: University of Oklahoma Press, 1990), Wright, *Comic Book Nation*, 30–55.

45. Peter Stearns, *American Cool: Constructing a Twentieth-Century Emotional Style* (New York: New York University Press, 1994), 109.

46. Parsons, "Batman," 70; Pustz, *Comic Book Culture*, 30–31; Hayes, *Republic Chapterplays*, 18; Zinman, *Saturday Afternoon*, 21–27; Goulart, *Comic Book Culture*, 60, 185–86.

47. Frank Jacobs, *The Mad World of William M. Gaines* (Secaucus, N.J.: Lyle Stuart, 1972), 54–55, and chap. 4; Pustz, *Comic Book Culture*, 40–41; Wright, *Comic Book Nation*, 77–85, 135–53. Interesting analysis of children's attraction to horror is found in Linda Christian-Smith and Jean Erdman, "'Mom, It's Not Real!' Children Constructing Childhood through Reading Horror Fiction," in *Kinderculture: The Corporate Construction of Childhood*, ed. Shirley Steinberg and Joe Kincheloe (Boulder, Colo.: Westview, 1998), 129–52; Mark Laidler, "Zapping Freddy Krueger," in *Wired Up: Young People and the Electronic Media*, ed. Sue Howard (London: UCL Press, 1998), 43–55.

48. Jacobs, *Mad World*, chap. 7; and especially Maria Reidelbach, *Completely Mad: A History of the Comic Book and Magazine* (Boston: Little, Brown, 1991); Wright, *Comic Book Nation*, 201–25.

49. Trina Robbins, *From Girls to Grrrlz: A History of Women's Comics from Teens to Zines* (San Francisco: Chronicle Books, 1999), 9–69.

50. Kelly Schrum, "Teena Means Business: Teenage Girls' Culture and *Seventeen Magazine*," in *Delinquents and Debutantes*, ed. Sherrie Inness (New York: New York University Press, 1998), 138, 146, 151–52.

51. Kate Kruckemeyer, "Future Pleasure, Present Danger: Conflicts over Sexuality in Girls' Popular Culture in the 1970s and 1980s" (paper presented at the meeting of the Organization of American Historians, Washington, D.C., April 2002); Mary Celeste Kearney "Producing Girls: Rethinking the Study of Female Youth Culture," in Inness, *Delinquents and Debutantes*, 285–99.

52. Quotation from Simon Frith, *Sound Effects: Youth Leisure and the Politics of Rock 'n' Roll* (New York: Pantheon, 1981), 228.

53. Dawn Currie, *Girl Talk: Adolescent Magazines and Their Readers* (Toronto: University of Toronto Press, 1999) 3, 24, 25, 31; Naomi Wolf, *The Beauty Myth* (New York: Vintage, 1991), 12; Douglas Kellner, *Media Culture: Cultural Studies, Identity and Politics* (New York: Routledge, 1995), chap. 8. See also Angela McRobbie, *Feminism and Youth Culture* (London: Macmillan, 1991); and, especially, Joan Brumberg, *The Body Project: An Intimate History of American Girls* (New York: Vintage, 1997).

54. Robbins, *From Girls to Grrrlz*, 70–120.

55. Jeffery Davis, *Children's Television, 1947–1990* (Jefferson, N.C.: McFarland, 1995), 97–104; Edward Palmer, *Television and American Children: A Crisis of Neglect* (New York: Oxford University Press, 1988), 22; Joseph Turow, *Entertainment, Education, and the Hard Sell: Three Decades of Network Children's Television* (New York: Praeger, 1981), 18.

56. Davis, *Children's Television*, 168, 174–75, 188–92, 249–54.

57. Turow, *Entertainment, Education, and the Hard Sell*, 18, 29–31.

58. Jerry Bowles, *Forever Hold Your Banners High* (Garden City, N.J.: Doubleday, 1976), esp. 16–17.

59. Parental and government pressure reversed this trend somewhat in the 1970s. Even Bugs Bunny was briefly edited for violence. And, of course, PBS continued to offer Sesame Street, the Electric Company, and Mr. Rogers. But none of the network's prestige programming was shown when most kids watched—Saturday morning. Davis, *Children's Television*, 174, 269; Hal Erickson, *Television Cartoon Shows* (Jefferson, N.C.: McFarland, 1995), 273, 332; Turow, *Entertainment, Education, and the Hard Sell*, 69–73, 96.

60. Brian Young, *Television Advertising and Children* (Oxford: Clarendon, 1900), 15; Ellen Seiter, *Sold Separately: Children and Parent in Consumer Culture* (New Brunswick, N.J.: Rutgers University Press, 1993), 115; Cross, *Kids' Stuff*, 162–71.

61. Steven Kline, *Out of the Garden: Toys, TV, and Children's Culture in the Age of Marketing* (New York: Verso, 1993), 170–71, 187–95.

62. "Bernard Loomis," *Toys and Hobby World*, Apr. 1976, 51; Daniel Cook, "The 'Other Child Study'": Figuring Children as Consumers in Market Research, 1910s–1990s," *Sociological Quarterly* 14 (2000): 487–507.

63. Bill Bruegman, *Toys of the Sixties* (Akron, Ohio: Cap'n Penny, 1992), 89–97; Forest Ackerman, *Famous Monsters of Filmland Magazine*, no. 3, *Monsters Strike Back* (New York: Paperback Library, 1965), quotation on back cover.

64. Bill Bruegman, *Aurora History and Price Guide* (Akron, Ohio: Cap'n Penny, 1992), 12–13; Carol Turpen, *Baby Boomer Toys and Collectibles* (Atglen, Pa.: Schiffer Publishing, 1993), 42–45, 92.

65. Bruegman, *Aurora History*, 3–4, 12–15, 35, 37, 59–64, 109, 119–20.

66. Turpen, *Baby Boomer Toys*, 42–50, 83–92; "Monstrous Christmas to All," *Nation*, 14 Dec. 1964, 463–64; Seiter, *Sold Separately*, 116–17. Allison James argues that penny candies blatantly break with the world of adults in taste, look, and emotional appeal. This culture has roots in school and independent play of kids but is exploited by merchandisers; James, "Confections, Concoctions, and Conceptions," in *Children's Culture Reader*, ed. Henry Jenkins (New York: New York University Press, 1998), 394–405. See http://www.amazon.com/exec/obidos/ASIN/B000067QXP/ref=cm_bg_f_1/104-0317603-3652738 for details on the Queasy Bake Oven.

67. Bruegman, *Aurora History*, 24–25.

68. Good sources include Pustz, *Comic Book Culture*, 43–49; Parsons, "Batman," 82–83; Carol Markowski, *Tomart's Price Guide to Action Figure Collectibles* (Dayton, Ohio: Tomart, 1992), chaps. 1–2; Steven Kimball, *Greenberg's Guide to Superhero Toys* (Sykesville, Md.: Greenberg,1988), 13–61; and Bruegman, *Toys of the Sixties*, 124–30.

69. Robbins, *From Girls to Grrrlz*, 81–141.

70. Sources include Ruth Handler, *Dream Doll* (Stamford, Conn.: Longmeadow Press, 1994), passim; A. Glenn Mandeville, *Doll Fashion Anthology and Price Guide*, 4th ed. (Cumberland, Md.: Hobby House Press, 1993), 1–33; Kitturah Westenhouser, *The Story of Barbie* (Paducah, Ky.: Collector Books, 1994), 5–15; A. Lord, *Forever Barbie* (New York: Avon, 1994); Kristin Noelle Weissman, *Barbie: The Icon, the Image, the*

*Ideal: An Analytical Interpretation of the Barbie Doll in Popular Culture* (self-published, 1999), 19–43.

71. Helen Gurley Brown, *Sex and the Single Girl* (New York: Avon, 1962); Mary Rogers, *Barbie Culture* (London: Sage, 1999), 37–40; Theodore Diehard, *Teenagers and Teen Pics* (Boston: Unwin, 1988), chaps. 1–3.

72. Patricia Adler and Peter Adler, *Peer Power: Preadolescent Culture and Identity* (New Brunswick, N.J.: Rutgers University Press, 1998), 39–56; Rogers, *Barbie Culture*, 61–66.

73. Billy Boy, *Barbie: Her Life and Times and the New Theater of Fashion* (New York: Crown 1987), 17–28, 40–44.

74. Vincent Santelmo, *The Official 30th Anniversary Salute to G.I. Joe* (Iola, Wis.: Kreuse, 1994), 1–17.

75. Susan Manos and Paris Manos, *Collectible Male Action Figures* (Paducah, Ky.: Collector Books, 1990), 20–33; Santelmo, *Salute to G.I. Joe*, 17–18, 66–72, 325, 343; Tom Engelhardt, *The End of Victory Culture: Cold War America and the Disillusioning of a Generation* (New York: Basic Books, 1995), 81–86, 300.

76. Santelmo, *Salute to G.I. Joe*, 17–18, 75–97, 412–13; Manos and Manos, *Collectible Male Action Figures*, 38–43.

77. "Star Wars," *Toys and Hobby World*, June 1983, 24, 26.

78. Cross, *Kids' Stuff*, 205–7, 213–14; Tyco Press Kit, Feb. 1988, box 8 (Please Touch Museum, Philadelphia, Pa.); also Sydney Stern and Ted Schoenhaus, *Toyland: The High-Stakes Game of the Toy Industry* (Chicago: Contemporary Books, 1990), chaps. 5, 11, 14, 17.

79. See Seiter, *Sold Separately*, 186, for an interesting discussion of the contrast between boys' and girls' fantasy in the 1980s.

80. Cross, *Kids' Stuff*, 211–12.

81. J. C. Herz, *Joystick Nation* (Boston: Little, Brown, 1997), 14–22, 33–37, 55; Geoffrey Loftus, *Mind at Play: The Psychology of Video Games* (New York: Basic Books, 1983), 100–101, 109; Eugene Provenzo, *Video Kids: Making Sense of Nintendo* (Cambridge, Mass.: Harvard University Press, 1991), 8–9, 31–35.

82. Provenzo, *Video Kids*, 34–35; Marsha Kinder, *Playing with Power in Movies, Television and Video Games* (Berkeley: University of California Press, 1991), 105, 118; U.S.. House, Subcommittee on Telecommunications and Finance, *Violence in Video Games*, 103d Cong., 2nd session (Washington, D.C.: U.S. Government Printing Office, 1994), 1–3.

83. "Interview with Martha Kinder," in *From Barbie to Mortal Kombat: Gender and Computer Games*, ed. Justine Cassell and Henry Jenkins (Cambridge, Mass.: MIT Press, 1998), 216–18; Provenzo, *Video Kids*, 16–17; Herz, *Joystick Nation*, 884–88, 140–44, 146–47.

Chapter 6

1. Hugo Munsterberg, *The Photoplay: A Psychological Study* (New York: Appleton, 1916), 95; Jane Addams, *The Spirit of Youth and City Streets* (New York: Macmillan, 1909), 75–76, 86; William Healy, *The Individual Delinquent* (Boston: Little, Brown, 1915), 307–8; Garth Jowett, Ian Javie, and Kathryn Fuller, *Children and the Movies: Media Influence and the Payne Fund Controversy* (New York: Cambridge University Press, 1996), 21–29.

2. Kathleen McCarthy, "Nickel Vice and Virtue: Movie Censorship in Chicago, 1907–1915," *Journal of Popular Film* 5 (1976): 37–55; Kevin Brownlow, *Behind the Mask of Innocence* (New York: Knopf, 1990), 4–20; Robert Fisher, "Film Censorship and Progressive Reform: The National Board of Censorship of Motion Pictures, 1909–1922," *Journal of Popular Film* (1975): 143–56; Mark Fackler, "Moral Guardians of the Movies and Social Responsibility of the Press," in *Mass Media between the Wars*, ed. Catherine Covert and John Stevens (Syracuse, N.Y.: Syracuse University Press, 1984), 181–97.

3. Henry Forman, *Our Movie Made Children* (New York: Macmillan, 1933); Richard Maltby, "The Production Code and the Hays Office," in *Grand Design: Hollywood as a Modern Business Enterprise, 1930–1930*, ed. Tino Balio (New York: Scribner's, 1993), 37–72; Paul Facey, *The Legion of Decency* (New York: Arno Press, 1974), 65–68; Jowett, Javie, and Fuller, *Children and the Movies*, 29–95, quotation on 96.

4. I discuss this more fully in *Kids' Stuff: Toys and the Changing World of American Childhood* (Cambridge, Mass.: Harvard University Press, 1997), 66, 67, 110–13.

5. "Toy Soldiers and Real War," *World Tomorrow*, Dec. 1931, 36; "Against War Games," *Rotarian*, Dec. 1933, 43; Rachel Palmer, *$40,000,000 Guinea Pig Children* (New York: Vanguard Press, 1937), 225–31; Nelson Crawford, "War Toys and War," *Literary Digest*, 4 Sept. 1937, 33.

6. "They're After the Toy Gun," *Toys and Novelties*, Jan. 1936, 30–40; "Readers' Protest," *Toys and Novelties*, Feb. 1936, 26–27; Adele McKinnie, "Shall I Let My Child Play with War Toys?" *Woman's Home Companion*, Nov. 1942, 52–53.

7. Marjorie Heins, *Not in Front of the Children: "Indecency," Censorship, and the Innocence of Youth* (New York: Hill and Wang, 2001), chaps. 3–4.

8. "Mothers Fighting Radio Bogies," *Literary Digest*, 15 Jan. 1933, 32, "Radio Horror for Children Only," *American Mercury*, July 1938, 294–301; "A United Front on Children's Radio Programs," *Parents*, June 1935, 23; Josette Frank, "These Children's Programs," *Parents*, Feb. 1939, 28–29; Sidonie Greenberg, "New Voices Speak to Our Children," *Parents*, June 1941, 23, 40; "Are the Programs They Like Bad for Them?" *Parents*, Apr. 1940, 32–33; "Much Ado about Programs," *Collier's*, 30 Dec. 1939, 50; "Children's Hour," *Time*, 24 Mar. 24, 1947, 63; Gladys Shultz, "Comics-Radio-Movies," *Better Homes and Gardens*, Dec. 1945, 22–23; Amanda Bruce, "Contesting the Boundaries of Childhood: Children's Radio and Parental Authority." Conference of the Society for the History of Childhood and Youth, 28 June 2003, Baltimore.

9. Jowett, Javie, and Fuller, *Children and the Movies*, 101–8, develops this theme. See also Mark West, *Children, Culture, and Controversy* (New York: Archon, 1988).

10. *New York Times*, 31 Mar. 1935, S7, 17; 4 July 1935, 35; 7 July 1935, S4, 10.

11. Roger C. Sharpe, *Pinball!* (New York: Dutton, 1977), 43–63; *New York Times*, 31 Mar. 1935, S7, 17; 4 July 1935, 35; 7 July 1935, S4, S10; 9 May 1917, S4, S12; 16 Aug. 1938, 6; 9 Oct. 1941, 13; 19 Oct. 1941, S7, S12; 24 Jan. 1942, 30; 10 July 1942, 17.

12. Roy Gay, "A Teacher Reads the Comics," *Harvard Education Review* 7 (1937): 206; "A National Disgrace," *Chicago Daily News*, 8 May 1940, 3, reprinted in *Parents*, Mar. 1941, 26; "Are Comics Fascist?" *Time*, 22 Oct. 1945, 67–68; Mary Mannes, "Junior Has a Craving," *New Republic*, 17 Feb. 1947, 20–23; Milton Klonksy, "Comic Strip Tease of Time," *American Mercury*, Dec. 1952, 93–99; Amy Nyberg, *Seal of Approval: The History of the Comics Code* (Jackson: University Press of Mississippi, 1998), 5–6, 37–38; Bradford Wright, *Comic Book Nation* (Baltimore: Johns Hopkins University Press, 2001), 26–29.

13. Frederic Wertham, "The Comics . . . Very Funny," *Saturday Review of Literature*, 29 May 1948, 6–7; Nyberg, *Seal of Approval*, 90–95; Samuel Berenberg, "Horrors a Dime Can Buy!" *American Home*, June 1949, 56–57; Judith Crist, "Horror in the Nursery," *Collier's*, 27 Mar. 1948, 22–23; Frederic Wertham, *Seduction of the Innocent* (New York: Rinehart, 1953), 2, 25, 43, 51, 381; Martin Basker, "Frederic Wertham—The Sad Case of the Unhappy Humanist," in *Pulp Demons*, ed. John Lent (Madison, N.J.: Fairleigh Dickinson University Press, 1999), 215–31; William Oakley, "The Destruction of an Industry: Dr. Wertham, the Hendrickson Committee, William Gaines and the Comic Book Controversy of the 1950s" (B.A. honor's thesis, Harvard University, 1988). An especially balanced treatment of Wertham is found in Wright, *Comic Book Nation*, 92–98, 157–64.

14. U.S. Senate, Committee on the Judiciary, *Hearing before the Subcommittee to Investigate Juvenile Delinquency (Comic Books)* (Washington, D.C.: U.S. Government Printing Office, 1954), 44–45; "Outlawed," *Time*, 19 Dec. 1949, 33; Wright, *Comic Book Nation*, 100–101.

15. Nyberg, *Seal of Approval*, 6–11, 15–16, 39; Harvey Zorbaugh, "What Adults Think of Comics as Reading for Children," *Journal of Educational Sociology* 23 (1949): 226–33; James Gilbert, *A Cycle of Outrage: America's Reaction to the Juvenile Delinquent in the 1950s* (New York: Oxford University Press, 1986), esp. chap. 6.

16. "What Is the Solution for Control of the Comics?" *Library Journal*, 1 Feb. 1949, 180; "Up, Up and Awa-a-y!" *New Republic*, 3 Mar. 1947, 15–17.

17. Frederic Thrasher, "The Comics and Delinquency: Cause or Scapegoat?" *Journal of Educational Sociology* 22 (Dec. 1949), 195–205; U.S. Senate, Committee on the Judiciary, *Juvenile Delinquency (Comic Books)*, 13, 23–25; "How about the Comics?" *Newsweek*, 15 Mar. 1948, 56.

18. Historian James Gilbert argues that this "moral panic" against the comic book was a reaction to a rising youth crime rate. There is also evidence that the save-the-kids argument was really an attempt to reassert the superiority of high over low culture. The trouble with this analysis, however, is that it does not take seriously the critics' goal of defending innocence. Gilbert, *Cycle of Outrage*, chap. 6. In the context of a later (1960s) attack on comic book culture, media scholars Henry Jenkins and Lynn Spigel

wrote that critics of comics "secured (at least temporarily) their own position as arbiters of good taste, giving moral purpose to their tirades against mass culture." Lynn Spigel and Henry Jenkins, "Same Bat Channel, Different Bat Times," in *The Many Lives of the Batman*, ed. Roberta Pearson and William Uricchio (New York: Routledge, 1991), 126–28. Important critics of comic book critics are Nyberg, *Seal of Approval*, viii, ix, 10–11, 18–19, 35–36; Ron Goulart, *Comic Book Culture* (Portland, Oreg.: Collectors' Press, 2000), 156–57; Matthew Pustz, *Comic Book Culture: Fanboys and True Believers* (Jackson: University of Mississippi Press, 1999), 33, 34.

19. U.S. Senate, Committee on the Judiciary, *Juvenile Delinquency (Comic Books)*, 1–2, 53, 56, 61, 162–63, 203.

20. Ibid. 79–90.

21. Ibid., 90–103.

22. Nyberg, *Seal of Approval*, x–xi, 81–84, 168–69.

23. "Suffer Little Children," *New Republic*, 4 Jan. 1960, 6–7; Frederic Wertham, "How Movie and TV Violence Affects Children," *LHJ*, Feb. 1960, 58; "The Real Scandal in Television," *New Republic*, 16 Nov. 1959, 21–22; Benjamin Spock, "Television, Radio, Comics, and Movies," *LHJ*, Apr. 1960, 60; Joseph Turow, *Entertainment, Education, and the Hard Sell: Three Decades of Network Children's Television* (New York: Praeger, 1981), 20–21.

24. "Your Child and TV," *Parents*, Dec. 1952, 36; Bruno Bettelheim, "Parents vs. TV," *Redbook*, Nov. 1963, 54–55.

25. There have been many congressional hearings and studies of television violence, beginning in 1952. Note, for example, the National Institute of Mental Health's publication *Television and Behavior: Ten Years of Scientific Progress and Implications for the Eighties* (Rockville, Md.: U.S. Department of Health and Human Services, 1982) (update of 1972 surgeon general's report). See also "Television at the Crossroads," *Society*, Sept. 1984, 6–40; "TV without Terror," *Parents*, July 1962, 42; "Crime Shows on TV: A Federal Crackdown Coming?" *U.S. News & World Report*, 9 Nov. 1964, 50–51; "The Mini Wasteland," *Newsweek*, 23 Jan. 1967, 93–94; "Batman and the Comic Profanation of the Sacred," *Christian Century*, 18 Oct. 1967, 1322–23; Joseph Seldin, "Saturday Morning Massacre," *Progressive*, Sept. 1974, 50–52; "Murder on Saturday Morning," *McCall's*, Sept. 1969, 72.

26. Richard Tobin, "When Violence Begets Violence," *Saturday Review*, 11 Oct. 1969, 69; *McCall's*, Sept. 1969, 72, 142.

27. "Video Game Rooms Targeted by Towns," *New York Times*, 13 Dec. 1981, sec. 2, 16; "Mesquite Texas vs. Evil Empire," *New York Times*, 23 Jan. 1982, sec. 1, 7; "Video Games: Diversion or Danger," *New York Times*, 17 Feb. 1983, C1; "Council Seeking Way to Curb Pupils' Overuse of Video Arcades, " *Washington Post*, 14 Apr. 1983, B13; Carl Rogers, "Nuclear War: A Personal Response," *APA Monitor* 13 (Aug. 1982): 6; J. C. Herz, *Joystick Nation* (Boston: Little, Brown, 1997), 183–95; Eugene Provenzo, *Video Kids: Making Sense of Nintendo* (Cambridge, Mass.: Harvard University Press, 1991), 93, 119, 132.

28. "Video Games Zap Harvard," *Newsweek*, 6 June 1983, 92; "Children and Video

Games," *New York Times*, 30 Sept. 1985, B11; "Children's Video Games," *New York Times*, 31 Aug. 1981, B4; Geoffrey Loftus, *Mind at Play: The Psychology of Video Games* (New York: Basic Books, 1983), 100–101 and chaps. 4–5; Provenzo, *Video Kids*, 53–54; G. D. Bigg, "Personality Differences between High and Low Electronic Video Game Users," *Journal of Psychology* 114 (1989): 143–52.

29. Gerald Kestenbaum and Kissa Weinstein, "Personality Psychopathology and Development Issues in Male Adolescent Game Use," *Journal of the American Academy of Child Psychiatry* 24 (1985): 329–37; "Interview with Martha Kinder," in *From Barbie to Mortal Kombat: Gender and Computer Games*, ed. Justine Cassell and Henry Jenkins (Cambridge, Mass.: MIT Press, 1998), 216–17; Herz, *Joystick Nation*, 2, 86–88.

30. U.S. Senate, Joint Hearing of the Judiciary Committee, *Rating Video Games: A Parent's Guide to Games* (Washington, D.C.: U.S. Government Printing Office, 19 Dec. 1993; 4 Mar., 29 July 1994), 2, 35, 36, 41–41; U.S. House, Subcommittee of Telecommunications and Finance, *Violence in Video Games* (Washington, D.C.: U.S. Government Printing Office, 3 June 1994), 4, 14.

31. Herz, *Joystick Nation*, 191.

32. Gilbert, *Cycle of Outrage*.

33. David Macleod, *The Age of the Child: Children in America, 1890–1920* (New York: Twayne, 1998), 111–18; Viviana Zelizer, *Pricing the Priceless Child* (New York: Basic Books, 1985), 13; Roland Marchand, "Precocious Consumers and Junior Salesmen: Advertising to Children in the United States to 1940" (unpublished manuscript).

34. Cross, *Kids' Stuff*, esp. chaps. 4, 6, 7; and Scott Bruce and Bill Crawford, *Cerealizing America: The Unsweetened Story of American Breakfast Cereal* (Boston: Faber and Faber, 1995), 103–214.

35. "Nostra Culpa," *Time*, 22 Aug. 1955, 47; "Television," *Nation*, 18 Aug. 1956, 146–47; American Character Dolls ads, *Toys and Novelties*, Aug. 1953, 14–15; June 1954, 10; Oct. 1954, 86; AMF ad, *Playthings*, Dec. 1957, 82.

36. Cy Schneider, *Children's Television: The Art, the Business, and How It Works* (New York: NTC Business Books, 1987), 41–45; Ruth Handler, *Dream Doll* (Stamford, Conn.: Longmeadow Press, 1994), chaps. 4–5; Mattel promotion, "Toy Fair," special issue of *Playthings*, Mar. 1959, n.p.; Ron Goulart, *The Assault on Childhood* (Los Angeles: Sherbourne Press, 1969), 103–7.

37. "Crime Shows on TV: A Federal Crackdown Coming?" *U.S. News & World Report*, 9 Nov. 1964, 50–55; Seldin, "Saturday Morning Massacre," 50–52; *Wall Street Journal*, 22 May 1974, 11.

38. "Caveat Pre-emptor," *Saturday Review*, 9 Jan. 1971, 37; Scott Ward, "Kid's TV—Marketers on Hot Seat," *Harvard Business Review*, July 1972, 16–28; Seldin, "Saturday Morning Massacre," 50–52.

39. Robert Choate, "Sugar Coated Children's Hour," *Nation*, 31 Jan. 1972; 146–48; Robert Choate and Nancy Debevoise, "Battling the Electronic Baby-Sitter," *Ms*, Apr. 1975, 91; "Sugar in the Morning," *Newsweek*, 3 Jan. 1978, 75; "Children's Crusaders," *Newsweek*, 4 Feb. 1974, 69. For an interesting critique of the rationalist assumptions of ACT organizers and their failure to understand ad appeals to children, see Ellen

Seiter, *Sold Separately: Children and Parents in Consumer Culture* (New Brunswick, N.J.: Rutgers University Press, 1993), 101.

40. *The Television Code*, 21st ed. (Washington, D.C.: National Association of Broadcasters, 1980); *Children's Advertising Guidelines* (New York: Council of Better Business Bureaus, National Advertising Division, 1975). Secondary sources include William Melody, *Children's Television: The Economics of Exploitation* (New Haven, Conn.: Yale University Press, 1973), 83–116; Edward Palmer, *Children in the Cradle of Television* (Lexington, Mass.: Lexington Books, 1987), 32–36; Marvin Goldberg, "TV Advertising Directed at Children: Inherently Unfair or Simply in Need of Regulation?" in *Marketplace Canada: Some Controversial Dimensions*, ed. Stanley Shapiro and Louise Heslop (Toronto: McGraw-Hill, 1982), 13 ff.; Barry Cole and Mal Oettinger, *Reluctant Regulators: The FCC and the Broadcast Audience* (Reading, Mass.: Addison Wesley, 1978).

41. Goulart, *Assault on Childhood*; Marie Winn, *The Plug-In Drug* (New York: Viking, 1977); Niel Postman, *The Disappearance of the Child* (New York: Dell, 1982); Postman, *Amusing Ourselves to Death: Public Discourse in the Age of Show Business* (New York: Penguin, 1985); Vance Packard, *Our Endangered Children: Growing Up in a Changing World* (Boston: Little, Brown, 1983).

42. *Newsweek*, 3 Jan. 1978, 75; Michael Pertschuk, *Revolt against Regulation* (Berkeley: University of California Press, 1982), 12, 69–70; "The FTC Broadens Its Attack on Ads," *Business Week*, 20 June 1977, 27–28.

43. Federal Trade Commission, *FTC Staff Report on Television Advertising to Children* (Washington, D.C.: FTC, 1978), 11, 20, 243, 267; Turow, *Entertainment, Education and the Hard Sell*, 119.

44. Michael Thorn, "Advertising," *Nation's Business*, Oct. 1979, 85–88; "If the Product Is the Problem," *Business Week*, 3 Apr. 1978, 90; Stephen Fox, *Mirror Makers* (New York: Morrow, 1984), 315–18.

45. Pertschuk, *Revolt against Regulation*, 69; "FTC and the Consumer," *Washington Post*, 28 Mar. 1978, C6.

46. Cross, *Kids' Stuff*, 185–86; "Post Publisher Troubled Last Week," *Washington Post*, 12 Nov. 1978, A11.

47. "FTC Curbs Are Adopted by Senate," *Washington Post*, 8 Feb. 1980; "Someone Does Need a Nanny," *Washington Post*, 16 Mar. 1979, A18; "Conferees Approve FTC Compromise," *Washington Post*, 25 Apr. 1980, E1; Dale Kunkel and D. Roberts, "Young Minds and Marketplace Values: Issues in Children's Television Advertising," *Journal of Social Issues* 47 (1991): 57–72; David Vogel, *Fluctuating Fortunes: The Political Power of Business in America* (New York: Basic Books, 1988), 168.

48. "Evangelist of the Marketplace," *Time*, 1 Nov. 1983, 58; "Fowler No Fan of Federal Pre-emption on Children's TV," *Broadcasting*, 14 Feb. 1983, 85; "Are Children No Longer in the Programming Picture?" *New York Times*, 25 July 25 1982, 2, 21; "TV View," *New York Times*, 17 Oct. 1982, 2, 29; "NAB Scraps Practice of Setting Standards," *Washington Post*, 6 Jan. 1983, D4; "FCC Weakens Policy for TV for Children," *Washington Post*, 23 Dec. 1983, B8; "Children's Television Labeled a Disaster," *Los Angeles Times*, 7 May 1985, 12.

49. "On the Air," *Washington Post*, 22 Oct. 1983, C1; Dale Kunkel, "From a Raised Eyebrow to a Turned Back: The FCC and Children's Product-Related Programming," *Journal of Communications* 38, no. 4 (1988): 91; "Toy-Based TV," *New York Times*, 23 Feb. 1986, A1; Nancy Carlsson-Paige and Diane Levin, "Saturday Morning Pushers," *Utne Reader*, 2 Jan. 1992, 68–69.

50. "Reagan Pocket Veto," *St. Paul Times*, 6 Nov. 1985, 1; "Shielding Children from TV Hucksters," *New York Times*, 6 Nov. 1985, A30; "FCC Ordered to Rethink Kids' TV Rules," *Washington Post*, 27 June 1987, B1; "Children's Television Act," *New York Times*, 15 Sept. 1990, S1, 22; "Pondering the Place of Children's TV," *Broadcasting*, 22 June 1987, 40; "Marketing to Children," *Across the Board*, Nov. 1992, 56–57; and "Selling Children Down the River," *Brandweek*, 12 Aug. 1991, 11.

51. "ACT Challenges Children's TV Rules," *Broadcasting*, 20 May 1991, 62; "FCC Issues Tighter Rules on Kids' TV," *Washington Post*, 10 Apr. 1991, C1; "On Kid TV," *Newsweek*, 30 Nov. 1992, 88; Dale Kunkel, "Crafting Media Policy: The Genesis and Implications of the Children's Television Act of 1990," *American Behavior Scientist* 35 (1991): 181–202.

52. Newton Minow, "Restore the Broadcast Code," *Washington Post*, 11 May 1999, A21.

53. I develop these points in my *All-Consuming Century: Why Commercialism Won in Modern America* (New York: Columbia University Press, 2000), chaps. 6–7.

54. "Federal Communications Commission v Pacifica Foundation," in *U.S. Reports, Judgements of the U.S. Supreme Court* (Washington, D.C.: U.S. Government Printing Office, 1978), vol. 438, 748–79, quoted in Goldberg, "TV Advertising Directed at Children," 25.

55. Heins, *Not in Front of the Children*, 6–7, 89–136, 157–200.

56. "Growing Militancy of the Nation's Non-Smokers," *New York Times*, 15 Jan. 1984, S4, 6.

57. "Surgeon General Says Second-Hand Smoke Endangers Children," *Washington Post*, 24 May 1984, A1; Erica Swecker, "Joe Camel: Will Old Joe Survive?" *William and Mary Law Review* 249 (spring 1995): 1519–58; Jennifer McCullough, "Lighting Up the Battle against the Tobacco Industry," *Rutgers Law Journal* 28 (spring 1997): 709–52; Food and Drug Administration (FDA), "Regulations Restricting the Sale and Distribution of Cigarettes and Smokeless Tobacco Products to Protect Children and Adolescents," *Federal Register*, 60 (1995): 41317, 41330, 41350.

58. "The Man Who'd Ban All Tobacco," *Adweek*, 21 July 1986, 3; "Mike Synar," *Adweek*, 31 July 1989, 2.

59. "Killer Billboards," *Washington Post*, 21 Feb. 1988, B8; John Pierce et al., "Does Tobacco Advertising Target Young People to Start Smoking?" *Journal of the American Medical Association* 266 (1991): 3154–58; "Joe Camel," *Los Angeles Times*, 1 July 1994, A3; "Ad Consultant Fires Shots at Camel Ads," *Adweek*, 4 May 1992, 2; Michael Pertschuk, "Fight Smoke with Fire," *American Prospect* 6 (summer 1995): 84; Paul Fischer et al., "Brand Logo Recognition by Children Aged 3 to 6 Years: Mickey Mouse and Old Joe the Camel," *Journal of the American Medical Association*, 266 (1991): 3145–48; "White House Rips GOP on Tobacco," *Los Angeles Times*, 22 Apr. 1998, A13.

60. Melvin Davis, "Developments in Policy: The FDA's Tobacco Regulations," *Yale Law and Policy Review* 15 (1996): 399–446; Claude Martin, "Ethical Advertising Standards: Three Case Studies," *Journal of Advertising* 23, no. 3 (1994): 17–25; O. Lee Reed, "Should the First Amendment Protect Joe Camel?" *American Business Law Journal* 32 (1995): 311–20; et al, "Strict Regulations," *New York Times*, 14 Sept. 1994, C10; "Attack on Teen-Age Smoking," *New York Times*, 11 Aug. 1995, A28; "FTC Takes Lump over Camel Ads," *Newsday*, 3 June 1994, A53.

61. FDA, "Regulations Restricting the Sale and Distribution of Cigarettes and Smokeless Tobacco Products," 41314–316, 41351.

62. FDA, Executive Summary, "The Regulations Restricting the Sale and Distribution of Cigarettes and Smokeless Tobacco to Protect Children and Adolescents," 7 May 1998, fda.gov/opacom/campgaigns/tobacco/ execrule.html

63. Pertschuk, "Fight Smoke with Fire," 84; "Clinton Tightens Tobacco Rules," *Chicago Sun Times*, 23 Aug. 1996, 3; "Kids and Tobacco," *New York Times*, 15 Apr. 1994, A1; "Tobacco Companies Fight Back," *St. Petersburg Times*, 3 Jan. 1996, 1A; "Regulating Tobacco," *Atlanta Journal and Constitution*, 26 Apr. 1997, 6A; "Tobacco Settlement," *Atlanta Journal and Constitution*, 9 Sept. 1997, 6C; "The Tobacco Agreement," *Journal of Commerce*, 4 Aug. 1997, 9A; Marvin Goldberg, "Loopholes and Lapses in the 1997 Tobacco Agreement," *Journal of Public Policy and Marketing* 16 (fall 1997): 345–47.

64. "Tobacco," *New York Times*, 28 Mar. 1998, A1; "Tobacco Strategy," *New York Times*, 19 Apr. 1998, sec. 4, 5; "Cigarette Makers and States Draft a 206 Billion Dollar Deal," *New York Times*, 14 Nov. 1998, A1; Susan Nielsen, "Though It Coughs Up Bucks, Big Tobacco Gets Last Yuks," *Seattle Times*, 6 Nov. 1998, B4; Michael Murphy, "Tobacco Accord Signed," *Arizona Republic*, 21 Nov. 1998, A1; "The Tobacco Bill," *New York Times*, 18 June 1998, A1.

65. Geneva Overholser, "Charlton Heston, Meet Joe Camel," *Washington Post*, 4 May 1999, A23.

Chapter 7

1. "Then and Now," *Parents*, Oct. 1946, 18, 127–29; "When and How Is a Child Spoiled?" *Parents*, July 1955, 38–39; "Are We Spoiling Our Kids?" *Parents*, Jan. 1967, 84–85, 88; Haim Ginott, *Between Parent and Child* (New York: Macmillan, 1965); "How to Raise Parents," *Newsweek*, 26 Feb. 1968, 54.

2. George Boas, "Century of the Child," *American Scholar* 7 (July 1938): 268–76. Note also his *Cult of Childhood* (London: Warburg Institute, 1966).

3. M. Harari, "Revolt of the Children," *Commonweal*, 17 July 1953, 363–65.

4. "Should Mothers Have Outside Jobs?" *Better Homes and Gardens*, Jan. 1952, 34–35, 105; Benjamin Spock, "How My Ideas Have Changed," *Redbook*, Oct. 1963, 51; Benjamin Spock and Mary Morgan, *Spock on Spock: A Memoir of Growing Up with the Century* (New York: Pantheon, 1989); Margaret Mead, "A New Kind of Discipline," *Parents*, Sept. 1959, 50, 84; Katherine Misher, "Why I Deprive My Children," *SEP*, 24 Feb. 1962, 10.

5. Benjamin Spock, "Bringing Up Children in an Age of Disenchantment," *Redbook*, Feb. 1966, 20, 135; "What's a Mother to Do?" *Newsweek*, 23 Sept. 1968, 68; "A Talk with Dr. Spock," *Newsweek*, 23 Sept. 1968, 71–72; Benjamin Spock, "Don't Blame Me!" *Look*, 26 Jan. 1971, 37–38; "Updating Dr. Spock," *Newsweek*, 3 May 1976, 86.

6. Examples of the attacks on permissiveness in the 1970s and 1980s include "The Cheated Generation," *Christianity Today*, 1 Aug. 1969, 7; "Sense and Nonsense about Being a Permissive Parent," *Redbook*, Nov. 1973, 95; "The American Family," *U.S. News & World Report*, 27 Oct. 1975, 45; "Permissiveness: A 'Beautiful Idea' That Didn't Work," *U.S. News & World Report*, 6 Sept. 1976; 54–55; "The Boom in Brats," *USA Today*, July 6, 1989, 1D; "Styles of Child Rearing," *Los Angeles Times*, 12 Dec. 1987, 5, 10; John Rosemond and James Dobson, *Dare to Discipline* (Wheaton, Ill.: Tyndale House, 1970).

7. "Bringing Up Superbaby," *Newsweek*, 28 Mar. 1983, 62; Barton White, *The First Three Years of Life* (Englewood Cliffs, N.J.: Prentice-Hall, 1975); Glenn Doman, *How to Teach Your Baby to Read* (New York: Norton, 1964).

8. "Boys and Girls Too Old Too Soon," *Life*, 10 Aug. 1962, 54–67; Joshua Meyrowitz, "Where Have the Children Gone?" *Newsweek*, 30 Aug. 1982, 13; "Where Have All the Children Gone?" *Reader's Digest*, Apr. 1966, 135–37; "The Plot to Abolish Childhood," *Reader's Digest*, Aug. 1962, 62, 86; Bruno Bettelheim, "When Should Parents Push?" *LHJ*, Mar. 1971, 56.

9. "I Do Not Like My Children," *American Mercury*, Aug. 1937, 423–29; letter to editor, *American Mercury*, Nov. 1937, 374–75; G. Shipman, "How to Make Your Son a Misfit," *American Mercury*, Mar. 1938, 283–86; "No Children for Me!" *American Mercury*, Apr. 1938, 412–14; Len Chaloner, "Why Have Babies?" *Parents*, Feb. 1939, 19; "I've Raised Three Selfish Little Savages," *American Home*, Apr. 1944, 70.

10. The difference between the satisfaction of parents and nonparents was not great: 78 percent to 72 percent of women and 65 percent to 64 percent of men. "Childless Bliss," *Newsweek*, 9 Dec. 1974, 87.

11. The total fertility rates of 3,339 (for 1960–64) and 1,774 (for 1975–79) represent the number of births for 1,000 American women had they given birth to all their children within this time frame. U.S. Census Bureau, *Statistical Abstract of the United States* (Washington, D.C.: U.S. Government Printing Office, 2000), 68.

12. "Those Missing Babies," *Time*, 16 Sept. 1974, 54–55; "Childless by Choice," *Newsweek*, 14 Jan. 1980, 96.

13. "Halloween Safety Guide," *Parents*, Oct. 1971, 20; *Newsweek*, 11 Nov. 1982, 33; *New York Times*, 31 Oct. 1982, 45; *Omaha World Herald*, 6 Oct. 1983, 23; *Seattle Times*, 11 Nov. 1984, B3; *Omaha World Herald*, 31 Oct. 1984, 34; *Dallas Morning News*, 31 Oct. 1989; *Seattle Times*, 1 Nov. 1984, B2; *Los Angeles Times*, 28 Oct. 1985, C3; *Washington Post*, 31 Oct. 1985, A21; *New York Times*, 27 Oct. 1985, 34; Jan Brunvand, *Curses! Broiled Again: The Hottest Urban Legends Going* (New York: Norton, 1989); *Seattle Times*, 30 Oct. 1990, B3; Nicholas Rogers, *Halloween: From Pagan Ritual to Party Night* (New York: Oxford University Press, 2002), 90–102.

14. *Toronto Star*, 4 Nov. 1987, 34; *Hackensack (N.J.) Record*, 24 Oct. 1985, 10; and *Hackensack (N.J.) Record*, 1 Nov. 1984, 10.

15. *New York Times*, 6 Nov. 1974, 63; *Newsday*, 30 Oct. 1986, 10; *Orange County Register*, 2 Nov. 1988; *New York Times*, 31 Oct. 1982, 45.

16. "Halloween's Changing Mask," *Christian Century*, 25 Oct. 1978, 1021–22; Ralph Forbes, "Protect Our Children from Halloween," *USA Today*, 30 Oct. 1987, 10; *USA Today*, 20 Oct. 1997, 2A; *USA Today*, 21 Oct. 1997, 3A.

17. *Washington Post*, 18 Oct. 1990, M1; *Washington Post*, 31 Oct. 1994, M1; *Los Angeles Times*, 30 Oct. 1995, 1; *Palm Beach Post*, 31 Oct. 1998, 1.

18. Examples of defenses of Halloween tradition include *Tulsa World*, 14 Oct. 1998, 1; *Denver Post*, 1 Nov. 1996, B1; *Washington Times*, 31 Oct. 1996, 1; *Kansas City Star*, 30 Oct. 1992, 14; *USA Today*, 30 Oct. 1987, 1 (for quotation); *Minneapolis Star Tribune*, 28 Oct. 1990, 6E; *Christianity Today*, 2 Oct. 2000, 34.

19. "Halloween, an Adult Treat," *Time*, 31 Oct. 1983, 110; *Washington Post*, 30 Oct. 1987, 1; *Wall Street Journal*, 22 Oct. 1999, 1; "PR Newswire" (via Lexus-Nexus), 13 Oct. 1999; *St. Petersburg Times*, 31 Oct. 1986, 1; *Houston Chronicle*, 30 Oct. 1988, 2; David Skal, *Death Makes a Holiday: A Cultural History of Halloween* (New York: Bloomsburg, 2002), 123–54; Rogers, *Halloween*, 125–38.

20. *Brandweek*, 24 Oct. 1994, 22–29; *Independent*, 17 Jan. 1999, 10; *St. Petersburg Times*, 16 Oct. 1996, 23; *Los Angeles Times*, 9 Apr. 2001, C1; *Minneapolis Star Tribune*, 8 Apr. 2001, 1G; *Los Angeles Times*, 20 Sept. 2001, C1.

21. *Boston Herald*, 25 June 1997, 1; *Minneapolis Star Tribune*, 20 Jan. 1998, 5B.

22. *Arizona Republic*, 18 July 1999, T1; *Boston Globe*, 28 June 1994, 17; *Houston Chronicle*, 16 June 1996, 1; *New Orleans Times-Picayune*, 4 Jan. 1998, 1; *USA Today*, 7 May 1999, 1; *Toronto Star*, 24 Feb. 1995, A15; *Houston Chronicle*, 17 Oct. 1999, T1.

23. "Charm of the Child," *House Beautiful*, Feb. 1902, 136–42, quotation 137; "Children Are Good for Parents," *Parents*, July 1943, 19, 41; Catherine Marshall, "What Children Teach Us about Christmas," *McCall's*, Dec. 1955, 23; Mark Hanchett, "Triumphs and Trials of Rearing Children," *Christianity Today*, 12 June 1981, 32–33; Mike Farrell, "Making the World Fit for Our Children," *National Catholic Reporter*, 24 Mar. 2000, 2.

24. Kay S. Hymowitz, *Ready or Not: Why Treating Children as Small Adults Endangers Their Future—and Ours* (New York: Free Press, 1999); for relevant publications of Commercial Alert, see the Web site: http://lists.essential.org/commercial-alert/.

25. Steven Allen, *Vulgarians at the Gate: Trash TV and Raunch Radio: Raising the Standards of Popular Culture* (Amherst, N.Y.: Prometheus Books, 2001); John Kozol, "Childhood Is for Children," *USA Today*, 1 July 2001, 66–67; "Forum Tries to Rescue Kids from the Advertising Flood," *Cleveland Plain Dealer*, 26 Mar. 2000, 9C; "Marketing to Kids: Who's Really to Blame?" *Business Week*, 21 July 1997, 12; *Los Angeles, Times*, 12 Sept. 2000, A1.

26. Marjorie Heins, *Not in Front of the Children: "Indecency," Censorship, and the Innocence of Youth* (New York: Hill and Wang, 2001), 8–12, 228–33.

# Index